Providential Accidents

Providential Accidents

An Autobiography

Geza Vermes

SCM PRESS LTD

0 334 02722 5

First published 1998 by
SCM Press Ltd
9–17 St Albans Place London NI ONX

Typeset by Regent Typesetting, London

Printed in Great Britain by
Biddles Ltd, Guildford and King's Lynn

Contents

Part Four: The Golden Years of Oxford
(1965–1993)

List of Illustrations

19 The author at an Encaenia procession. Fergus Millar (capless) is on his right

20 After the honorary degree ceremony at Durham University, 5 July 1990. From left to right: J.M. Young (Hon. MA), Dame Margot Fonteyn (Chancellor of the University), Toru Takemitsu (Japanese composer, Hon. DMus.), Crown Prince Hassan of Jordan (Hon. DCL) and the author (Hon. DD)

21 Margaret, Ian and Geza (Oxford 1997)

Prologue: 10 June 1993

Shortly before midnight on 9 June 1993 I realized that my wife was dying. Not having previously witnessed death, I was dreading the moment during the last months of her illness, but it did not turn out to be frightening at all. It was really an uplifting experience.

That morning Pam did not want to get up. She did not appear to be particularly poorly. Only two days earlier, she was her usual critical and inventive self when both of us worked non-stop on putting the finishing touches to an article of mine and successfully met the deadline set by the *New York Review of Books*. As her coughing signalled another infection, I decided to call her doctor, who dutifully came along in the early afternoon, examined her and prescribed a course of antibiotics. As usual, she was teasing him and they laughed. I accompanied the doctor to his car and asked how Pam was. 'She has a significant infection,' he said. Should I telephone Tina, my stepdaughter, in the United States and tell her to come at once rather than the following month as she intended? 'There's no need to do so,' I was told. The doctor believed that the medication would again pull her back from the brink.

I felt that something was unusual and called off an important appointment with a publisher. Pam was concerned, as always, and asked me to ring up a school friend of hers to postpone her visit to us arranged for the next day. I did so, but before I put down the receiver, Pam felt the need to speak to her. 'I hope you haven't cooked a meal for us,' she said. 'I'm afraid I have,' was the reply, 'but don't worry, we'll eat it.' Pam was very upset that she had prevented someone who had put herself out to be kind from showing her kindness. A couple of minutes later she picked up the telephone to revoke the cancellation: 'I'm sure I'll feel better by tomorrow.'

Pam had had lung troubles for years. In 1991 her condition so deteriorated that she was put on oxygen for fifteen hours out of twenty-four and later continuously. She bore the constraint with remarkable courage. She had regular two-monthly visits as an outpatient to the chest clinic of the Churchill Hospital in Oxford. I always went with her, as she needed a driver. (The last time she drove herself was on the day she *passed* the driving test. That was in 1959.) Most of the time spent with the consultant was devoted to talk about music (or about my occasional television appearances) until finally she was asked, 'And how are you?' 'Not too bad,' was her usual very English reply, but she was far from being all right.

She was told that she suffered from chronic bronchitis, a neutral-sounding condition. Then one day in March 1993 when she arrived for a normal check-up, her consultant was off sick. The doctor on duty, the consultant's registrar, looked at her and decided to hospitalize her without further ado. Next day, when I visited her, the same registrar came to see us in the large mixed ward where Pam had been put as an emergency case. He pulled the curtain around the bed before informing us that in fact she had lung cancer. We froze but remained composed. What do you say when you are suddenly confronted with such news? Pam simply asked: 'What's next? Surgery?' 'You would not leave the operating table alive,' she was told. Possible chemotherapy was mentioned. I would have accepted the diagnosis without further question had it had come from the much-respected consultant. 'Did he know?,' I asked the registrar. I was assured that it was he who had spotted the fateful shadow on an X-ray some nine months earlier, and that our doctor had been informed about it too. 'Why weren't we told?' 'It wouldn't have done any good.'

Pam and I were left alone in that makeshift tent. I remember my words: 'We always knew that your condition was grave. The only difference now is that it has been given a new name.' We held each other close. 'You behaved marvellously,' I said. 'So did you,' she replied. She was not frightened of death.

Pam responded astonishingly well to massive antibiotic treatment. Chemotherapy, with its likely side-effects, was postponed and she was discharged a couple of days later, though I had to wheel her back from the car park to the ward because the nurse forgot to remove the intravenous needle from her wrist. (There was pandemonium in the ward with the sister on maternity leave and the consultant convalescing after heart trouble.) Pam returned again to the Churchill in late May for another routine check by the same registrar. She described to friends the conversation between them with her typical dry humour. 'They know they can't do anything for you, but they go through the old routine questions. How are you? *Fine.* Do you have any pain? *No.* Can you sleep? *Yes.* How is your appetite? *Not bad.* You see how hard they are trying to convey some comfort, but nothing worthwhile is said. Finally: See you in two months' time. *If I'm still here.* Oh you will be.' She wasn't.

The late afternoon of the last day was peaceful. A woman friend came and brought a vitamin drink at my request as Pam could not eat anything. She drank it, was very grateful, but asked her to go so as not to catch her infection. 'Don't leave me,' she asked me later in the evening, surely sensing the approaching end. It was marvellously peaceful. She gave no sign of fear or of agony. I kept on repeating her favourite verse (23) of Psalm 73:

Va'ani tamid 'immakh; 'ahazta beyad yemini
I am with You always; You hold my right hand.

I like to think that she heard these much-loved words. Then the breathing stopped and I found myself alone with a future hard to imagine.

During the thirty-six years that we shared, we always worked together, and at the final stages the prospect of co-operation with me seemed miraculously to revitalize her. She was delighted to see the publication of the third volume of my (or rather our) Jesus trilogy, *The Religion of Jesus the Jew,* just over three months before she passed away, and visibly enjoyed what turned out to be her last appearance at a public event, the party given by the publishers, SCM Press, in my Oxford college on 1 March 1993. So whenever sickness appeared to weaken her resolve to live, I tried to fortify her with the idea of some new task for which her help was essential. 'You must give me a hand when I finally turn to my autobiography,' I told her a month or two before she died. She shook her head, and with a mixture of smile and sadness on her tired face she told me: 'You'll write your memoirs when I'm gone.'

'What will you do when I'm no longer here?,' she once asked me. 'I can't think about that,' was my truthful but evasive answer. Pam continued: 'I'll tell you what you'll do. First you'll grieve, but you must pull yourself together and deal with all the unfinished business.' Finally, prophetically, she added: 'In time, I hope someone nice will turn up to take care of you.'

Sixteen months have passed since that fateful night, and now here I am, recently turned seventy, seeking to piece together and make sense of my life story, which I can best sum up, mixing religious and secular imagery, as an amazing series of providential accidents.

Part One: From Makó to Budapest

(1924–1946)

I

Roots

Uncle Pista (Steve), my mother's half-brother, was my last blood relation. In 1986 he suddenly decided to pay us a first visit in Oxford. He arrived at Heathrow airport from Budapest on his eightieth birthday, a shortish, bald, lean, erect and lively figure, totally oblivious of the handicap of not knowing a single word of English. I watched him walking into a London shop a few days later to buy a navy sports jacket. Without the slightest hesitation, he addressed the salesman in French and went on talking until someone was found with a smattering of French who could deal with him. He had left Hungary after the First World War for Germany, where he qualified as an engineer of some sort. He fled to France when Hitler came to power and joined the French Communist party. 'I wanted to save the world,' he remarked with melancholy when we were last together in the summer of 1992, 'and look what they have done to my socialist ideals.'

As a youngster I first met him in extraordinarily tragic circumstances. His wife and their only little daughter were visiting her parents in Budapest, but one night her father, a well-known painter, went berserk, murdered his wife together with his daughter and granddaughter (Pista's wife and daughter), and finally killed himself. Pista flew from Paris to Budapest for the funerals and afterwards travelled to Gyula in south-east Hungary, where we lived, to meet my mother. She was his elder sister and he had not been in touch with her for more than twenty years. I can still see her lying on a sofa after an afternoon rest and conducting a jolly conversation with Pista in French. (She had a French governess as a girl and tried to reawaken her dormant knowledge of the language.) Aged fourteen, I was amazed by the strange-sounding and to me incomprehensible chat, but would have been even more astonished had I been told that from 1946 to 1957 French would be my prime vernacular, and the language of my first book in 1953.

In 1939 Pista volunteered for the French army; he was captured by the Germans, but as a prisoner of war escaped the fate of ordinary Jews. He returned to Paris after 1945 and spent another three years there before migrating back to Hungary. I tried to contact him on my first trip to France in 1948, but must have missed him by a few weeks. As a fluent French and German speaker (and a party member of some years standing!), he was recruited for the Hungarian foreign service as a commercial attaché. He married again and was widowed a second time. However, he shared the last few years of his life with a 'girl friend' who made him very happy. When I was in Budapest in the summer of 1992 and gave a well-advertised public lecture at the Hungarian Academy of Sciences, followed by press, radio and television interviews, I took Uncle Pista wherever I went. He was enthralled by the shared limelight, and did not miss an opportunity to tell all and sundry that I was his nephew. Two months later he had a heart attack and died in his eighty-seventh year. With him disappeared the last direct family link with my Hungarian past.[1]

I was born on 22 June 1924 in Makó, a county town of southern Hungary, famous for its onions and its garlic. Their horrible smell filled the streets where the warehouses stood, and to this day garlic strikes me with nausea. According to my birth certificate I was the 'Israelite' son of Ernő (Ernest) Vermes, aged forty-six, of 'Israelite' religion and by profession a journalist, and Terézia Riesz, aged twenty-nine, also 'Israelite'. (The words 'Jew' and 'Jewish' were thought offensive in those days and were not used in official terminology.)

Until the summer of 1994, when I spent a day there, Makó remained a hazy notion for me, consisting of a few early childhood memories, all antedating my fourth birthday. By that time my parents had left the place. Makó's most famous son was Joseph Pulitzer, born there in 1847, the later American newspaper magnate after whom the Pulitzer prize is named. Today the city seems extremely sleepy and remote, justifying the Hungarian proverb, 'It is as far as Makó from Jerusalem' (or from Oxford, as I might put it). But in the 1920s Makó was intellectually more alive. The local high school counted among its members two nationally famous poets: Gyula (Julius) Juhász, a school-master, and Attila József, a pupil, today the dominant figure of twentieth-century Hungarian poetry. Both ended their lives by their own hands. Juhász was a friend of my father. My mother smilingly told me later how embarrassed she was when one day I did what babies are wont to do right in the lap of the poet. Attila József, some of whose early poems were published by my father in the *Morning News of Makó* (*Makói Reggeli Ujság*), where he worked, had some distant family links with my mother. A cousin of hers married the poet's sister.

My mother, a qualified school teacher, was a local girl. She was tall by Hungarian standards, about 5ft 8, with long jet-black hair, black eyes and a fine complexion. She was always very thin. Her grandfather and father were corn merchants. She never knew her father, who died of pneumonia before her first birthday. Her mother, widowed at the age of twenty-two and dead when she was thirty-two, married again and moved to another part of the country. She bore four more children to her second husband, of whom Uncle Pista was the youngest.

For reasons unknown to me, my mother was left behind in Makó, and was brought up by her paternal grandmother. My beloved great-granny was in her mid-eighties when I was born, and had been a widow for nearly thirty years. She spoke the local dialectal form of Hungarian, and still could remember the patriotic songs she learned during the great national uprising against the Austrians in 1848. I recollect her elderly handwriting on postcards addressed to my mother, always formally signed, 'Your loving grandmother, the widow of Bernard Riesz, née Sarah Strausz'. (The fact that neither she, nor any of my grandparents or my parents, spoke, or even understood, Yiddish shows how deeply assimilated was the layer of Jewish society to which both my mother and my father belonged.) Great-granny was a practising member of the Jewish community. I remember her regularly reciting the daily prayers, but I think she felt too old to attend synagogue services. She died of pneumonia in her one hundred and first year in the cold January of 1940, thus escaping the Holocaust which engulfed most Jews, including my parents, in provincial Hungary four years later. My mother travelled from Gyula to attend her funeral in the large Jewish cemetery of Makó, situated a couple of miles' distance from the city in the middle of fields and approachable only by unmade paths. In the autumn of 1996 I spent half a day in Makó, intending to visit the grave of my great-grandmother. Alas, this turned out to be an impossible task. The Jewry of Makó, which numbered 3,000 souls in 1944, is today reduced to five. The cemetery is completely neglected and overgrown with weeds. So in the absence of records indicating the site of the individual graves – all the synagogue registers were destroyed over fifty years ago – I prayed there in the sure knowledge that her remains, and possibly those of her husband and her son, my grandfather, lay not far from the spot where I stood. It is odd to realize that the death of the cemetery soon followed the disappearance of the community.

My mother went to school in Makó and later attended a teachers' training college in Szabadka (Subotica, in what was soon to become Yugoslavia). If she ever received any traditional Jewish education, I cannot recall any trace of it in her behaviour. The same is true of the members of her fairly large family, all of whom, uncles and aunts as well as her half-brothers and sisters, with the exception of Pista, soon followed the path of upward-moving Jewry and settled in Budapest, mostly as fairly prosperous businessmen or wives of businessmen. An aunt of hers married a highly trained and cultured mechanical engineer-factory owner who in his young days lived in France and built locomotives for the French railways. A cousin was a successful lawyer. Most of them were polyglots, equally at ease with Hungarian, German and French. They all cut themselves off from Jewish observances, and almost the whole family embraced Christianity for social reasons, naively or optimistically believing that a baptismal certificate would protect them from rampant Hungarian antisemitism. They formed a close-knit and loving family and were very helpful when after the enactments of anti-Jewish legislation in the late 1930s my parents found themselves in financial straits. Like a good many Budapest Jews, with three exceptions they survived the real hard times. These started late in Hungary, on 19 March 1944, when Hitler's armies moved in and replaced the half-hearted Germanophile government with dedicated Nazis.

I loved my mother for her warmth and kindness and solid practical touch; I admired my father for his intelligence. I do not know how the two of them met in 1923, when he wrote for or edited one of the local dailies, but from a letter written by one of the sisters of the poet Attila József to another it seems that their wedding plans did not meet with great-granny's approval.[2] I am not sure how much earlier my father joined the paper or where he came from. He did not stay for long in any place in those days. He led a bohemian life before my mother succeeded in anchoring him down.

He was born Ernő Weisz in 1877 in Miskolc, north-east of Budapest. Like many assimilated and patriotic Jews, he 'Hungaricized' his surname to Vermes in the late 1890s. His father, Lajos (Louis) Weisz, was a railway hotel manager; like trains, he seemed to be moving from one place to another. My paternal grandmother came from a Bohemian (Czech) Jewish family. She was the only grandparent still alive when I was born, but died when I was one year old without ever seeing me. To bury her, my father travelled to the northern city of Kassa, then Kosice in Czechoslovakia, now in Slovakia. My only paternal uncle, a deaf-mute and I believe a jeweller by trade, also died before I was born. Grandmother, Amelia Weinberger, must have been a native German speaker, judging from letters written by her to her husband; however, he answered them in Hungarian. Both my parents spoke German, and my father also had some Italian, which he picked up in Fiume (now Rijeka in Croatia) during the years of the First World War, when he edited a paper in old Hungary's only seaport. English was generally unknown in Hungary in those days. I first started to learn it as a twenty-four year old university student in 1948. My Hungarian school curriculum of foreign languages included German, French, and of course Latin.

My father spent his childhood in Transylvania, then part of Hungary, now a province of Romania, and attended a college of commerce in Nagyvárad (Oradea to the Romanians), a city where I found myself just after the last war. But business was not his cup of tea, and from his late teens he joined the literary and journalistic circles in Budapest. By the age of twenty he had a collection of poems published. He worked for various daily newspapers, and was acquainted with leading writers, poets and theatre personalities. He married for the first time in 1905. Neither he nor my mother ever mentioned this to me. I discovered it one day as a naughty child opening an old suitcase in the attics and tumbling on an invitation to the wedding of Ernő Vermes and a woman whose name I cannot remember. I have no idea how long this marriage lasted. As I found out about it illicitly, I didn't dare enquire. I think I also felt embarrassed to do so, and preferred not to know. In retrospect, I wish I had, though if this first marriage had produced children, I imagine I would have been told that I had siblings.

In the early years of this century my father decided to leave Budapest and settled for a while in the southern city of Temesvár (now Timisoara in Romania) as a staff writer for the local daily, the *Temesvár Newspaper* (*Temesvári Hirlap*). It was there that in 1909 he published the second volume of his verses. As a child, I found a fairly worn copy in his library and soon could recite every poem by heart. He played a leading role in a literary society, called 'The South' *(A Dél)*, formed by young writers and poets of the region. He was in charge of arranging lectures, and proudly told me his greatest achievement, the organization of an evening of poetry reading by the idol of the generation, Endre Ady. My father, acting as the host, stayed in the same hotel as Ady and some thirty years after the event told me with visible emotion how Ady, suffering from insomnia, came to his room in the middle of the night wearing just his pyjamas, and sat on the edge of his bed discussing literature, poetry and politics until dawn.

I believe it was in Temesvár that my father applied formally to be registered as belonging to no denomination. Though he always moved in Jewish company, Judaism as a religion never made any impact on him, and since those Hungarians who were classified as affiliated to a religious body had to pay a special 'church' tax collected by the state, he thus found a way, he thought, to make some small savings. About fifteen years later, in order to have a synagogue wedding with my mother, he re-declared himself Jewish. This was to pacify my great-granny.

He was in his thirty-seventh year at the outbreak of the Great War, a tall (5ft 11) and well-built man; he was mobilized as a private, but apparently displayed no martial talents and was soon released to go back to his newspaper in Fiume. Military drill was obviously not his forte. He laughingly reported the sergeant major's screams in his direction: 'Mr Journalist ... (expletives), *left*, right, *left*, right!'

Politically he was a liberal, and throughout his whole career as a journalist in right-wing Hungary he always supported the opposition parties. He was a bit of an adventurer by nature: he loved cards and gambling, especially horse-races. Apparently he wanted to call me Anton Oscar, the name of the winner of the Hungarian Derby a few days before I was born, a horse on which I believe he made some money. But my sensible mother got the better of him and I was named Geza after her late father. In his heart of hearts, Ernő Vermes was a dreamer and a poet. He wrote his last piece when he turned fifty and dedicated it to me. Here it is in a lame English rendering.

Fifty

Spring twilight. I'm sitting in silence.
Faraway mountains are shrouded in blue mist.
Old memories come to life in me,
O pensive dreams, call me! I'm on my way.

On the azure mirror of the Adriatic
My ship sails towards a distant new goal.
It proudly lurches forward as it used to,
And as in old times, it never reaches the shore ...

The giddy old dreams are driving me
And the goal beckons from the distant blue,
And while I'm racing with head intoxicated,
The winter turns my hair ash-coloured.

Spring twilight. I'm sitting in silence
And I perceive that time is rushing.
But my little son, while I'm staring at the past,
Runs after a pretty, colourful butterfly.

O my little son, chase the colourful dream.
Go on, your father did the same.
While I fall out of the line, follow my footsteps
Towards unattainable beauties.

Seek beauty as your father sought it
And after being beaten by a hundred heavy storms,
You too will enjoy peace on the approach of evening
In a cosy armchair smoking a good cigar.

2

Childhood Memories

(1926–1937)

When I was a few months old, my mother dropped me at bathtime and my head hit the concrete floor. She thought I would die or at least become mentally deficient, and needed much reassurance and cheering up, but her fears seem to have been exaggerated. Despite the fall, the mark of which is still detectable today, I turned into a round-faced, black-haired, brown-eyed, happy little fellow.

The tragic events of the war deprived me not just of the people I loved but also of the warmth of objects which were known as home, including photographs. But thanks to an aunt and an uncle of my mother, I possess three precious mementoes. The first is a picture of my mother, still unmarried, wearing the most inappropriate fancy dress of a devil. The second is my parents' wedding photograph, which I hold especially dear. Finally, there is a portrait of my father with me standing next to him, curly-haired, at the age of about two and a half. Each of us has a pipe in his mouth. We both look very jolly, but in truth I have no recollection of the scene.

I also treasure a single heirloom, great-granny's watch. After her death in 1940, my mother gave it to me, and it remained with me intact through all the upheavals of the war years. The heavy silver pocket watch, with its front cover inlaid with gold, actually belonged to my great-grandfather, whose name is calligraphed on it with blue indelible ink: 'Bernard Riesz, Makó'. This Longines model won a gold medal at the 1889 Paris World Fair six years before my great-grandfather died. It is still ticking away, marking the inexorable continuity of the family time.

Only three memories have actually survived of my earliest childhood spent in our house in Makó, which I left in 1928. The first is connected with tears; the second with disappointment and anger; and the third with a feeling of blissful security.

In reality, the sad episode is rather funny. I was given a chocolate rabbit and adored it. Then, ignorant of the consequences, I began to chew it with the utmost delight. However, when realizing that in the process my rabbit friend had lost its head, the sight broke my heart. Inconsolable, I cried for hours. A short while ago, someone very close to me who had heard the story smilingly presented me with another chocolate creature, but to this day it has remained intact. I could not bring myself to repeat the deed which had such a shattering outcome.

The next story is connected with our garden, my favourite place as a toddler. In my memory it was quite large, but a recent return to the ancestral home rather cut it down in size. One day after lunch I escaped from the house to play instead of having my usual siesta. Precociously blessed with foresight, I did my best to keep my mother out. As the garden gate had no latch or lock, but only a nail and a string, I tied it to the nail as tightly as a two-and-a-half to three year old could. It is easy to guess my despair when I saw Mummy undoing my fortification. She carried me under her arm, kicking and yelling, to my bed. This, I believe, was my first experience of 'unfairness'.

The blissful third image, sharp, perfectly in focus, still warms my heart, yet in my adult mind it is mingled with something unbearably sad. I can see myself in an early afternoon standing in the large window overlooking the broad street.¹ Safely held by my mother, I was watching my father, his left hand clutching his right wrist behind his back, walking away slowly towards the newspaper office after his lunch break. I knew that he would come back and meanwhile my mother was there to look after me. It was late spring or summer, warm, sunny, heavenly, the quintessence of happiness.

But this vision of a beloved parent going away later became linked, first in my subconscious and then in my conscious mind, with a negative mirror image. I could see myself seventeen or eighteen years later, in late May 1944, watching my mother walking away in the afternoon sun ready to set. I was watching her from the basement window of my hiding-place. Tall, holding herself straight, but bearing the burden of the world, she walked slowly. She wore a yellow blouse to conceal the compulsory distinguishing mark of the yellow star of David. My father had already been taken. She was returning to her solitude in the improvised ghetto. There was no real Jewish quarter in Gyula. 'I thought that at least *you* would be safe,' she told me during our brief *tête-à-tête*, but her hope was manifestly shattered. I watched the yellow figure of my beloved mother until it reached the corner of the street and disappeared. I never saw her again.

I do not know why my parents left Makó and great-granny, whom I remember only from later sporadic visits. I believe that they moved in early 1928 to nearby Szeged, the second largest city of Hungary. Our stay there was short, and no memories have survived except that of an accident. I felt hungry and decided to cut a slice of bread with a large knife; in the process I managed to inflict a deep wound on my left thumb. A faint trace of the scar is still visible today. I imagine my father must have taken up an appointment with the big regional paper *South Hungary* (*Délmagyarország*),[2] but judging from the fact that a few months later the family was on the move again to a county town, Gyula, some fifty miles to the north-east, the Szeged job must have been only temporary.

Gyula, where I lived between the ages of four and eighteen, personifies pre-war Hungary for me. Two recent short visits, the first in 1992, forty-six years after I left it for good, and the second in 1994, revived its fading image, but the modern reality is very different from the city with which I was familiar. In my time the inhabitants numbered about 25,000 , but being the administrative centre of the county of Békés, the town was full of offices and civil servants; it had also a court of law, and a variety of schools. During the Communist era, the county hall and the connected offices were transferred to neighbouring Békéscsaba. However, almost simultaneously hot therapeutic springs were discovered in the park; in my time this used to belong to a local count, but was confiscated after the war. Since then the quiet little city has developed into a popular spa with much cultural activity, an open-air theatre, museums, picture galleries, etc. My father ran the local daily for a while before setting up his own twice-weekly *Lowland* (*Az Alföld*), popularly known as 'The Yellow Paper' on account of the colour of the newsprint. His mordant leaders, which bore the title 'With the sharp point of the pen', were highly popular, except with those whom they left bleeding. He had to face a good many libel suits, but won them all, sometimes taking the case to the appeal court in Szeged, or even to the supreme court in Budapest. I remember how once an irate army officer, disdaining civil justice, provoked my father to a duel. They did not come to blows; the seconds settled the differences to everyone's satisfaction. Military honour was safe and, more important, my father, who was neither a virtuoso swordsman nor a sharp-shooter, remained unharmed.

Of the two years spent in Gyula before I reached pre-war Hungary's primary school age of six, few details are clear beyond a general recollection of total contentment. I am not aware of any misery caused by my being an only child. On the contrary, I could always amuse myself and was the sole beneficiary of the undivided attention of doting parents, proud of their 'clever' boy. Living in a house full of newspapers, I soon learned to read headlines printed with capitals and to write with big letters. My parents often asked me to perform before their guests. Once I wrote to Father Christmas listing my requests. My father volunteered to post the letter. However, when he came home in the evening, he learned that I had been naughty and needed a talking-to. Father Christmas had to be warned, I was informed, as he accepted letters only from good children. Wide-eyed, I watched Daddy fiddling with the knobs of his primitive radio set, which ran on a kind of car battery. He reported to Father Christmas my disobedience or rudeness, or whatever it was. Then the drama heightened as he put his left hand into his jacket pocket, and lo and behold out came my letter, returned to the sender by Santa Claus. So I had to learn that being good was more important than being clever and able to write at the age of four. I have no doubt that in the end the presents materialized all the same.

Another episode has remained deeply engraved on my memory. Uncle Joe (Jóska), great-granny's widower son-in-law who continued to share a house with her after his wife's death, came to stay with us for a couple of weeks. He must have been nudging eighty and, since he was quite traditional, he decided to go to the synagogue on Saturday. He thought that it would be only proper if I went with him. I did so, though not without being admonished by my mother not really to kiss the scroll of the Law as it was unhygienic! I do not remember much of this service and perhaps another one which I attended, except that I was with other children. What the very learned local rabbi had to say was clearly above my head. He was deported at the same time as my mother. Later I found out that he was the uncle of a dear friend, the greatest Hungarian Jewish scholar of the post-war years, Professor Alexander Scheiber. In any case, these were my first and last visits to a synagogue for the next forty years.

After the two Sabbaths, Uncle Joe returned to Makó; he died a year or two later. Superstitious neighbours believed that I was responsible for his demise. One day, after a storm, I found a dead sparrow. I felt very sorry and wanted to bury it. The young woman who worked for us decided to provide an appropriate ceremony; she mimicked the burial service, sang hymns, and interred the little creature, surrounded by all the children of the neighbourhood. Some of the parents strongly disapproved: one should not play with death. A few days later my mother heard that her uncle was gone. I do not believe I felt dreadful, but I was a bit disturbed by the death of the dear old man to whom I owe my first awareness and experience of Jewishness.

I used to spend my days playing at home or in the garden of a neighbour, the wife of a printer with an adopted daughter about two years my junior. The idea that I should go to nursery school came as a shock. I was not used to mixing regularly with crowds of children. Still, at the age of four or five, one's resistance is rarely effective, and one day I found myself in their company and that of a young teacher, Aunt Mimi. I took a liking to her and put up with the other children. But soon a double disaster hit: Aunt Mimi was replaced by the elderly Aunt Rose, and from the word go I could not bear her. Worse still, one day we were all sent to the school yard during the break. Hungry, I took out my snack from the bag, but very clumsily let it fall to the ground. Aunt Rose's cockerel, also in the yard, was quick to notice the sandwich and beat me to it, running away with the booty. I furiously chased it without success while the children looking on roared with laughter. That was the last time I attended the nursery school. Indeed, I thought that going to any kind of school was a dreadful idea.

Yet in September 1930, shortly after my sixth birthday, whether I liked it or not I had to join the local elementary school. It was a Roman Catholic institution – all the better schools were denominational. I learned very fast and – in those days – had an exceedingly retentive memory. Once, with older schoolchildren, I volunteered to attend a talk organized by local wine-growers. 'What was it about?,' my parents asked me on my return. 'It was about a nasty little bug called phylloxera which is destroying all the vine-yards,' I proudly explained. My report sounded good enough for my father to risk a short article in the next issue of his paper. This was my first venture in journalism; the next came six years later when I was commissioned by my father twice a week to write brief notices on the Berlin Olympic games based on radio reports and cuttings from national newspapers.

The story of the vine louse recalls a dinner to which years later my wife Pam and I were invited by a Middle-Eastern princely pupil of mine at the Restaurant Elizabeth in Oxford. The wine served was an old claret. It tasted out of this world. And thirty-seven years after the 1930 lecture I still knew why. Château Mouton de Rothschild 1929 was *real* French wine of the last *pre*-phylloxera vintage.

In the early 1930s my mother toyed with the idea of returning to part-time teaching, though in fact this came to nothing. She registered for a refreshers' conference and I was determined to go with her. To explain the presence of a six- or seven-year-old, she told the organizers that I also wanted to be a teacher. I did not protest against this prediction, although in those days, like most boys, I first hoped to be an engine driver and later a doctor. Another twenty years had to pass before I began to dream of a university professorship. However, my teaching career started much earlier. From the age of twelve, I acted as a home tutor to pupils in need of help. As the years passed, I was more and more in demand and earned a respectable amount of pocket money, most welcome when circumstances were getting tougher in the late 1930s. One more 'prophetic' sign is preserved in my memory. It concerns our doctor, who was also a family friend. He used to arrive in a horse-drawn cab before acquiring his first car. Misfortune followed. He had an accident and died of blood poisoning.

I vaguely knew that he had a brother or cousin who taught Scripture in a theological college, but obviously could not guess that some fifteen years later it would be when tidying up the library of this professor, after a visit by drunken Russian soldiers, that I would have the first inspiration that I ought to study Hebrew and become what I am.

In the late spring of 1931, my school teacher took me aside after a (Catholic) religion class and asked: 'Are you going to be baptized or not? I will soon have to fill in your papers. What shall I put in the box, Israelite or Roman Catholic?' What he actually wrote was RC. My parents finally decided to cross the Rubicon. Bound by law, they had to inform the rabbi of their intention to convert, and subsequently they received instruction (in great secrecy, I think) from the parish priest of Gyula. He belonged to one of the oldest Hungarian aristocratic families, and was soon to become bishop of Győr in western Hungary. In 1944, he saved my life before losing his own a few months later when he tried to protect a group of women from Russian soldiers. The christening of the family took place, quietly without witnesses, in June 1931, a week or so before my seventh birthday. Thereafter I was brought up as a little Catholic boy, but was never allowed completely to forget my origin. My mother forbade me ever to mention the change to great-granny. Whether great-granny found it out or not, I have no idea. I hope she didn't. But some friends of my mother in Makó were privy to it. One of them, the wife of a barrister, reproached me for having done something unforgivable.[3] Didn't I realize that Abraham was the first founder of religion and Jesus the first heretic? Aged eight or thereabouts, I was not yet in a position to query her history, but I was mature enough to sense the unfairness of her question. However, it stuck in my mind.

How did conversion affect my parents? My mother became a devout Catholic; she prayed daily, attended mass in church every Sunday, ate no meat on Friday, and moved almost exclusively in Christian circles. What happened to her piety in the hell of Auschwitz or whichever hell she had to pass through, God alone knows. I only hope it helped her. My father, by contrast, showed little change. Very occasionally he went to church if my mother or I insisted for some reason. But otherwise he seemed to be no more interested in Christianity than he was in Judaism. He allowed himself to be baptized to give me a chance. The large majority of his friends were Jewish, and he carried on with his journalism as before. For some years he was also busy writing several volumes of local history, describing the state of three or four Hungarian counties ten years after the 1920 peace treaty, each volume ending with a kind of who's who of notables (who were all expected to buy their own copy). I attended religion classes, learned the catechism by heart, and had to go to church with the rest of my class on Sundays and feast days as part of my obligations during the twelve years of my Catholic primary and secondary schooling.

The school where I started had its problems; the classes became too large and the teaching suffered. So I was taken to another primary school in the centre of the city. I still have a memento of the first one, a class photograph which I was given on one of my return visits to Hungary in the 1960s or 1970s. I am immediately recognizable as almost the only boy with a decent length of hair. Three other faces figure on the same photograph, those of lifelong friends who at a later moment of crisis were brave enough to risk their own reputation and support me.

I was happy at home and in my new school. At meals I heard the latest news told by my father to my mother. The prime minister had resigned and a new more right-wing government had been formed. A little later I sensed anxiety in my father's voice as he announced that someone called Hitler had been made Chancellor of Germany by Hindenburg. Hitler was a nasty man, I gathered.

At the second school, too, I got my usual top marks, and when I reached the age of ten, I had no difficulty in gaining admission to the local Roman Catholic gymnasium, the grammar school where I was to spend the next eight years. Though among the best from the start, I was not conceited or cocky. A kind of self-effacement was no moral virtue on my part, but derived from an innate shyness. One day in my first year a master asked us to memorize in class a short poem some twelve lines long, and let him know when we thought we knew it. After a couple of minutes I could recite it to myself, but did not want to be the first to raise my hand. Perhaps five minutes later another boy timidly volunteered but broke down half-way through. This gave me the green light, and a smooth and perfect delivery followed.

In the gymnasium, I was most attracted to literature and languages. In addition to Hungarian, I did Latin, German and French. Greek was no longer taught, and what I know of it I had to learn much later the hard way. I coped sufficiently with mathematics and science and, always one of the tallest in the class (1m 85.5 or 6ft 1), was moderately good at sport, especially athletics and skating. One of my classmates, a very gifted boy from an uneducated background, was my chief rival. He beat me in maths and sciences, and above all in sport – he became a champion sprinter and only illness stopped him from representing Hungary in the 1948 London Olympics – but I was ahead of him in humanities. Our lives ran their separate paths for half a century but when we met in 1992, on the fiftieth anniversary of leaving school, one of the leading Budapest architects greeted an Oxford professor and Fellow of the British Academy.

Outside school activities, which almost exclusively occurred in the morning, from 8 a.m. until 1 or 1.30 p.m., my life was gently monotonous. My parents took no regular summer vacations, and apart from a few short visits to Makó before great-granny died in January 1940, in her one hundred and first year, and two or three trips to Budapest to visit the many aunts and uncles of my mother, I spent my time at home mainly reading and going to the cinema all year round, and to the theatre in the summer, the only time when it functioned. I began my acquaintance with movies at a very early age, in the era of the silent film. In fact, I remember my first experience of a talkie. I went to the cinema with a heightened anticipation which was totally disappointed. I could not imagine the purpose of those funny noises. It took me years to realize that the gibberish perceived by my child's ears was in fact English! As a teenager, I never missed a film or a play. The question of money to buy tickets did not come up. My father had free press passes for himself and his family. I regularly flouted the high school's strict rules about frequenting cinemas, but miraculously I was never caught.

By the mid-1930s the glorious days of contentment began to fade, replaced by greater intellectual demands and a short phase of what I thought was a poetic vocation (verses which, I am sure, are not to be reproduced even in Hungarian, let alone in English). Then in the late 1930s the clouds of war began to gather: they foreshadowed doom and disaster for most of the Jews of Hungary.

Childhood was over.

3

Unread Signs of Doom

(1938–1942)

In the second half of the 1930s, like most young Magyars I was a fervent patriot. I considered myself a Catholic Hungarian, and found it both incomprehensible and hurtful when working-class children, who imbibed antisemitism with their mother's milk, called me a Jewboy who should go to Palestine, or, worse still, sang the horrid little song, 'Jew, destined for the string. There's a pole in Pest, waiting for them all.'

We young Hungarians deeply resented the injustice inflicted on our defeated nation by the Western victors of the First World War, and were continuously encouraged to voice our protest. The hated 'Trianon' peace treaty, signed in the Trianon palace at Versailles in 1920, deprived Hungary of two-thirds of its traditional territory, and handed over large chunks of the northern, eastern and southern regions of the fatherland to the disdained Slovak, Croat and Romanian minorities who triumphantly joined the freshly created states of Czechoslovakia and Yugoslavia, and Romania, which we much despised. We were brought up on nationalistic slogans: 'Truncated Hungary is not a country, complete Hungary is heaven' [or in rhyming Hungarian, *'Csonka Magyarország nem ország, egész Magyarország menyország'*]. 'Trianon [*tria non* = three noes]: no, no, never', we loudly proclaimed, punning in Latin.

At first this irredentism seemed just a dream, but from 1938 onwards Hungarian government sympathies with Hitler and Mussolini were rewarded, and part of the lost areas were returned to Magyar rule. The whole school marched in candle-lit processions, we sang patriotic songs, and in 1940 a day-trip was organized to nearby Nagyvárad, freshly 'liberated' from the Romanians. This was the city of my father's student days, where a little later I was to spend two crucial years of my life. The atmosphere was one of elation shared by us all, but it soon began to evaporate for the Jews in the wake of the antisemitic laws enacted between 1938 and 1941 by an increasingly pro-German government.

The first anti-Jewish measures hit hard, but were not yet bloody. The so-called 'balancing' laws, promulgated in 1938 and 1939, aimed at restricting the participation of Jews in the political, academic, intellectual and professional life of the nation. At these early stages of repressive legislation Jewish identity was still defined by religious affiliation, although among the baptized Jews only those who converted before 1919 counted as Christians. According to the 1938 legislation, Jewish intake at the universities, and Jewish membership of the officially created professional bodies for doctors, lawyers, journalists, etc., was not to exceed twenty per cent. This was a relatively generous figure, but was reduced next year to six per cent, corresponding to the Jewish share of the total population of Hungary.

In the light of what was in store, these acts may appear 'mild', but for those who fell foul of them, they were not just detrimental but also deeply humiliating, since most Hungarian Jews defined themselves as Magyars of Israelite religion. Our baptismal certificates were never of any practical use to my family, as they bore a post-1919 date. Consequently, from the word go the anti-Jewish laws were a threat to my father's professional status and to our livelihood. As the owner and publisher of a weekly newspaper, the *Echo* [*Viszhang*], which he had launched a year or two earlier, when political machinations deprived him of his previous editorial position, he had to seek admission to the officially controlled association of journalists. I can no longer be sure of the date (was it in 1938 or in 1939?), but I still remember the day when the fateful letter was delivered by the postman: Ernest Vermes was refused admission to the guild of journalists, and as a result his permit to publish the weekly was revoked.[1]

It is not difficult to imagine what this blow meant to a man already in his early sixties, who had been a journalist all his life. From then on, my father remained unemployed until the day of his deportation and subsequent death in 1944. The pattern of his external behaviour changed completely. He got up late in the morning; he spent part of the afternoon in his favourite coffee house, reading all the newspapers and playing cards with his Jewish friends at weekends. At home, he buried himself in books and, true to his character, kept on dreaming of rosier days.

Once more, it was my mother who had to shoulder the burden of the blow and find ways and means to make ends meet. The occasional income my father gained from free-lancing for Budapest newspapers – which he still could do – and from sporadic consultancy work for commercial firms was neither sufficient nor regular enough to form the basis of a family budget. So my mother buried her pride and turned to her well-off relations. They provided her with a monthly allowance, enough for the essentials. In one of the first poems I ever wrote, dated 1939, I stood beside my mother, who was asleep on the sofa, placed a warm kiss on her worry-wrinkled forehead, and promised her prompt solace amid her anxieties and misery.

By then in a way I was self-sufficient, earning a decent sum, at least by teenage standards, through tutoring up to four or five pupils. I paid my school fees (I had a scholarship worth half the tuition fees), was able to clothe myself and still kept some pocket money. From time to time, especially in the last week of the month, my mother asked me to 'lend' her a few *pengő*s to tide her over until the arrival of the next money order from Budapest. More often than not, the 'loan' was not repaid. I should have felt glad that I could help, but to my deep shame I must admit that I was sometimes resentful. Why was my father so helpless? Why didn't he pull up his socks and find some work? The very thought of such unkindness now makes me shudder. I prefer to recall another 1939 poem in which I presented as a fact what in truth was only a wish and an encouragement, namely that in spite of his age, he should go on fighting and singing the praises of life.

I can still clearly recall the September day in 1939 when the radio announced the outbreak of the war. As Hungary was not yet involved, it only produced an odd feeling without immediate consequences. At home, we thought that the British and the French with their world empires would make mincemeat of the Germans, but this turned out to be just wishful thinking. One of my great-uncles, a little less starry-eyed, seriously suggested that my parents should send me to London, where one of his friends would look after me and would train me in the clothing business, a trade that knows no national boundaries! Whether I would have made a good tailor I have reason to doubt, but in any case I thought that the idea was quite insane. Neither my childhood dream of foreign travel, nor even the undeniable lure of England, made any impact on me. I was determined to stay with my family. Had I agreed to sail to Britain in 1939, the most likely advantage I would have gained would have been a quasi-native English pronunciation without the noticeable accent I am lumbered with. People who know my background claim that it is Hungarian, though I prefer to describe it as cosmopolitan.

Incidentally, my only contact with Britain in the war years was through the Hungarian news service of the BBC, nicknamed 'Vitamin J' because of its beneficial effects on Jewish morale. The star performer was a Professor Macartney, who broadcast once a week. In those days he was just a name for me, a name that sank into oblivion after the war. However, more than twenty years later, shortly after my arrival in Oxford, I was invited to dine at All Souls on a Sunday. Wearing my first, freshly acquired dinner jacket to conform to the custom of the college, I found myself seated between the Warden, John Sparrow, and a tall elderly man by the name of Dr C. A. Macartney, an expert on Austro-Hungarian history. 'Would you be by any chance ... ?' To my amazement, he was. Afterwards, each time I met him, usually at the local garage where he was filling his decrepit car with petrol, I remembered his voice echoing in the streets of Gyula in the early 1940s, listened to, despite the strict prohibition against tuning in to the BBC, by all and sundry, including rabid Nazis, because of his unbelievably funny Hungarian accent.

My last years at the gymnasium began with late-adolescent rebelliousness and culminated in an experience of 'excommunication' inflicted on me by the majority of my classmates.

Throughout my schooldays I was known as a well-brought-up and law-abiding schoolboy. My general behaviour mark was as good as those I obtained in all other subjects, except on one occasion. When I was approaching sixteen and thought that by being such a goody-goody I was missing out on something, I decided to be more unruly than usual. But when at the end of the term the form-master read out the marks of each of us before the whole class and I heard that despite my unruliness I had been given 'excellent' for behaviour, I burst out laughing. The master noticed it, and no doubt made up his mind to teach me a lesson, so on the following occasion I was given a '2' instead of a '1'.

It was about the same time that I nearly got into serious trouble with the school authorities. A group of youngsters from my home neighbourhood, about half of them pupils of the gymnasium, used to meet on Sunday mornings to gamble in a workshop belonging to the father of one of us. Strictly speaking, our card game was illegal since the workshop counted as a public place, where no gambling was permitted. The father of one of the participants, in despair because of his inability to control his son, decided to report the matter to the police. Two detectives raided the 'casino' and our names were taken. In the normal course of events, the matter would have been brought to the knowledge of the headmaster, who would have taken a rather dim view of it. So I thought I'd better confess to my father, who had a word with the local chief of police. We all had to turn up a few days later at the police station, were firmly told off and dismissed with 'Don't you dare do it again!' I took this to heart, and since then have generally been law-abiding.

In 1941, a third series of anti-Jewish laws was enacted. By this time Jewishness was defined on a racial basis and not by religious affiliation. Restrictions deriving from it did not apply to secondary education, but some oppressive measures slipped in through the back door. A weekly session of pre-military training was made compulsory for boys over sixteen, and since the new laws demanded that in the army Jews should serve in special labour units, the teacher in command of these military classes decided to apply the same kind of discrimination to us. He was a brilliant sports instructor, admired and liked by all of us, but he suddenly turned into a self-important despot. So while the 'Aryan' boys received their army drill and patriotic indoctrination, the three Jews of my form were given manual work to do. My two friends, who incidentally survived the Holocaust and with whom I am still in contact,[2] had to sweep the school courtyard or engage in some similar labour which was more demeaning than exhausting. I, in turn, was borrowed by the Catholic chaplain and religion teacher who out of kindness requisitioned me to do some futile clerical work for him in the office of the school janitor. As I 'worked' indoors, I was not exposed to the gaze of the rest of the school. Nevertheless I was deeply distressed by this undeserved indignity and dreaded the Mondays of shame, despite the sympathy shown to the three of us by some of the teachers and, at the beginning at least, by many of our class-mates.

However, a number of them whole-heartedly embraced the Nazi ideology of the new era and were determined to extend the discrimination in force during the premilitary practice to the everyday life of the school. At some secret meeting to which, apart from the sports instructor, no teacher was privy, they resolved that a complete boycott should be applied to the Jewish members of the form. We were to become nonentities who were not to be greeted or spoken to in any circumstances. What I found particularly wounding was that the ringleader used to be a friend who in previous years had sat next to me in class. The move could not be ascribed to stupidity as the fellow, whose surname was Ördög (=Devil) – '*Nomen est omen*', one might say! – was among the top students of the class, though I would characterize him as a fairly gifted plodder rather than a truly clever boy. I prefer not to speculate on his motivation, as he has been dead for more than half a century. He was the first of our group to fall on the Russian front.[3]

Since the boycott was not inspired from higher up, being exclusive to our form in the whole school, I am sure I am not over-neurotic or conceited in suggesting that it had something to do with me. The other two Jewish pupils did not play a sufficiently high-profile role in the life of the class to have accounted for this unparalleled manoeuvre.

Being a loyal comrade and a top performer, I was reasonably popular among my peers. To explain what I mean by loyal comrade, it is necessary to sketch the general ethos – if this is the right word for it – that prevailed in our gymnasium, and probably in all other similar institutions in Hungary. It was the extreme opposite of the spirit of honour and fair play that used to characterize school life in Britain. Here, until recent times, cheating was thought despicable. I know of a fourteen-year-old boy who tore up the essay written for him by his over-ambitious father, preferring punishment for failure to produce his homework to dishonestly gained kudos. My comrades would have called him stupid.[4] In our Central European world, teachers and pupils belonged to opposite camps and were in open warfare with one another. The student's job was to obtain the best possible result by whatever means, whereas the masters' duty was to prevent irregularities. Those who were caught could blame only themselves. By contrast, the successful had nothing to be ashamed of; on the contrary, they could pride themselves on their cleverness.

Utterly unethical though they may appear to me today, these unorthodox means seemed perfectly acceptable in my schooldays. Indeed, provision of help to the less fortunate in any possible way was a kind of social responsibility for a good student. The main opportunity for such assistance arose on the occasion of regular written tests conducted under the supervision of a teacher, especially tests in Latin, German, French and mathematics. My task was to draft a translation or solution as fast as possible, reproduce it in half a dozen carbon copies and pass these on without being noticed by the teacher – the 'professor', as secondary school masters were called. I have no recollection of ever being caught. Once the drafts reached their destination, it was up to each client to make sensible use of them. It would have been counter-productive for a mediocre pupil to hand in a faultless paper. There were occasional hiccups when a mistake in the master copy was reproduced by all and sundry. I have no doubt that the teachers guessed what was afoot, but they too played the game.

The boycott of course deprived the beneficiaries of the help on which they had previously relied. Yet such was the influence of the bullies – who improvised a new system of 'assistance' – that only three boys, Steve Lang, Louis Pfaff and Francis Tarnay by name, had the courage to resist. They did not do so for selfish reasons; having been my friends from primary school days, they rebelled against the unfairness of it. Their bravery offered some solace during those harsh months. So also did the continued friendship of the one girl, Kate Vincze, who attended the classes as a private pupil and of whom I was particularly fond. Those four were the only ex-classmates whom I contacted on my first return to Hungary in 1968 after twenty-two years of absence. Kate was by then the wife of Steve, and a qualified paediatrician. I have remained in touch with all four of them to this day, although we have little in common apart from memories of youth.

The approach of the school-leaving examination brought home to the majority of the form that they needed me more than I needed them and the ostracism disintegrated. I reverted to my old role, and one day I overheard two former boycotters admitting that I was 'a decent chap after all'. It gave me some comfort and a quiet feeling of victory. However, for a long time I remained bruised, and the wound did not completely heal until 1992, when I first revisited my old school on the fiftieth anniversary of our leaving it. Reconciliation with my erstwhile 'enemies' was made easier by the knowledge of imminent public recognition in Hungary. Two days later I was to deliver a major address in the main auditorium of the Academy of Sciences in Budapest.

The *matura*, corresponding to British A-levels but twice as broad, took place at the end of the eighth year in the gymnasium. For me this was in the early summer of 1942. It constituted the essential part of the final year's school result and qualified the successful candidates for university entrance and in due course, provided you were not Jewish, for a commission in the army. I was given top marks in every subject, though my success in mathematics was due half to luck, half to a good acting performance. During the oral examination I was asked to demonstrate some theorem which I had not had time to revise during my final preparation for D-day. I knew how to start off, but felt sure that beyond a certain point I would get lost. Concealing my worries, I went to the blackboard firmly determined to appear cool as cucumber, in full command of the situation. At the same time, I kept on repeating to myself: 'Don't rush! It's essential to gain time.' So I proceeded unhurriedly. I avoided easy short cuts, calmly spelling out every detail of the demonstration. At the penultimate line before my knowledge ran out, the external examiner intervened. 'I think this will be enough,' I heard him saying, 'You seem to be familiar with this problem.' An enormous invisible sigh of relief followed. I passed the examination with the highest honours.[5]

With the completion of my gymnasium education, the next step towards the future had to be decided. The matter was in the forefront of my and my family's thinking during the final school year. I certainly wanted to carry on with studies, but the general view was that in the prevailing conditions I had no chance of being admitted to a university. In other circumstances I think I would have chosen Hungarian literature, as I was still dreaming of a vocation in poetry and *belles lettres*. But to the great surprise of many, I opted for the Catholic priesthood. With its six-year philosophical and theological curriculum, this seemed to provide the only real prospect for higher education.

I truly cannot remember when this idea was first mooted; I believe it came from one of my very practical great-aunts, who thought that a seminary would offer me not just an opportunity for further study, but also security if the bad times continued, since ordained Christian ministers of Jewish origin enjoyed exemption. The idea of becoming a priest did not strike me as extraordinary, since despite my recent experiences of discrimination I still saw myself as a Catholic, albeit with Jewish ancestry. The implications of celibacy did not act as a deterrent. I knew that final commitment was still years ahead, whereas the urge to go on studying was irresistible. Learning was my primary aim; the rest formed the necessary means, which I accepted in all honesty.

With hindsight, I would love to know what exactly went through my mind in those days, but my recollections are hazy. I would say that at the age of eighteen Catholicism for me was part of twelve years of upbringing, a reality taken for granted rather than an external object of analysis and reflection. I was not fired by curiosity about great theological issues. I don't think I was aware of them. The religious teaching we received in school from Father Anthony Szabados, a very gentle middle-aged ailing priest (he had only one lung), was of a traditional, non-exciting, indeed pedestrian kind. We were told that religion was something to be learned from the church and practised, not something to be discussed. By the way, during the eight years of religious instruction in the gymnasium, I had never been given a Bible; it was for Protestants. We had to have a prayer book and a rosary instead. I attended mass on Sundays and feast days, occasionally even during the week; also afternoon litanies in honour of the Virgin Mary, Mother of God, every day in the month of May. I recall the strange smell that prevailed in the churches: a mixture of the scent of spring flowers and incense. Naturally, I abstained from meat on Friday, and tried to obey the church rules as well as I could, as far as my not very religious surroundings and the urges of adolescence allowed.

I was interested in the opposite sex and learned to dance at the age of fourteen or fifteen; I went to school balls and had some girl friends, but this did not lead to any deeper involvement. So when I decided to apply for entry into a theological college, I had some idea of what I was going to miss. We must have discussed the matter at home because I can still see tears in my mother's eyes and hear her muttered complaint: 'But then I won't have any grandchildren.'

In my position, thinking of a clerical future was one thing, realizing it was quite another. I had a talk with my teacher of religion, who listened very kindly and encouraged me to go ahead, promising his support. Looking for intellectual challenge, I first approached the Jesuits, reputed for their excellence. By return came a polite but terse note of rejection. Naturally I did not know then that in those days the Society of Jesus refused in principle to tolerate Jewish converts among its ranks.

This first rebuff did not discourage me; I have always been rather tenacious. I lowered my aim, and sent an application to the theological college of the local diocese of Nagyvárad, then in Hungary, now again in Romania. I explained my circumstances and was delighted to receive an invitation to an interview. No doubt the warm recommendation from Father Szabados, a priest of the same diocese, was largely responsible for this initial success. I was to show my knowledge of religion, answer questions about myself, and – the sting in the tail – sing a hymn of my choice.

The day of the interview arrived and I travelled by train to Nagyvárad. I was warmly received by the professors of the seminary and one or two grandfatherly canons of the cathedral. I met the other candidates, perhaps half a dozen in all, and to my astonishment I discovered that they included another of my kind, i.e. of Jewish origin, Miki Frank, who became a close friend for many years. He is still a priest. For years he was attached to the charitable organization Caritas, in Rome. He visited me once in Belgium in 1948 and a couple of times in Oxford, but afterwards we somehow lost touch until in 1997 I bumped into him in Munich. He now commutes between Budapest and Munich as director of Caritas in both places.

The interview took place in a large eighteenth-century room. I was perfectly composed and handled all the questions, including those relating to my family background, to my, and apparently the committee's, satisfaction. But then I was faced with what I most dreaded: the singing test. The truth is that I cannot sing. More exactly, my singing is completely unpredictable. To my surprise, I performed my chosen hymn faultlessly, but when the cathedral organist played a note on the harmonium and asked me to sing it, the result was disastrous. He tried again and the outcome was the same. 'How extraordinary!', I heard him commenting, 'This young man can sing a hymn, but is unable to repeat a note.'

I thought that was the end of my career as a seminarian. I was soon reassured, however, and told that I was expected to report in September of that year (1942), not to Nagyvárad where theology was taught during the final four years of training, but to the philosophical college in Szatmár, for the first two years of study. At home we were delighted. For a short while it was forgotten that Hungary had entered the war; that the Nazis, already masters of Western Europe, were triumphant on the Eastern front, and that Rommel's tanks were approaching Alexandria.

In our momentary fool's paradise we could not imagine the horrors that lay ahead.

4

From Boredom to Nightmare

(1942–1944)

All that has been written so far derives from patchy recollections occasionally assisted by photographs and poems. My account of the two years which start in September 1942 in dull Szatmár, where my first theological college was situated, and ends in Budapest, besieged and conquered by the Red Army in December 1944, suffers more than the previous chapters from a lack of documentation: notes, letters or diaries. Nine months of Nazi tyranny are to be blamed for their absence. Also, a mechanism of self-protection seems to have deleted many important details from my memory. However, some of these resurfaced when I stared at photographs dating from that period which almost miraculously survived.

At the end of the summer of 1942 I collected my belongings, mostly clothes and books, and filled several suitcases with them, in readiness for a 100-mile journey to Szatmár, a city in north-eastern Hungary regained two years earlier from Romania. This was the first time that I was leaving my parents for a lengthy period, nine months to be precise. Seminarians were not allowed to go home at Christmas and Easter – they were too busy during those festive periods; they could return only for the summer vacation between the end of June and the first week of September. Naturally I was a little nervous, but also anxious to embark on a voyage of discovery. And a voyage of discovery it was, though not quite what I had imagined.

Szatmár (Satu Mare in Romanian) was a largish county town and the seat of a bishopric. The seminary was, if I remember correctly, part of a large complex, most of which was occupied by the offices and residential quarters of the bishop. It provided for two years of philosophical study; the four years of theology was taught in Nagyvárad. The college offered living accommodation of a fairly primitive kind for the twenty-five or so students, the majority of whom came from peasant stock and were used to an unsophisticated existence. Apart from myself, only two seminarians had an educated background: Nicholas 'Miki' Frank, the 'Jewish' boy whom I had met at the interview session, whose father was a consultant physician in

Budapest, and another who was the son of a primary school teacher. After a couple of weeks came the great day when for the first time we donned a soutane. It was blue, not black, to distinguish us from real priests, and we also had to wear a black bowler hat. Imagine an eighteen-year-old in such an outfit. The photo which shows me so equipped, standing in the snow, still makes me laugh.

We slept in a communal dormitory where not even a curtain separated the beds. After an early rise (at 5.30 a.m. I reckon) and a few minutes of physical exercises directed by one of the students, we went to the chapel to spend about ninety minutes there in prayer, meditation and attending the daily mass. On Sundays and festivals we were led to the nearby cathedral for a solemn sung service at which two of the more senior seminarians, dressed as deacon and sub-deacon, assisted the celebrating canon. This odd custom – normally only ordained sub-deacons and deacons would be permitted to perform those offices – deserves mention because of its significance at a later stage of this story.

Meals, quite decent ones by wartime group standards, were served in the refectory; study and reading took place, not in private, but in a common hall. Only the theology students in Nagyvárad were granted the privilege of individual study/bedrooms during the last four years of the six-year pro- gramme. I was greatly looking forward to the classes given by the director of the college and two or three other teachers. In addition to the main subject, philosophy, the first two years of the curriculum included courses on apologetics and church history. The lectures were not particularly excit- ing, to put it mildly. Philosophy and apologetics were taught in Latin. This caused me no problem, but most of my colleagues found the language hurdle placed in front of an already difficult subject unreasonably tough. They were given remedial classes and we all were ordered to converse only in Latin during the morning break. I don't think Cicero would have been impressed.

The professors seemed to be bored and consequently were boring. Most of their lectures consisted in reading aloud from a textbook, with a comment here and there. They made no attempt to interest us in the mysteries of thought, let alone wisdom. Church history, the subject of the director, a mild, short and rotund priest in his fifties, was taught in Hungarian out of a multi-volume popular work. We were given an abridged version. After the class, we borrowed the teacher's volume in which the relevant sections were underlined with pencil and marked our copies accordingly. Needless to say, I coped without much effort, making some of my hard-working colleagues not a little jealous. I finished the first semester, and those which followed, with top marks. At that stage I was not particularly upset by the primitiveness of the lectures. Finishing the course-work in no time, I used most of my days to read literature and literary criticism, enjoying and still writing poetry of some sort, and taking an interest in modern philosophy, particularly in Henri Bergson. I was not desperately bored yet.

Recreation consisted in ball games, football and especially volley-ball, which was new to me. However, for a novice I did not do too badly at the net, perhaps because of my height. In the winter I could return to my favourite skating on the ice rink of a neighbouring school. Almost every day we went for a walk in a group. This often took us through the ghetto of Szatmár. I had never seen the like of it before. Gyula had no Jewish quarter. In Makó there were two streets familiarly known as Little Jewish Street and Great Jewish Street, but we did not live there, and I have no recollection of them.[1] However, Szatmár had a Jewish population of some 13,000, of whom a good many were 'Satmarer' Hasidim. The sight of the small pale-faced boys with long and curly side-locks, each of whom wore a small caftan plus a skull cap *and* a hat upset me, but I was also secretly fascinated by this strange but intense world. My first visit to the extreme orthodox Meah Shearim quarter of Jerusalem ten years later brought back to me the image of the by then annihilated Jewish streets of Szatmár and their sombre-clothed inhabitants.

Half way through the first semester I caught scarlet fever from another student and we were quarantined for a number of weeks in the infirmary. This accidental seclusion from the outside world turned out to be providential. For it was during that period that young men born in 1924 were summoned to be registered with the army and were provided with military identity papers. Had I read the street posters and obeyed the call, the cover of my recruitment booklet (like that of Miki Frank, which I saw much later) would have borne a large *ZS* (for *zsidó* =Jew) on its front cover. But the contagious disease kept me indoors in happy ignorance of my duty to enrol, and no one told me about it. This in turn meant that the army had no formal knowledge of my existence, nor was I ever called up for compulsory labour service.

Seminarians, like all other young people, had to take part in pre-military training. In Szatmár, the weekly sessions were conducted by a young Jesuit. He was not greatly concerned with theory or drill and we used him as our window on the big world outside. We had no access to newspapers or to the wireless. It was through this man that I learned that the war was reaching a turning point in the Allies' favour; that Montgomery had routed the Afrika Korps at Alamein and that the advancing German armies in the USSR had first been halted at Stalingrad, and then forced into a retreat which proved unstoppable. I was only too ready to believe in the imminence of a sunnier future.

The first year in Szatmár ended and I was glad to return home, little suspecting that this would be for the last time. I took up tutoring again and had the immense pleasure of helping (gratis, it goes without saying) a close friend to pass his repeat A-level examination, to his elderly father's immense relief. As was expected of me, I took part in various religious ceremonies on the occasion of feasts occurring in those months, unaware of the rumours this provoked in certain circles. Another episode which had unforeseen consequences happened when the Italian army was on the point of surrendering in the late summer of 1943. My father, a steady pipe and cigar smoker all his life, stopped one day to buy cigars at a tobacco shop run by the mother of one of my schoolmates. There was a shortage and he either met with a blank refusal or was given fewer cigars than he thought he was entitled to, which made him angry. Implicitly hinting at the events in Italy, he told the woman that no doubt soon life would change in Hungary, too, putting an end to the kind of nonsense of which he had been the victim. We all thought that his outburst, attributable to the heat of the moment, would soon be forgotten. We were wrong.

By the time I rejoined the seminary in the autumn of 1943, my intellectual patience with the pedestrian teaching was completely exhausted. In the end, I screwed up courage and asked for a transfer to the Central Theological College attached to the University of Budapest. I explained in all honesty and modesty that in order to give the diocese my best, I needed a greater challenge. I was firmly put in my place by the authorities in pious jargon: I should consider my situation a test of my humility; also, in a true spirit of obedience I had to accept the decision of my superiors. And this decision was negative. On that occasion, or perhaps a little later, I was told that my high-profile presence in church services in Gyula during the previous summer had upset some of the parishioners imbued with the spirit of the new Hungary. My superiors did not share their views, but in the circumstances I ought to be more circumspect, ought I not? Also, did I know that my father had been charged with slandering the nation? I did not. My parents obviously wanted to spare me the embarrassment. I never learned the details; all I know is that the case was connected with the argument in the tobacco shop. My father's words to the owner about impending changes were interpreted as an announcement that Hungary would soon lose the war. I was reassured by my mother that there was nothing to worry about. The best lawyer in the town who, although a Jew, was universally respected, had volunteered to defend him and he was bound to be found not guilty.[2] The case never reached the courts: it was overtaken by darker events. Suddenly I came to realize that beyond the appearances of relative security, danger was looming on the horizon.

Compared to the Nazi treatment of the Jews in the rest of occupied Europe, the situation of Hungarian Jewry was extraordinarily privileged up to the spring of 1944. Members of the professions and other persons in leading positions had had their freedom of action curtailed, but Jewish existence as such was not formally threatened. Young men called up for auxiliary military service on the Russian front were exposed to danger – not just from the enemy, but also, and often in particular, from their Hungarian guards. But at the beginning at least the numbers were limited: the upper age limit was originally twenty-five; it was raised to thirty-seven in April 1943. Taking into account Hungarian corruption, no doubt a good many exemptions could be negotiated. There must have been much administrative incompetence, exemplified for instance by officialdom's failure to notice that I did not register with the military.

Most assimilated Hungarian Jews simply did not believe that the hard times could be anything but a passing ordeal. They were just a little worse than the periodic antisemitic outbursts of the past. What with the war going as it did in North Africa, Italy and Russia … A little more patience and the troubles would all be over. Meanwhile they could cheer themselves up as usual with a good Jewish joke. I first heard of systematic murder in death camps in the summer of 1944, when my beloved great-aunt Gizi, her eyes filled with tears, asked me whether I thought that we might all end up as soap. Even then, in much worsened circumstances, this seemed inconceivable.

I have recently discovered a few precious mementoes, the only surviving specimens of my parents' handwriting: two cards for my name's day (26 February 1944), more important than a birthday in Hungary, and two delivery forms of food parcels – containing delicacies rather than essentials – with mini-messages scribbled on the back to 'darling Geza'. 'With much love Mummy and Daddy', concludes the one signed by my mother; 'With many kisses Your Father', reads the other. They are dated 13 January and 15 February 1944 and mark the end of an era.

By the early spring of 1944 German defeat on both the Eastern and the Western fronts appeared inevitable, and rumours were circulating that the Hungarian government was looking for ways and means to extricate the country from the war. As a counter-measure, on 19 March German forces moved into Hungary. The prime minister was removed and replaced by a puppet of Hitler, until then Hungarian ambassador to the German Reich in Berlin. On the same day SS Obersturmbannführer Adolf Eichmann arrived in Budapest to organize the final solution for the Jews of Hungary.

A few days later a government decree compelled every person classified as a Jew to wear a canary-yellow star of David. Plans were laid out for the deportation of more than half a million people. The real nightmare started.

I was stunned and felt completely helpless. With the church authorities' connivance I decided not to put on the yellow star. Another parcel delivery form, dated 4 April, brought me food and 'kisses' from 'Mummy'. She promised a letter and suggested that I should find out how the Budapest relations were coping. They were as all right as possible in the circumstances, and a few days later I received a relatively substantial money order from them, no doubt intended for my parents. The next message (6 May) accompanied a large parcel containing the best part of my parents clothes' and read: 'My darling Geza, We are going to be removed from home. This is why I am sending the clothes. Thank God, we shall remain in Gyula. Send no money! I have got over it by now. Kisses. Mummy.' How typical of her, that penultimate phrase. *She* was trying to reassure me.

Another letter, which I no longer have, followed soon afterwards. In it she informed me that my father had been arrested and taken to a concentration camp in a village called Csertő in north-eastern Hungary. Would I send him food? I did, but the parcel was returned with the notice 'addressee unknown'. My father was apprehended in a first raid on 'unreliable elements' of potential influence: politicians, journalists, known Communists, etc. That he was a Jew was an additional black mark, but not the essential reason for his removal. That he no longer had a newspaper in which to vent his 'subversive ideas' did not seem to bother the authorities.

Shortly after the war had ended, by chance I met in a village near Gyula an agricultural labourer, who was a leading local Communist and long-standing Party member. My clerical garb did not endear me to him, but when he heard my name, his attitude changed. He told me that he had been picked up by the police at the same time as my father and for a short while shared the hardships of the Csertő camp with him until the Jews were rounded up and dispatched towards an unknown destination. He remembered my father well as the man who always used to walk up and down with a book in his hand, reading. When he learned that my father did not come back, he looked into my eyes and said, 'If you will allow me, I will be your father. That's the least I can do for a comrade prisoner who is dead.' Such a manifestation of genuine and spontaneous goodness by this warm-hearted simple man deeply moved me.

In the streets of Szatmár I saw groups of stunned Jews herded by the gendarmes in the direction of the railway station. People looked on, showing no compassion. I think most Hungarians would have disapproved of gas chambers, but would not have objected to a forcible removal of the Jews to some distant foreign land. Even one of my colleagues in the seminary showed such insensitivity that when one day a young Jew was given temporary shelter among us, this prospective priest set out to explain to this bewildered boy whose family had just been deported that the Jews were just getting what they had bargained for. Weren't they? I gave him a very dirty look, but he was impervious. Most of the others appeared embarrassed, but said nothing. Even my world, protected by the walls of a church institution, began to shake. I felt dazed and could not believe what was happening before my eyes. With hindsight, I suppose I should have rebelled. I didn't. Instead I was praying for the horrible dream to go away. It didn't.

About the end of May one of my superiors – I cannot remember which one – gently informed me that for the sake of my own safety it would be better if I left the seminary and remained out of sight, preferably in some place where I was not known, until things had calmed down. I was to report to the authorities of my diocese at Nagyvárad for further instructions.

In Nagyvárad I was told that in the first instance I should quietly go to Gyula where the Fathers of the Salesian order would hide me, and arrange a meeting with my mother. They would then direct me to another house of theirs. I was also provided with a document which I was to show only if challenged.

This sheet of yellowing paper, still in my possession, is a masterpiece of double-talk in splendid officialese. It claims that I was qualified for exemption from the anti-Jewish decrees on account of being an ordained deacon in the Catholic Church. Of course I was not an ordained deacon, as I was only in my second year of training and one did not reach deacon status until the sixth year. But I was allowed to act as a deacon more than once in cathedral services at Szatmár. This is implied by the legal mumbo-jumbo, which I find rather hard to put into intelligible English.

From the Office of the Bishop of Nagyvárad of the Latin Rite

2760/1944
CERTIFICATE ISSUED BY THE CHURCH AUTHORITY

I, the undersigned, have the honour to certify that Geza Vermes, of Jewish origin, seminarian of the Latin Rite diocese of Nagyvárad, and at present student in the seminary at Szatmár, having performed by virtue of an official decision, after his investment in 1942 as a student priest, the office of deacon at the altar, is for the competent ecclesiastical authority an

ordained deacon and is consequently entitled to the exemption stated in the ministerial decree 1460/1944. M.E. 1.§.1 [1].
Nagyvárad, 25th May 1944

Dr Béla Schriffert
Episcopal Deputy

I don't suppose I would have dared present this paper to anyone, but during the seven months of incessant peregrination and semi-clandestine existence that followed, fortunately I was never asked to produce any identification.

I am unable to recall how I travelled to Gyula, but I arrived at the students' home of the Salesians, an order dedicated to religious education, still in one piece. I was kept away from the gaze of the pupils. My meals were brought to my room and I remained out of sight even during mass. Under some pretext, the superior obtained a permit for my mother to leave the ghetto. I have already sketched our heartbreaking last encounter, and I cannot bring myself to repeat it. During my 1994 return visit to Gyula, I suddenly found myself in front of the unchanged Salesian convent building and my heart overflowed with sorrow.

After a stay of three or four days in Gyula I was despatched to another Salesian institution in Ujpest, a northern suburb of Budapest. I was well received by a friendly Salesian priest – his name escapes me – who was the director of the school and residential home. The place was empty of students, who had already gone home for the summer. The director obviously enjoyed the reputation of being kind and generous and I often saw him in the company of people who were visibly upset. One day I accidentally overheard the plea of a Catholic woman asking him for help because her Jewish husband had been taken by the police to a fairly distant detention camp. The director agreed to do what he could, but shocked me when he audibly muttered to himself, still within the earshot of the distraught wife, 'If you had listened to our warnings against mixed marriages ...' However, a quarter of an hour later I saw him, with a rucksack on his back, on his way to find the missing husband.

I lived from day to day in total insecurity and prayed to stay sane and alive. Being discovered by the authorities was a permanent danger, but in a way it was less acute than the threat to life and limb from American and Soviet bombers. This was the summer of 1944, with twice-daily air raids on the Hungarian capital. Between 10 and 11 a.m. the American planes arrived from Italy and pounded the place. Late in the evening came the Russians, creating a conflagration with their incendiary bombs. The US Air Force was the more dangerous, and when I decided to go to central Budapest, which was almost every day, I saw to it that I was in an area of tall buildings with reasonably reliable shelters. By that time the Allies dominated the skies. We noticed German fighters only before and after the bombings. Despite the massive daily destruction, people somehow managed to go to work and do their shopping.

Again I cannot remember how, but I met and became attached to an impressive Dominican professor of theology by the name of Father George, and was thereafter a daily visitor in the convent's library. At last, in those terrible times, I was given a first inkling how I might stretch my mind. But this was not the moment for intellectual pursuits. However, this Dominican connection had later reverberations.

After a short period of acclimatization, I gained enough courage to go and investigate what was happening to my Budapest family, to my mother's relations. Compared to the utter devastation of the provincial Jews, who were all removed, mostly to Auschwitz, in the early summer, the large Jewish population of Budapest was relatively unharmed. It suffered no deportation, nor was a ghetto established in the capital until much later. Instead, individual houses were designated for Jews, usually apartment houses with mainly Jewish tenants. The authorities apparently imagined that Jewish presence throughout the capital would deter the allies from attacking the city from the air. This miscalculation allowed a substantial proportion of Budapest Jewry to survive the war.

I found two of my great-aunts and their husbands apprehensive, but fairly comfortable. To their enquiry whether I had any news of my parents, the answer was a sorrowful no. They shared a single rather luxurious flat and did not seem to lack food or other essentials, thanks to a large extent to Miki (Szántó – not to be confused with Miki Frank), the no-good son of my great-aunt Minus (Hermina). He was seven years older than I; as a child, I used to inherit his expensive toys and equally expensive clothes. He was spoiled in every way. He spoke three foreign languages like a native, having learned German from a living-in *Fräulein*, French from a *Mademoiselle* and English from a *Miss*. He went to the most expensive boarding school run by a Catholic religious order, although he and his parents were baptized Calvinists (for purely social reasons). Miki entered the Technical University in Budapest to read mechanical engineering and after graduation was meant to inherit the directorship of his father's factory. He failed his first-year examination and dropped out, secure in the knowledge that his doting mother would provide him with money. It goes without saying that he did not declare himself Jewish and put on the yellow star. Instead, he went into hiding. I met him on my first visit to the family. 'I have chosen the safest possible hiding place where no one would search for me:

I am sheltering in the lion's jaws.' With his fluency with the language, and no doubt furnished with false documents, he sought and found employment with the Germans as an interpreter. After the liberation, rumour had it in family circles that he was seen working with the Gestapo. After the German withdrawal he had to run. Two years later, at the time of my exit from Hungary, his distressed mother asked me to look for him in Vienna, but he was unknown at the address she gave me. According to the family, he successfully escaped to South America. I never heard from him or tried to discover his whereabouts. His one known good deed was to look after his family in those hard times.

My mother's remaining relations, two uncles and their wives and a widowed aunt, her two half-sisters Rose and Martha, and a half-brother, Alex, were also managing at that time. Martha, Alex and a cousin, the lawyer Feri (Francis), were murdered, and Feri's sister, Betty, committed suicide in the last months of 1944, during the terror unleashed by the Hungarian Nazis. They were known as the 'Arrow-cross' men, after the Magyar version of the swastika which they wore on their arm-bands.

My safe stay in Ujpest lasted about two months; by August 1944 I was again in Nagyvárad, in the senior seminary. How this came about I can no longer recall, but I must have been called back there by the authorities, who judged that the heat was no longer on. All I do remember is that there were numerous air raids by the Russians during which the enormous cellars of the episcopal palace were filled with all the neighbours. Luckily, we were never hit. By contrast, my college in Szatmár was completely demolished by Russian bombers in September 1944. One of my former teachers and two fellow students were killed and a third one was pulled out alive from the rubble. If I had not been sent away from there three and a half months earlier, I would almost certainly have been sheltering in the same cellar.[3]

Every night, even when there were no bombings, we could hear Soviet transport planes flying over the city. They were nicknamed 'Tito-buses', carrying supplies to the Yugoslav resistance. I distinctly remember also listening to a BBC broadcast in the home of a Szatmár colleague who was a Nagyvárad boy, announcing the liberation of Paris on 25 August. The future once more appeared promising. In the West, the British and the American forces were approaching Germany; in the East, two Soviet armies were practically on the Hungarian border. Little did I suspect that what for me would be the worst two months of the war still lay ahead.

Why I left Nagyvárad some time in September is unclear. I guess it must have been my own decision to return to Ujpest and the Salesians. As my next port of call was the city of Sopron in the extreme west of Hungary on the Austrian border, my links with the Dominicans whose theological college was situated there must have been the incentive for this move. With the assistance of Father George, the professor whom I had befriended earlier that summer, I was given permission to attend their theology lectures without being a member of the order. I timidly enquired whether I might join them, but was told that such plans should await more opportune times.

The Dominicans found a family willing to provide me with bed and board. No doubt I received some money from my church authorities and, I believe, also from my family, so that I was able to finance my stay. I hoped that it would be of limited duration as the Russians were already in eastern Hungary. The higher quality of teaching did not make up for the lonely existence in a totally unknown place. I had to be continuously on my guard lest compromising words should escape my lips. This happened once in the presence of my landlady and I was truly frightened. In the middle of October, I believe it was the 15th, out of the blue the Hungarian radio broadcast an order from Nicholas Horthy, the head of state known as the Regent, instructing the army to cease fighting the Russians who had already occupied the eastern third of the country.[4] I naively imagined that the war and the German oppression were over, was overjoyed and did not conceal my delight. Extreme concern appeared on the face of the landlady, whose husband was a civil servant. What I did not know was that as soon as his proclamation to the Hungarian forces was released, Horthy was arrested by the Germans and political power was handed over by them to Ferenc Szálasi, leader of the extreme Nazi Arrow-cross party. Instead of peace, we were facing bloody terror. Living alone in Sopron spelled danger. Once more I had to get on the move and run fast. But where to?

From the moment I left Szatmár at the end of May, I had been heading westwards, ending up in Sopron, within miles of the German Reich. Now I had to travel in the opposite direction: salvation (through the Russians) was beckoning from the east. I had to reach Budapest again but it was now the centre of the Arrow-cross power. The only relatively safe place there would be the Central Theological Seminary, with a large number of students among whom I could disappear.

Roughly half-way between Sopron and the capital lies the city of Győr where my former parish priest from Gyula, Baron William Apor, was then the bishop. I decided to knock on his door in the hope that he would remember me. I packed my suitcase, got on a train and turned up at the palace without an appointment. I timidly requested to see the bishop and was received at once. He could not have been kinder. He was genuinely sorry to hear what happened to my parents and I had to tell him about my wanderings. He was curious to see the exemption certificate which I was carrying and read through its roundabout verbiage with an increasingly perplexed look on his face. It would never have occurred to this noble but simple man to invent something so circuitous. In fact, his inability to twist the truth meant that he had lost the only Jewish convert student of his seminary. (He was the brother of Joseph Stiassny, a future colleague of mine among the Fathers of Notre-Dame de Sion. What a small world!) Bishop Apor probably felt a little guilty, so, if possible, he was even more generously disposed towards me. Could he do anything for me? Yes, help me to be admitted to the seminary in Budapest. Without hesitating for an instant, he picked up his notepaper, wrote a letter in longhand and gave it to me with his blessing. Overwhelmed, I expressed my thanks and took leave of him. I never saw him again. As I have mentioned earlier, he was shot dead by Russian soldiers on 2 April 1945 for his gallant defence of a group of women sheltering in his palace. He was fifty-three years old. A plaque with a dreadful bas-relief of his bust can now be seen on the wall of the parish church of Gyula, and a dreadful portrait of him hangs in the dining-room of the presbytery. He was beatified in Rome on 9 November 1997. I think he would be embarrassed if he knew. But he surely deserves pride of place in the annals of human nobility, goodness and courage.

Thanks to Bishop Apor's letter of recommendation, I was accepted in the Central Seminary without further ado. I found well over a hundred students resident there, among them my Szatmár friend, Miki Frank. Outside, terror reigned. Jews were forced into a ghetto and hundreds of people were led to the banks of the Danube and shot. A small number, including the majority of my family, managed to acquire and enjoy diplomatic (Swedish, Swiss and Vatican) protection in specially designated houses. But with gun-waving Arrow-cross men on the rampage, the streets were not a secure place for anyone, let alone for a Jew. There were three or four of us in the seminary. I know of one who was caught and considered himself extremely lucky when he got off with only a bad beating. His captors were no doubt in a generous mood. The nearest I came to serious peril was on the occasion when I was posted as guard at the lodge of the seminary. I heard a loud knock on the door. When I opened it, I found myself face to face with a uniformed and armed Arrow-cross man. My heart sank. I was in civilian clothes, wearing an open-necked shirt and unshaven. I did not look a clergyman. 'Brethren, come and bury the dead!', he shouted. Then his eyes met mine and for a moment he seemed puzzled. Fortunately the man was very drunk. Later I heard one of the officials of the seminary telling off the senior student who was in charge of allocating jobs: he was never to put me on guard duty again.

War noises became more and more deafening as December progressed.

First the Red Army abstained from launching a frontal attack on Budapest. Instead, they crossed the Danube south and north-west of the city and in a fast pincer movement cut off the retreat route of the Germans towards the west. The fate of some 50,000 SS soldiers was thus sealed. They fought desperately street by street, house by house, as they knew they would receive no quarter. Situated close to the Danube in Pest, the seminary was in one of the last sectors to fall. There was nothing to do but wait, hope and pray. We had several Russian speakers among the students, Ruthenians from north-eastern Hungary, who belonged to the Oriental Rite of the Roman church.[5] They were to explain to the Russian soldiers that we were no threat to them.

For a number of weeks the cellars of the college had been turned into a dormitory with rows of couches in every direction. On Christmas Eve, 24 December 1944, I went to bed still a marked man. The lights were extinguished. Around midnight I woke. There was pandemonium. A group of Red Army soldiers burst into the cellar with their submachine guns at the ready. One of our interpreters rushed to parley with the officer. He shouted something to his troops in Russian to the effect that everything was OK, these sleeping men were harmless.

After seven months on the run I was at last free, liberated, thank God. The roles were reversed and it was now the turn of the Nazis to flee. The worst of the nightmare was over.

5

From Darkness to Light

(1945–1946)

For days, even weeks, I felt completely stunned after that Christmas Day. It was hard truly to realize that, apart from unruly and often drunk Russian soldiers, there was nothing to fear any longer. It became possible to venture out into the streets. And what a mess they were in in those cold winter days! Everything lay in ruins after the fighting all over the place. There was no public transport. All the Danube bridges were floating in the water, blown up by the Germans as soon as they withdrew from Pest to Buda on the right bank of the river. Not that I intended to visit the older hilly part of the city where the battle was still raging. From the liberated east bank, one could watch with detached, almost cruel, eyes the bombs falling on the buildings in the area of the royal castle and hear the explosions. They were not aimed at us any more, but were directed towards the SS soldiers dug in in the hills who went on resisting to the last – until April, I think.

I was waiting for the first opportunity to get away. In miserable Budapest chaos reigned, and food was in short supply. With an anxious heart, I rang the bell at the door of the flat of one of my great-aunts, but found it occupied by Russians. There was no need for alarm. The two sisters and one of their brothers, and their spouses, all moved into another apartment, that of great-aunt Gizi, just a minute's walk away. They, the members of the older generation – in their sixties at the time – all survived, but three younger relations, an uncle, an aunt and a cousin, mentioned earlier were missing. They had been taken away and killed by Hungarian Nazis. A good deal of the survivors' belongings were destroyed or stolen by the men of the 'glorious Red Army', the commonly used official designation of the Soviet liberators.

The moment to get out of the city came in early February; the destination was Gyula, which used to be my *home*. But how to get there? There were no trains from Budapest, so with a small group of seminarians heading towards the east and the south, I walked about thirty kilometres in melting snow and mud before reaching the first active railway station, from which goods trains departed. I climbed on to an open wagon full of scrap metal and off we went. Each station we stopped at looked like a busy market-place. The local farmers offered food at exorbitant prices to the famished refugees from the capital. We would have paid any money for delicacies such as fresh milk, butter, cheese, home-baked bread and the like. Lack of hygiene and the fact that we were unaccustomed to rich food caused many a stomach upset, with easily imaginable consequences in the travelling conditions of those days. Later I graduated from my goods wagon to a train made up of decrepit passenger coaches. These became so full, especially close to the doors, that the crowds waiting at the later stations were all left behind except for the occasional individuals who managed to fight their way in, amid shouting and cursing, or were helped to climb in through a window. These abominable conditions characterized train travel for at least the best part of a year. Owing to a flourishing black market in food stuff, the space destined for passengers was occupied by pigs, chickens, ducks, geese and rabbits, and resembled a smelly and noisy farm-yard. The very idea of travel, first with non-existing and later with largely imaginary time-tables, filled me with nausea.

The 130-mile trip took the best part of a week, but finally, exhausted and filthy, I arrived in Gyula. Outwardly, the war had hardly touched the town. It escaped the bombings and was taken without a fight. Most of the people were the same. Only some of the younger men were missing, captured or killed on the Russian front. But *all* the Jews were also missing. The two months I spent there, housed in the Catholic presbytery, were occupied in a constant, but not very fruitful, effort to discover where I was, what I was to do and where.

Although the horrors perpetrated against the Jews by the Germans and their acolytes were known, the magnitude of the devastation was as yet unimaginable. I still entertained a genuine hope of my parents' homecoming. Home? I was told by local officials that all Jewish property had been confiscated by the former authorities, and what had survived destruction and plunder was kept in a depository. But the man in charge declared that he had no record of anything belonging to the Vermes family. Not only my parents, but also our goods and chattels were missing.

Postal and telephone services were non-existent between Hungary and the outside world, so there was no alternative to waiting, however painful it was. Nor could I communicate with my seminary in Nagyvárad, which by then was in a no man's land: it was due to revert from Hungary to Romania and be renamed Oradea once again. In early April, I decided to explore the situation there. I travelled with a haulier in his horse-drawn wagon and found the college still standing, but in a chaotic state inside, because of several months of occupation by Russian soldiers. The courses were just starting and I was summoned back. Still in a dizzy state, without a clear vision of my future, I decided to obey. Having obtained a promise from the clergy in Gyula that they would inform me at once if any news reached them of either of my parents, I packed up again and returned to the theological school.

Among the small number of students, I again met my friend Miki Frank and another Jewish convert, Andrew (Andy) Villányi. He was an extraordinary character, over twenty years our senior, with a doctorate in economics, a reserve lieutenant of the pre-Nazi army. The prime achievement in his life – or so he thought – was that he attended the wedding of King Zog of Albania and a Hungarian countess in Tirana at the end of the 1930s as a semi-official military delegate. Though already in priestly robes, he had been picked up together with the Nagyvárad Jews in the previous summer and put into a train for deportation, but escaped and nonchalantly retraced his steps to the seminary. It did not occur to anyone to look for him again there. The professors treated him more as a colleague than as a pupil and held him slightly in awe. For Miki and me, he was a worldly-wise benevolent avuncular figure who insisted on turning us into old-fashioned *gentlemen*. He remained a cherished friend over the years.[1] If I were asked now why as a Catholic seminarian I chose two seminarians of Jewish ancestry as my closest confidants, my honest conscious answer would be that I was not particularly aware of their Jewishness, but found them personally and intellectually more congenial than the rest. No doubt, subconsciously there was more to it than that. These friendships marked the start of a slow internal metamorphosis which took more than twenty years to mature.

Of that first term in the seminary in Nagyvárad, apart from the increasing worry and depression caused by the lack of news about my parents, only two matters have been clearly preserved in my memory. The first was a growing realization that even if I were to become a Catholic priest, ordinary church ministry in provincial Hungary would not be my cup of tea. I needed a more scholarly future environment, something the Dominican order could provide, I thought. This, needless to add, turned out to be a red herring.

With hindsight, I can identify the other experience which occurred in that Nagyvárad spring that actually contributed to the transformation of my ideas and aspirations. By that time I had reached the point where I knew that I would not make a good poet and thought, equally mistakenly, that my vocation was philosophy. A kind old canon of the cathedral presented me one day with a full Latin set of the works of Thomas Aquinas, of which I became an avid reader. Then, one day, early during my stay, I accidentally

entered a large room which used to be the study of the director of the
college, Dr Geza Folmann, the only teacher from Nagyvárad whose name
I still remember. I mentioned him earlier as the relation of our first doctor
in Gyula. The room was in total disorder brought about by Soviet soldiers.
Books and papers lay all over the place. It was quite a substantial library,
many of the volumes were in French, and the main subject was the Bible,
Old and New Testament, since Folmann was the professor of scripture in
the college. He willingly gave me permission to try to bring some order into
the chaos. I spent many a happy hour there, more in reading than in tidying up the place. For the first time I saw a Hebrew Bible. (The only Hebrew
book I remember having held in my hand was great-granny's prayer book.)
Several of the large pink-covered French tomes, the well-known series
Études Bibliques, were full of Hebrew quotations, as were also the issues of
the very learned periodical *Revue Biblique,* thrown all over the place. Both
the series of Bible commentaries and the journal were issued by the École
Biblique of the Jerusalem Dominicans. All this filled me with fascination
and an irresistible urge to learn Hebrew. In keeping with my pre-scholarly
views of the time, my conscious reason for this desire was to read Moses'
own words in the original language, but again, who knows what was going
on in my subconscious? To this experience, which had no immediate
consequences, I can confidently trace the origin of my future academic
vocation. I can no longer recall Folmann's lectures on the Bible, but his
continuous reminiscences of two years spent at the École Biblique in
Jerusalem just before the First World War, his travels in Palestine and the
Sinai peninsula, and unending stories about the founding fathers of the
School, the French Dominicans M.-J. Lagrange, H. Vincent and F.-M.
Abel remain vividly engraved on my mind. So too do the numerous
anecdotes concerning Brother Matthieu, a lay-brother, who befriended the
foreign students at the École. Vincent and Abel were still alive when I
stayed at the same École seven years later in 1952, and so was Frère
Matthieu, the only one to remember Folmann, who never made a name for
himself in the world of biblical scholarship.

The short session at the college ended at the beginning of July and I soon
found myself in Budapest, staying with my generous and long-suffering
great-aunt Gizi. Her flat housed herself and her husband, a sister and a
brother with their respective spouses, and penniless me. The main purpose
of the visit was the follow-up of my contacts with the Dominicans during
the previous year. When I tried to join them in Sopron in October 1944, I
was turned away with the comment that the moment was inopportune.
Times had changed since, and I felt I had to make a fresh attempt. The
Provincial of the order did not have the courage to turn me down straight

away – in fact the Dominicans were traditionally as unwilling to admit Jewish convert candidates as the Jesuits – and I wrote without delay a letter applying to become a postulant among the Dominicans. I was told that it would take a month or two before I was informed of their decision.

A three-week stay in Gyula in the middle of the summer brought no comfort. By that time, survivors of the Holocaust began to trickle home. My parents were not among them and no one had anything to report except one family friend, who as owner/manager of a printing firm, used to produce my father's newspapers. He returned from a labour camp in Austria, in reasonably good condition given the circumstances, and was waiting for his wife, who never arrived. When I asked him whether he knew anything about my father or mother, he first said no. Then, seeing the sadness on my face, he added, 'No, wait a second, I now remember that I saw the name of your father signed on the wall of the station in Vienna as well as that of David Szobel (a Jewish physician of Gyula)!' I think this was pure invention on his part, just to give me a grain of hope.[2] By that time, though not yet quite dead, hope was already waning.

My expectations for a Dominican future were also shattered. Shortly after my return to Budapest and the family, I received an icy letter of rejection. 'I regret to inform you that the council of the novice house has decided against your admission. Your brother in Christ,' signed the Provincial. That was that. It was then for the first time that the idea of the order of the Fathers of Notre-Dame de Sion, founded by two French Jewish converts, the brothers Ratisbonne, fleetingly crossed my mind. I had learned of their existence during my stay in the Central Seminary in Budapest the previous year. The Jesuits and the Dominicans were not interested in me, and I found diocesan priesthood more and more unappealing. Might Sion *in France* provide me with a home? I did not pursue the matter. I was too depressed to think constructively. For a few days I even toyed with the idea of giving up theology and a priestly career altogether, and entering the law faculty in Budapest instead. This was just a passing thought, but sufficiently powerful while it lasted to share with Miki Frank's father, who understandably was not quite sure how to react. I did not entertain it for long either. Nor did my burgeoning friendship, definitely no more than a friendship, with a girl whom I remember only as Magdi without a surname, have any serious influence on my planning. She was a neighbour of Miki Frank; I met her in the Frank's house and visited her a number of times. We enjoyed talking about poetry. During the intervening years her image had completely faded until I re-read my Budapest diary of the summer of 1945.

The month of September came, and with it the start of a new academic

year at the university. So I sought escape in study. Since direct communication with Nagyvárad was still impossible, I journeyed once more to
Gyula, obtained permission and a pittance of support from the local church
authorities, sold some of our goods[3] to supplement my finances, and
returned to Budapest. At long last I was able to become, to use the local
jargon, a citizen of the university, founded by a seventeenth-century cardinal, Peter Pázmány, through registering as a member of the theological
faculty.

My Hungarian university education lasted only a few weeks. Of the
lectures attended, I can only recall the Hebrew classes taught by an internationally known orientalist, Professor Joseph Aistleitner.[4] One of my
great-uncles wryly remarked when he saw me studying a Hebrew grammar:
'I see you're now busying yourself with what you should have learned as a
child.' The family was as loving and kind as ever, but I felt that any prolonged stay in those cramped conditions would be a serious burden on
them. I was very concerned because my 'capital' was insignificant and I
doubted whether I could earn enough money as a student to support
myself. So when out of the blue a letter came recalling me to Nagyvárad,
though unenthusiastic, I did not have the guts to say no. In my confused
thinking of the time – my surviving notes are full of pious, and indeed
embarrassing, platitudes – I persuaded myself that I was following the will
of God. Maybe I was, but not in the sense I imagined. Also, an entry of my
diary of 11 October notes that, according to Miki Frank, my friend Magdi
wanted to talk to me 'at any price'. I did not propose to leave without
saying good-bye, but no meeting could be arranged. So I hurried off to my
boring seminary and reached it after several days' journey on 19 October
1945.

Continuous self-examination and thinking during the next seven and a
half months in Nagyvárad enabled me to make some progress for the
future, mostly by way of elimination. More than ever before I became
convinced that ordinary parish priesthood was not for me, either in the
Nagyvárad diocese or anywhere else. Next, the Dominican fiasco brought
home to me the truth that anti-Judaism was still consciously or subconsciously at work in some of the leading organizations of the Catholic
Church. This realization, together with the experiences of the Nazi years,
nurtured my Jewish awareness deep down, although at that time I could not
imagine myself as anything but a Christian and was still set on continuing
my ecclesiastical studies. But I was longing for a congenial setting where
my Jewish origin would not be a disadvantage and where my intellectual
aspirations would be allowed to develop unhindered. Finally, having by
then accepted the idea that my parents were no longer alive, I wanted to

leave Hungary behind with all the horrors of the past, and start a new life in the West.

The Congregation of the Fathers of Notre-Dame de Sion appeared more and more the answer to my dreams. Erroneously I assumed that it was largely filled with converts. I knew that it was a French institution, with its centre in Paris, and I imagined (wrongly) that my French was quite good. I also learned from my seminarian informant in Budapest that the study house of the order was in Louvain in Belgium, next to a famous university, and that the congregation had establishments not only in France, Belgium and America, but also in Jerusalem. But what could I do, shut up in godforsaken Nagyvárad, which was being more and more re-Romanized?

For several months the dream remained a dream, but it inspired an increasing zeal to improve my French. I went on reading one book after another, irrespective of content, as long as they were written in French. I was also desperate to discover the address of the 'head office' of the Fathers of Sion. In a pre-war encyclopaedia I came across one. I did not know whether it was still valid or not, but I treasured it for weeks or months before I plucked up enough courage to sit down and compose a letter of application in French. Then came the greatest hazard: I had to entrust it to the care of the Romanian postal service, unreliable at the best of times even inland, let alone abroad. I had no choice. I prayed, bought a stamp, stuck it on the envelope and dropped it into a letter-box.

With the despatch of the letter, in March 1946 I guess, a long waiting period began. One after another the weeks passed, and I was close to despair. The examinations came, and arrangements had to be made for the return home of the seminarians from Hungary, including the trio Villányi, Frank and Vermes. By that time the Romanians were guarding the borders, and from their point of view we were illegal residents. My first clandestine frontier crossing took place during the night of 3 June. We were led by a hired guide along unmade paths and across fields until we reached Hungary. Each of us had to carry his luggage during the three-hour walk. Mine contained most of my worldly goods, but something I valued even more lay in the inside pocket of my jacket. By providential accident, the very morning of my departure a letter was delivered to me, written by hand by Père Paul Nicolas, Superior of the seminary of the Fathers of Sion in Louvain, informing me that my application had been favourably received, but that they needed answers to a few further questions before I could formally be accepted. Hallelujah, I exclaimed, realizing that if that precious letter had spent only one more day in transit, it might never have found me. I said goodbye to the authorities, thanked them for their help and told them that I was unlikely to come back. They showed understanding and wished me all the best.

After eighteen months of groping in darkness, light was shining at last and pointing towards what I thought was my *final* destination. I need hardly add, though, that the destination was not final; it covered only the next decade, the ten years spent in Louvain and Paris, or, as I later used to refer to it, my 'French period'.

My last three months in Hungary were mostly taken up in hectic preparations for the great departure. Going abroad in those days was no simple matter. I arrived in Budapest on 5 June, welcomed by my family, who were truly delighted by my news. I read and re-read the letter from Louvain and hastened to send my reply. Then, without waiting for an answer from Louvain, which in fact arrived on 13 July and formally notified me of my acceptance by the Fathers of Sion, I set in motion the Hungarian administrative machine which had the reputation of moving slower than a snail. I needed a passport. To obtain it, I had to go from one ministry to another, from office to office, from lower civil servant to higher official, before I was allowed to submit an application. Thereafter matters could stretch out for months and I was in a hurry, since I was expected in Louvain by the beginning of October. I was experienced enough to know that in Hungary, whether before or after the war, one needed 'protection', friends in high places, if an application was to receive expeditious treatment. Fortunately for me, the Minister for Foreign Affairs was Ferenc Gyöngyösi, a former journalist from a town close to Gyula and a friend of my father. I called on him and he warmly commended me to the head of the passport department: as the son of a journalist who had perished in the deportation by the Germans, he informed his underling, I was above political suspicion. A note from Gyöngyösi ensured that I would receive a passport, though even with such support it took another fortnight to reach me.

The passport was only the first step. I needed not only a Russian exit permit to leave Hungary, but also a Belgian entry visa and a French transit visa. Here I faced an apparently insoluble conundrum. With the strong support of the Foreign Minister the Russian permit would have been fairly certain, except that the granting of it presupposed a Belgian visa in my passport. The same went for the French transit visa. But Belgium had no proper consular representation in Hungary at that time, and the whole process was halted. On the last day of July I asked the superior of the Louvain house to expedite matters and had to settle down for another wait. My formal entitlement to a Belgian visa did not arrive until 2 September, but there was still no one to process it. Another crisis point was reached.

A few words need to be said about my circumstances during this last

Hungarian summer. Although I had generously been given a bed by my family, I did not wish to abuse their hospitality. Following the advice contained in the letter from Louvain, I paid a visit to the Mother Superior of the Sisters of Sion, who before the change of regime in Hungary used to run a classy girls' school in a rather select area of Buda. She at once invited me to stay in their convent. The invitation was gratefully accepted and I stayed there during the best part of that summer. An elderly French nun kindly gave me daily conversation classes and I felt that I was making noticeable progress.

In the middle of August I revisited Gyula, the last time for the next forty-six years. I said goodbye here and there and had the pleasure of learning that a dear school friend of earlier years, the one whom I had successfully coached for his repeat A-levels, had come back from Russian captivity and had already left to enter university. Would we ever meet again?, I queried in my diary. So far we haven't.

Back in Budapest, I made my rounds to take leave of the family, whose members were by then living in their own separate homes. On the spur of the moment, I decided to call on a journalist cousin of my father, Gustavus Földes (Uncle Gus). I had met him only once before the war, but kept fond memories of the occasion. He and his wife had survived the ordeals and were getting ready to emigrate to the United States, where their son lived. They were a delightful elderly couple, and from then on I shared their lunch and charming company almost daily. Uncle Gus took the initiative and approached his brother who lived in Cleveland, I think, and asked him to help me financially. I was told that he had agreed, but in fact nothing ever happened.[5] Gus and Liz Földes left for Baltimore a few weeks later, and both dear creatures were dead within a couple of years of their arrival in the dreamland of their imagination.

In Budapest I also met up with Andy Villányi and Miki Frank. They, too, were making preparations for leaving Hungary. Miki was sent to the University of Innsbruck in Austria to complete his theological studies. The most traditionally-minded of our threesome, he gained a doctorate there, was ordained priest in 1950, and spent the best part of his life in Rome doing charitable work. Andy, truthful to his eccentric self, started off on a collision course with the authorities, ecclesiastical and secular. Nevertheless, he too became a priest: in 1948 in Morocco. As a result of his expulsion by the French from North Africa in 1954, he landed in Rome determined to live in style, acquiring the nickname of *spendereccio* (squanderer) in the Hungarian circles of the Vatican. Miki, who was always kind, looked after his ageing and ailing friend during the last years of his life. Andy's life tragically ended in 1973, two months after a collision between a rogue Roman bus and a car driven by Miki with Andy in the passenger seat.

Having consulted the Mother Superior of the Sion Sisters, who knew all about the complications of my exit permits and visas, I resolved to take another risk and attempt to slip out of Hungary without Russian authorization. I had to travel light, so the Sisters arranged for my luggage to be sent to their house in Vienna by courtesy of the French embassy. One of my great-uncles wrote to a friend who was the station master in Sopron; he promised to intervene with the passport control people on my behalf and put me on a train for Austria. Andy, still in Budapest, suddenly decided to join me, so that we would escape together. We were to meet up in Sopron, the town from which I had fled eastwards two years earlier to the relatively safe haven of Budapest.

During the last few days before my exodus from Hungary, I again stayed with my family and with their blessing set off on the great adventure on 14 September 1946. In Sopron, which is not my favourite place, everything went haywire. Andy did not turn up. The 'friendly' station master, who had reiterated to me personally that he would speak up for me, could not be found when he was needed, and the Austrians who checked the passengers' papers at the station in Sopron did not let me board the train as my passport contained no Russian exit permit. There was only one thing to do. A local priest put me in touch with a smuggler in a neighbouring village. We agreed on a fee, and on 18 September 1946, in broad daylight, he safely led me across the Austrian border. I spent the night in the nearest village and next day took the train to Vienna. Here I found hospitality in the Pazmaneum, the residence of Hungarian theological students attending the University of Vienna. The college was neglected and the sheets I found on my bed were dark grey, unwashed after umpteen previous uses by a succession of guests. The streets in the evening were eerie; this was the Vienna of *The Third Man*, but for me it was the city of the ultimate promise soon to be fulfilled.

At the convent of the Sisters of Sion I retrieved my suitcases, which had travelled from Budapest in the French diplomatic bag. At the Belgian consulate I was granted my visa of provisional residence and, assisted by a French Sister of Sion at the French embassy, I also obtained a *visa de transit sans arrêt* through France. All was set for safe sailing ... provided that I managed to cross from the Soviet to the French zone of occupation without the confounded Russian stamp on my passport. The train departed from Vienna on 30 September at 12.35 p.m. An hour or so later a Red Army officer perfunctorily stared at my papers and gave them back without comment or question, and moved to the next compartment.

That was that. I entered French-occupied Austria in the free world of the West.

Totally exhausted, I slept for most of the journey through devastated southern Germany, and really became conscious again at the Rhine bridge at Kehl, leading to Strasbourg. FRANCE at last. I caught a train for Belgium. At one of the first Belgian stations, Bastogne I think, I was struck by an extraordinary sight. Was I seeing visions? On the platform stood three men wearing black caftans and black, hard, broad-rimmed hats. But wait: something was wrong. They had no beards or side locks! This was my first encounter with Belgian Catholic priests, with their overcoats as long as their soutanes and their clerical headgear. Soon I, too, would look like one of them, I muttered. I was amazed and amused, but was even more fascinated by the abundance of oranges and bananas, luxury food which I had not seen for years. Had I entered paradise?

I reached my goal, Louvain, via Brussels, on 2 October 1946. To my surprise, I was greeted at the Sion noviciate by a Hungarian-speaking and unmistakably Jewish-looking priest, Paul Démann, formerly an architect from Budapest. He was to become a friend, confidant and elder brother, as well as my chief intellectual support for the next ten years. Everything seemed marvellously smooth. I was elated and was tempted to intone *Te Deum laudamus*. I abstained for fear of hitting the wrong note.

Part Two: At Notre-Dame de Sion

(Louvain-Paris 1946–1957)

6

The Fathers of Notre-Dame de Sion:
Prelude

(1946–1948)

49 rue des Moutons, Louvain, and 68 rue Notre-Dame des Champs, Paris 6: ten and a half crucial years of my life are linked to these two addresses. Louvain was my base from 2 October 1946 until the completion of my studies in 1952. Then, after a brief visit to Jerusalem, from September to the end of December of that year, on 1 January 1953 I was assigned to the central institution of the congregation of the Fathers of Sion. There I remained until the big turning point in my destiny, the start of my 'British period', on 10 March 1957.

How did the new setting impress me? As a town, Louvain was totally beyond my previous experience. Having never left Hungary before, I found it strange to be in a truly old city. Because of wars and a century and a half of Turkish occupation, ancient buildings still in use were rare, and whole streets or quarters quite exceptional in the region where I grow up. Yet in Louvain the Middle Ages and the Renaissance were staring at you from right, left and centre. In those early days I did not know that some of the antique-looking edifices were replicas, constructed after the devastation caused by the Germans in the First World War. Old churches, convents and monasteries stood in every street. The university itself was founded in the mid-fifteenth century. As in Oxford, it did not lie within the boundaries of a campus, but all over the place.

The Louvain/Leuven of the mid-1940s was a bilingual city, with street name plates in Flemish and French. However, one could easily get by just with French, there and in any other town in Flanders. The present linguistic chauvinism limiting the use of the two official languages to officially designated areas was introduced long after my time in Belgium. I never bothered to learn Flemish.

In this beautiful town the convent of the Fathers of Sion, situated in a largely working-class street (rue des Moutons: Sheep Street, Schaapen-straat in Flemish), was something of an anti-climax. It was a two-storey jerry-built house, uncomfortable and cold, but conveniently placed close to the centre and with a largish garden. The community was not quite what I had imagined. It was small, almost minuscule. The superior *cum* novice master was Father Paul Nicolas, the signatory of the letters I received in Hungary. He was French with, I guess, not a drop of Jewish blood in his veins. He was sixty, kind, pleasant, a do-it-yourself person rather than an intellectual, yet appreciating academic achievement. During the six years which we spent together, for some extended periods with just the two of us occupying the building, I learned to appreciate him, and he seems to have taken a liking to me. This survived even after I broke away from Sion and the church. The greatest period of his life was the four years of the First World War, during which he served as a stretcher-bearer. I heard unending stories, many of them repeated often, about life in the trenches at Verdun or in the Somme. Over meals he entertained us with all the gory details of the experiences of a *brancardier* among the *poilus* (hairy men), the colloquial designation of the French soldiers, fighting the *boches* (the Huns). This was 1914-18 French, which was innocent of the present-day, politically correct, conventions of the European Community.

Father Paul Démann, who greeted me on my arrival, was Hungarian, Jewish, blessed with all possible talents including mobility. Usually he was on his way from one place to another, hitch-hiking most of the time, considering himself the itinerant ambassador of the message of Sion. However, this message, as will soon appear, was more his own than that of the order. My association with him, which continued until the late 1960s (by which time he, too, had left the congregation and the church and was married with a child), was a source of intellectual and mental salvation during my Sion years.

The junior section of the community consisted of one French student theologian already at the end of his training and, I believe, three French novices, none of them of Jewish origin. We were soon joined by a short, round, Jewish convert from Egypt in his forties; Greek was his mother tongue, but he had a Levantine linguistic ability, with fluency in French, English and Arabic. Since he had formerly been a lawyer, we usually called him '*Maître*' – the title of an advocate in French – rather than 'Brother'. This dear fellow, something of a figure of fun, did not last long as a novice, but apart from me none of the 1946 intake ran the full course.

The Louvain house was a faithful reflection of the general state of the Congregation of the Fathers of Sion outside Brazil. (Their success in South America was probably due to the fact that instead of being devoted to Jewish-Christian matters, they were simply engaged in ordinary parish ministry.) If I remember rightly, the sum total of the membership did not reach three figures. Throughout the one hundred years' history of the congregation, while the Sisters flourished, the male branch remained stagnant. Indeed, it was declining, with the middle-aged and elderly largely outnumbering the young.

The order of Notre-Dame de Sion was founded in the middle of the nineteenth century by Théodore Ratisbonne, an Alsatian Jew converted to Catholicism and subsequently ordained priest. He and his brother, Alphonse, who claimed to have had a vision of the Virgin Mary in Rome in 1842, founded a congregation of nuns; their aim was to provide Christian education for girls and pray for the conversion of the Jews. A small body of priests joined the new society to serve as chaplains to the Sisters, but the vagueness of their religious aspirations and perspective no doubt explains why the institution of the male group made little or no progress. When I arrived, the majority of the Fathers were associated either with parishes or with schools, and their specific 'Sion' activity consisted in organizing and leading pious associations belonging to an 'Archiconfrérie de prière pour Israël' (Confraternity of Prayer for the Jews). Earlier on, a few half-hearted attempts at proselytizing the Jews were made in Paris, London and Jerusalem, but in general they ended in failure; this progressively led to a tacit shelving of the project. Of course, these details were unknown to me on my arrival; I learned about them bit by bit during my noviciate year and later. But even had I been better informed, I do not think that it would have cooled my ardour. Louvain was welcoming, and I was thirsty for knowledge. The apparent lack of importance of the group to which I chose to belong, disappointing though it may have been, did not really matter as long as my ultimate goal remained within reach.

The first hurdle to cross was the noviciate, which lasted for twelve months. I accepted the spiritual training as a necessary stage in my progress, tried to absorb as much French as possible, and put up with the monotony of our daily life and the syrupy taste of nineteenth-century spirituality which was poured down our throats. In any case, offered in French it felt less sugary. The day involved mass and several sessions of prayer and meditation in the chapel, as well as regular daily instruction from the novice master who, when short of ideas of his own, read out extracts from the writings of the founder (referred to as Père Théodore) and like-minded authors of that age. Meals were eaten in silence, while we listened to the monotonous voice of one of the novices reading from a religious book. We had to perform a fair amount of chores: washing up after the meals, sweeping and dusting rooms and corridors, and work in the garden, once including the transfer of the contents of the cesspool to Père Nicolas' favourite vegetable plot.

Every afternoon we went for a walk in town, an exercise which I greatly enjoyed because of the beauty of the old streets and ancient buildings. After lunch and dinner, we had recreation in the garden. The only sporting opportunity was tennis on an un-maintained court, just to allow us to stretch our legs. A year or two later a new novice arrived from Manchester who found life intolerable without football. Our sympathetic Father Superior arranged for him to play once a week with the team of another religious order, but the English brother was probably so disgusted with the quality of Belgian seminary football that after a few months he packed his boots and returned to Britain.

In contrast to Szatmár, ascetic training in Louvain did not go as far as to put us into a communal dormitory, but our private bedrooms were not exactly luxurious. They lacked both running water and heating. A communal bathroom at the far end of the building offered a hot bath once every two or four weeks. As a daily routine, before going to bed we had to collect water from a tap in the corridor for our morning ablutions. The winter of 1946/47 was exceedingly harsh, and the water which was poured into my porcelain washbasin was regularly covered with ice by the morning. However, I discovered that I could prevent it from freezing if I kept the jug in my wardrobe. Throughout the winter I and most of my fellow novices suffered from chilblains. It was a delight to get up at the crack of dawn (5.30 or 6 a.m.) and go to the heated parts of the house, the chapel and the refectory. The Belgian-style breakfast, often consisting of coffee, bread and butter and a bar of Côte d'Or chocolate, struck me as original but wholly acceptable. Sister Bernarda, a jolly, fat, elderly Flemish nun, mistress of the kitchen, lovingly looked after us and provided us with copious if not exciting meals.

After breakfast and lunch, the refectory was transformed into a classroom where the novice master delivered his instructions every morning. Each day a couple of hours were set aside for correspondence and private study. Our letters were handed over unsealed to the Father Superior, who may or may not have glanced at them. Likewise the incoming mail arrived open. For me this made no great difference, as I dare say Hungarian was not one of Father Nicolas's languages. In any case, I had nothing to hide, and my correspondents, the Budapest family and the my expatriate clerical friends, Andy and Miki, had no great secrets to impart either. I did a great deal of reading and writing in French, but the lion's share of my free time was dedicated to Hebrew. I found a grammar in the library and continued my study where I had left off a year earlier at the University of Budapest. My aim was to acquire sufficient competence to handle texts by the time I was to attend lectures on the Bible. I was the only novice to show such an

interest, and this was noticed with approval by Father Nicolas and especially by Father Paul Démann, who soon detected in me a potential ally in
his dream of reforming the outlook and objectives of the order. I began to
learn New Testament Greek, too, but it lagged behind Hebrew and my real
scholarly encounter with the Gospels did not occur for another twenty
years, long after my theological studies and my breach with the church and
subsequent reassessment of the Christian religion. I was getting ready for
the fast approaching great moment of freedom when I could lose myself in
learning all about the Hebrew Bible, and whatever else was necessary in
pursuit of the prescribed theological curriculum.

My noviciate was completed in October 1947, and I became a temporary
member of the congregation of the Fathers of Notre-Dame de Sion.
Permanent commitment would follow three years later. So the great day of
return to study was approaching. I was to seek admission to a theological
course given by the Jesuits, primarily for their own scholastics. I consulted
Paul Démann, who had been through the same programme – in theory he
was working on a doctoral thesis on Saint Paul's teaching on Jewish destiny
in Romans 9 to 11, but he never managed to complete it – and with the
ready consent of Father Nicolas I opted for the '*grand cours*', the honours
course. This led to a degree, while the '*petit cours*' provided a mere professional qualification for a priestly career. My sparsely furnished and
uncomfortable bedroom was turned into a study, containing a desk and a
bookcase, and thank goodness also a gas fire. Good-bye chilblains.

The Jesuits had two provinces in Belgium, one for Flemings and one for
Walloons, but in 1947 students from both branches were taught in a single
bilingual establishment in Louvain itself. Next year they split up to form
two institutions, and I joined the French-speaking section. The new college
was located in a suburb; according to the good Belgian custom, I was to
travel there daily by bicycle. The four-year programme was divided into a
first preliminary year with an examination and the main part with a final
examination at the end. During the last two years, degree candidates were
also to produce a dissertation to qualify for the 'licence', more or less the
equivalent of a British BA.

With all those (meaningless) top marks obtained in Hungary, I was not
only accepted for the '*grand cours*', but also dispensed from sitting for the
first examination. I started on the second-year programme with dogmatic
theology, church history and New Testament as the core subjects. All these
courses were given in Latin, and dogmatics included regular mediaeval-
type Latin debates. The professor designated a student to propose and
defend a thesis against the objections advanced by two appointed opponents. Here I cannot resist revealing that, as in my Hungarian schoolboy

past, cheating was the order of the day, in that the objectors and the defender colluded in working out their line of argument. On the day of the battle, umpired by the relevant professor, they pretended to improvise the whole discussion, but in reality they performed according to a pre-arranged scenario. I was called on once to act as objector and did as I was expected. However, during the 'improvisation' I could not refrain from pointing to a flaw of logic in my opponent's dialectic which I had previously failed to notice. Not surprisingly, this threw him off his stride and resulted in a very dirty look in my direction. But I apologized afterwards, and all was well.

The level of teaching was incomparably higher than anything I experienced in Szatmár or Nagyvárad. If my Jesuit professors read out of a book, it was one which they had written, and many of their lecture notes appeared in print sooner or later. Some of the professors were quite renowned in Jesuit circles and beyond. Fathers L. Malevez and E. Dhanis were well respected theologians; Dhanis later became Rector of the Gregorian University in Rome. Father Pierre Charles invented the so-called science of missiology; he was also a famous wit and, closer to my own interests, was among the first Christians to denounce *The Protocols of the Elders of Zion* as a forgery. It was a meritorious effort, yet without the learning and sophistication displayed twenty years later by my future colleague at the University of Newcastle and life-long friend Norman Cohn in *Warrant for Genocide* (1967).

Stimulating though they were, the lectures of that first academic year (1947–48) made no special impression on me. Neither dogmatic theology nor church history interested me greatly and, curiously in the light of later developments, the New Testament also left me cold. What I was subjected to was a theologically inspired course on Saint Paul without the slightest hint of things Jewish, the exploration of which fired my desire for learning. I was longing to begin the study of the Old Testament the following year. Needless to say, I had no idea that a few months earlier a young Arab shepherd had accidentally stumbled on ancient Hebrew manuscripts in a remote cave of the distant Judaean desert which were soon to attain fame as the Dead Sea Scrolls.

At the same time, life at Notre-Dame de Sion was also undergoing significant changes, at least from my point of view. In 1947 a new periodical, entitled *Cahiers Sioniens,* was launched at the Paris house; this subsequently played a momentous role in the development of my thinking and scholarly activity. The new journal was to replace the organ of the Archconfraternity of Prayer for the Jews, *La Question d'Israël*, which died a non-untimely death when the Germans entered Paris in 1940. The first couple of issues of the *Cahiers* were still imbued with the old spirit, but due partly to the impact of the Holocaust, and even more to the paramount influence of Paul Démann, the publication shifted direction: instead of focussing on the theological problem of conversion, it began to turn its guns on Christian anti-Judaism. Many of the old subscribers dropped out, disappointed or disgusted. Some of the Sisters and the older generation of the Fathers grumbled, but slowly a new readership emerged in progressive Catholic and Jewish circles. They warmly welcomed the Sion revolution represented by such articles as 'Anti-Semitism and Christian Conscience', 'Are the Jews cursed?' and 'At the Christian Sources of Anti-Semitism', all written by Paul Démann between January 1948 and January 1949.

On the sudden death of the first editor, Father Marcel Leroux, the heir apparent, Paul Démann, took over the direction of the journal and transformed it from an irregular publication to a not quite regular quarterly. The *Cahiers* threw itself behind the cause of Christian-Jewish understanding championed by Jules Isaac, renowned and admired in France and elsewhere for his greatness as a historian and even more as a human being. He played a leading part in the Seeligsberg Conference convened by Christians and Jews in the summer of 1947, whose ten-point manifesto[1] sought to combat religious antisemitism and promote a new spirit of friendship, the *Amitiés Judéo-Chrétiennes*. The substance of the ten propositions was borrowed from Isaac's epoch-making, beautifully written and deeply moving book *Jésus et Israël* (1946),[2] which received whole-hearted acclaim in the *Cahiers* in a long review article signed by Démann.

These new developments reassured me that the apparently failing Notre-Dame de Sion order could serve as a platform for a reform aimed at changing the church's ideas and attitudes towards Israel. Consequently I had to persevere in this seemingly unimpressive congregation.

Two new personal contacts, with Joseph André and Kurt Hruby, which date back to this period, have left a lasting mark on me. In the summer of 1948 I spent a few weeks in the house of Abbé Joseph André of Namur. This saintly Belgian cleric, a close friend of Paul Démann, was renowned for having saved many Jewish children during the years of German occupation at the risk of his life. Even in 1948 his house was full of orphans and uncared-for youngsters, some of them Jewish, whom he managed to feed and clothe without regular funding from anyone. He said that God looked after them. In 'Monsieur le Vicaire', as we used to call him, I encountered goodness incarnate.

During that summer I was invited to accompany him and his boys on a holiday to Spain. It was a memorable journey. It was then that in France, close to the Spanish border, I saw the sea for the first time. I was also overwhelmed by the beauty of Spanish art in the Prado in Madrid and in

Toledo, where I also encountered the relics of mediaeval Jewry. I was persuaded by an old Spanish nun to go to a bull fight, but it made me sick. Finally, it may be noted in passing that in the Basque country I nearly lost my life. During a walk in the mountains, to which as a child of the Hungarian plains I was completely unused, I found myself lagging behind my group. As I tried to catch up with them on a steep downhill slope, I suddenly realized that I was gathering more and more momentum. 'I must stop,' I said to myself. 'If necessary, I must fall. A fractured leg is preferable to a broken neck.' But I did not know how to slow down or fall. The edge of the slope came nearer and nearer and I had no idea what lay beyond it. A precipice? Thank goodness, it was not a precipice, but another rather abrupt slope and I literally took to the air. Fortunately the branches of a large, recently felled, tree cut my flight short and I landed with only a few bruises and torn garments. It was a narrow escape.

On the return journey I stopped in Paris and had plenty of time to visit it as a tourist. I saw many of the famous sights only on that occasion, despite the four years I was to spend there in the 1950s. My dear friend and research colleague, Renée Bloch, about whom I will have much to say later, always claimed that, although a *Parisienne* born and bred, she had never been inside the Sainte Chapelle. But she may have been pulling my leg. It was on this occasion that I tried to meet up with my uncle Pista, but he no longer resided in the rue du Paradis where I was supposed to find him.

Back in the Louvain house itself another welcome change occurred. While the novices who started with me in 1946 withdrew one after another, new recruits replaced them. One of these was Kurt Hruby, who was to become a dear friend for many years. Son of a Christian father and a Jewish mother, Kurt was born in Austria in 1921, and migrated to Palestine with his mother after she was divorced by her husband following the *Anschluss*, the annexation of Austria by Hitler in 1938. For a time Kurt worked in a religious kibbutz. His modern Hebrew was fluent and his knowledge of traditional Judaism very extensive and profound. To him I owe my first initiation into spoken Hebrew and rabbinic literature. In Palestine he became a Christian and found a job as a journalist at the French news agency (Agence France-Presse) before coming to Louvain.

His formal link with Notre-Dame de Sion was of short duration, but for many years he remained a close associate of Paul Démann in the Paris house, where I renewed contact with him between 1953 and 1957. In due course he was ordained priest by the Belgian bishop of Liège; he opted for an academic career, but till his dying day he stayed inside the church. He taught Jewish studies at the Institut Catholique in Paris, published widely, and for the last twenty-one years of his life edited *Judaica*, a German-language quarterly, in Zurich. Although his genuine attachment to Christianity cannot be doubted, those who were as close to him as I was knew that in his heart of hearts he felt like, and probably considered himself as, a nineteenth-century Orthodox Jew. I used to enjoy his newsy letters enormously, pages and pages of them written in the German of a traditionalist last-century rabbi, letters replete with biblical and talmudic quotations, among which were interspersed arcane Hebrew and Aramaic abbreviations. I will never forget one particular episode in the house of the Fathers of Sion in Paris in the late 1950s, by which time I was no longer an insider but a passing visitor. Though not a member of the order, Kurt Hruby had been put in charge of the place as Paul Démann's substitute during a summer vacation. As a capable handyman, he undertook the renovation and redecoration of the interior of the Sion chapel, which in my time used to be filled with awful traditional plaster statuary. Kurt decided to get rid of the lot. I can still see him in shirt-sleeves, standing in the garden on a sunny afternoon. Dozens of angels, apostles, a Jesus with a sacred heart painted on his chest, and several Virgin Marys wearing a white robe and a blue cape, were lined up on the ground against the wall of the chapel. No doubt incensed by the sight of those horrors, Kurt lifted a monumental sledge hammer and with a naughty twinkle in his eye smashed the statues, one after the other, into thousands of pieces. While doing so, he recited in Hebrew with old-fashioned traditional Ashkenazi pronunciation a conflated text of Psalm 96.5 and 135.15:

Eloyhey ha-goyim elilim, maase yedey odom.
The gods of the nations are idols, the work of man's hand.

Kurt Hruby was a kind, humorous, big-hearted, friendly and helpful giant of a man. Pam and I met him in 1964 in Paris and she took an instant liking to him. Our paths parted in the late 1960s and thereafter the correspondence became sporadic. I was planning to revisit him, but alas the angel of death beat me to it. Kurt died, aged seventy-one, on 5 September 1992. I treasure the memory of our days in Louvain and will never forget the great support which I received from him there and later in Paris when I arrived at my parting of the ways.

7

Discovery of the Bible

(1948–1950)

By the end of my first year at the Jesuit college, I was already firmly set, at least in intention and imagination, on my life task among the Fathers of Sion. I planned to join a new crusade, led by Paul Démann, against the age-old Christian anti-Judaism in the Catholic Church. I saw my role as that of a student of the Bible and of the history of Jewish-Christian relations, fighting on the academic battlefield and not in the arena of religious politics. The latter was Paul's preserve. So the next step was to find out all I could about the Bible, that is, the *Hebrew* Bible. I had no idea of the dangers involved in the enterprise on which I proposed to embark.

The new academic year of 1948-49 entailed a change of scenery. I had to migrate from the Louvain house, henceforward the home of the Flemish-speaking Jesuits, to Eegenhoven, where the French branch of the Belgian province of the Society of Jesus moved. The man who had previously taught Old Testament in the joint French-Flemish college, Father Gustave Lambert, was a Walloon, and with all his Francophone colleagues had to vacate his rooms in the old establishment and join the freshly formed College of Saint Albert of Louvain a few miles outside the city. For me, this was another lucky stroke of fate, because it was Lambert who was to mould me into a Hebraist and biblical scholar, and launch me on my future career. We happened to suit one another splendidly.

Gustave Lambert (born in 1894) was by then in his fifties, a tallish, broad man, warm and often amusing, with grey crew-cut hair and large spectacles. He was also a highly learned person, trained in Rome at the Pontifical Biblical Institute. For a chosen minority of pupils he was an admirable teacher, and in those whom he judged receptive he instilled a real enthusiasm for his subject. I found Father Lambert at his best in private meetings and passed many happy hours in his office, enjoying the freedom I was given to browse among the thousands of volumes on his shelves. It was there that I realized that a good proportion of academic literature on the Old Testament and related subjects was in English. So at once I set out to gain a reading ability of this strange language with the help of a teach-yourself book which had a lying title, *L'anglais sans peine*, or 'English without trouble'. A couple of years later, through a strange quirk of destiny, I acquired a native tutor, but thereby hang numerous crucially important other tales which I must not anticipate.

Father Lambert's style of teaching may not have been ideal for the common-or-garden variety of theologian who expected a proper introduction to all the major issues of Old Testament literature, history and doctrine. What his audience received instead was an extremely detailed reading and exposition of short, but important, texts. Lambert devoted a full year to covering the first two chapters of the Book of Genesis, that is to say the two accounts of the creation, and next to no time was left to examine the story of Adam, Eve and the serpent in chapter 3. In the second year, we proceeded faster by Lambertian standards, and were given a somewhat 'cursory' reading of the whole of the admittedly short Book of Amos. However, the lack of breadth in the survey was more than compensated by the wealth of detail and the depth of the analysis. An entirely new world, that of the ancient Near East, was opened up to me: in it the Jewish Bible appeared in its historical reality side by side with the heritage of Babylonia and Assyria, with the antecedent culture of Sumer on the one hand and that of Egypt on the other. To become a real Old Testament scholar, one had to be initiated in these mother civilizations, we were told. Father Lambert's words were music to my ears, but few of my co-students welcomed such non-theological ideas.[1] I, however, was totally captivated; I hoped to follow in my master's footsteps and learn all the skills which a competent Bible interpreter needed. Indeed, two years later, fascinated by the cultures of the ancient Near-East, I registered, *inter alia*, as a student of Assyriology. With hindsight, I know that this was a mistake. A more thorough initiation into Arabic would have served my future interests better.

Gustave Lambert was a born rebel but his Jesuit training weakened the courage of his convictions. Those who respected him less than I did, called him a grumbler because in class he frequently let out words of dissatisfaction aimed at the ecclesiastical authority in general and the Biblical Institute, his *alma mater*, in particular. To understand him, some knowledge of the state of Catholic biblical studies in the first half of the twentieth century is required.

Church directives issued in scriptural matters prior to the Second World War not only hindered, but to all intents and purposes destroyed, freedom of enquiry into the Bible among Catholic students. These students were prevented from focusing on truth with an open mind and behaving as genuine scholars. Enquiry without fear or favour, *sine ira et studio*, was not for them. Their church-given job was faithfully to echo traditional doctrine and abstain from teaching anything that might *appear* to detract from it. The powers that be in Rome saw modern Bible research as a direct threat to their doctrinal authority.

This state of mind resulted from the fact that in the Europe of the nineteenth century, under the impact of German liberal Protestantism and French rationalism, the scientific study of the Old and the New Testaments had progressed by leaps and bounds. Textual, literary and historical criticism, enhanced by a fresh investigation of ancient manuscripts and a whole wave of archaeological discoveries in Palestine, Egypt, Mesopotamia, Greece and Rome, provided a new historical perspective in which Scripture lost its unique status as the oldest document of human civilization. Parallel accounts of the venerable stories of the creation of the world and of the flood were found on the clay tablets yielded by archaeological excavations in the land between the Tigris and the Euphrates. Peculiarities of New Testament Greek, rather than expressing something special and sacrosanct, turned out to reflect the *koine* or vulgar Greek of the papyri of Hellenistic and Roman Egypt dealing with the commonest everyday subjects. If Catholic biblical scholars were to gain respectability, urgent re-adjustment was required: they had to come down to earth.

Two brilliant late nineteenth-century French *savants* set out to achieve such a reform: the Abbé Alfred Loisy (1857–1940) and the Dominican Father Marie-Joseph Lagrange (1855–1938). Loisy, professor of Scripture at the Institut Catholique in Paris, soon fell foul of the church hierarchy and was downgraded from a teacher of the Bible to being a professor of harmless oriental languages. Further clashes followed, leading to some of Loisy's works being placed on the Index of prohibited books, and finally in 1908 to his public excommunication from the church.

Lagrange, whose name is primarily linked to the creation, in 1890, of the famous Catholic research institution the École Biblique in Jerusalem, and in 1892 of the highly influential and still flourishing quarterly the *Revue Biblique*, managed to steer clear of trouble, though not without some nerve-racking moments of tight-rope walking. The École has remained to this day the standard-bearer of Catholic scriptural learning, and has shown enough academic excellence over the years to be recognized by the secular French state as its own École Biblique et Archéologique *Française*. A kind of rival establishment, entrusted to the Jesuits, was founded in 1904. Its title, the Pontifical Biblical Institute or *Pontificium Institutum Biblicum*, and its location in Rome itself, make plain that this school was intended to serve as an ultimate mouthpiece of orthodox scriptural exegesis. By the time the Biblical Institute was born, an ecclesiastical supervisory body was already fully engaged in issuing dictates so primitive and old-fashioned as to put Catholic exegesis beyond the pale of academic respectability.

In its fight against the dangers of modernism, in 1902 the papacy established the Pontifical Biblical Commission, a watchdog of cardinals and 'consultors' endowed with quasi-dictatorial powers. Its aim was to ensure that Bible scholars subject to its jurisdiction would not adopt and disseminate the errors of the 'critics' and 'modernists', which were actually or even potentially harmful to the traditional teaching of the church. The Commission set out without delay to order Catholic exegetes to turn their back on all the major advances of scriptural research.

For instance, in the field of the Old Testament Catholic writers were forbidden to question the Mosaic authenticity of the Pentateuch (Decree of 27 June 1906). The thesis of the great German scholar, Julius Wellhausen, claiming that the first five books of the Hebrew Bible developed from pre-existing sources and could not have had Moses as their author, was declared contrary to the testimony of both Testaments, the perpetual conviction of the Jewish people, and the constant tradition of the church, and no Catholic author was therefore allowed to profess it.

It was forbidden, furthermore, to see in the story of the creation of the world and of Adam and Eve in the first three chapters of Genesis an edited and expurgated version of ancient cosmogonies (i.e. the Mesopotamian creation myths); indeed, the biblical narrative in its literal sense was to be accepted as historical in conformity with the uniform tradition of the church (Decree of 30 June 1909).

Likewise, it was forbidden to subscribe to the thesis commonly embraced by 'the critics' that the Book of Isaiah was the work of two or three authors (First, Second and Third Isaiah); in other words, all sixty-six chapters were to be attributed to the one and only prophet Isaiah who lived in the eighth century BC (Decree of 29 June 1908).

It was also laid down – against the consensus of all enlightened opinion – that David was the author of most of the Psalms, and in particular that the Davidic authorship of those poems which are explicitly cited in the royal Psalmist's name in the Old or in the New Testament could in no way be queried (Decree of 1 May 1910).[2]

Three decades of such high-handed and unwise decretomania on the part of the most stubborn Pontifical Biblical Commission[3] had predictable consequences. A tiny group of Catholic authors took a radical step and left the church or, like Loisy, were forced out of it.[4] Some of the leading experts, e.g. the professors of the Dominican École Biblique in Jerusalem and some of the teachers at the Biblical Institute in Rome, chose diplomacy. They shied away from 'dangerous' topics or had recourse to equivocation.

Yet others moved into safe areas such as the study of Hebrew grammar or the ancient translations of the Bible. Many tried simultaneously to save their scholarly conscience and their skin by teaching orally what they actually believed, but without going into print.

Father Lambert, an ex-pupil of the Pontifical Biblical Institute under the directorship of the then arch-conservative Father Augustin Bea, strongly resented the stringent control exerted by the Vatican on the practitioners of biblical exegesis, and enthusiastically preached the necessity of an unblinkered approach in Old Testament study. However, he too belonged to the class of non-publishers. His only notable piece of work predating 1948 was a philological investigation into the meaning of the expression 'to bind and to loose' which appeared in the 1944 volume of *Vivre et penser*. This was the renowned *Revue Biblique* of the Jerusalem Dominicans compulsorily renamed, like all the other existing periodicals, during the German occupation of France. In 1948, my colleague Paul Démann persuaded him to publish in our *Cahiers Sioniens* a paper on the restoration of the Jewish state under Cyrus in the sixth century BC, to serve as a prelude to the establishment of the modern State of Israel. Both articles were on doctrinally innocuous subjects. His lack of output may have been partly due to his natural reluctance to exert himself. When he suddenly became productive from 1949 onwards, rumours began to circulate among his Jesuit brethren that the change was due to my influence![5] Be this as it may, Father Lambert advised us to be *cautious*.

In fact, by the late 1940s, the circumstances in which Catholic Bible interpretation operated seemed more tolerable and propitious. The extreme conservatism of the Vatican had already begun to slacken when in 1938 the renowned orientalist, Cardinal Eugène Tisserant, formerly Professor of Oriental Languages at the Institut Catholique in Paris and for a time the learned prefect of the Vatican Library, was appointed president of the Pontifical Biblical Commission. Lambert told me a very revealing story about how Tisserant attempted to turn on the green light in connection with the old decree of the Commission concerning the authorship of Isaiah. In the first decade of this century, a major study of Isaiah was prepared by a French Jesuit, Albert Condamin, to appear in the influential series, *Études Bibliques*, issued by the Jerusalem École Biblique. A first massive volume containing a French translation of Isaiah was duly published in 1905, and a second, offering a full critical introduction to all the literary and historical problems raised by the book, was soon to follow. But although the manuscript was complete, the learned tome remained hidden under a bushel because its open scholarship fell under the prohibition of the Biblical Commission's 1908 decree against the theory of the plural authorship of Isaiah. Tisserant was convinced that time had come for Condamin's long-withheld introduction to see the light of day, and in his private capacity suggested that action should be taken. As a result, the volume was promptly typeset and printed in Rome. Lambert had an unbound copy of it which he lent me, and I read it. By mid-century academic standards, its views were in no way sensational, let alone revolutionary. Yet, despite Tisserant's sponsorship, Bea stopped the binding and distribution of the book because its message infringed the Commission's thirty-year-old unrevoked edict.[6] The outraged Cardinal Tisserant apparently conveyed his disapproval by paying the printer's bill out of his own pocket.[7]

A further signal indicating that the highest church authorities were no longer opposed to some moderate progress in Catholic biblical scholarship was given by Pope Pius XII in his encyclical letter *Divino afflante Spiritu* (By the Inspiration of the Divine Spirit), published in 1943. For, while still insisting on the literal interpretation of Scripture, the document recognized the existence of literary forms and thereby left the door ajar for a more liberal scientific approach to biblical studies.

While extolling the virtue of the positive aspects of the encyclical, Father Lambert retained many misgivings about the Biblical Commission. Hence he encouraged me to specialize as an Old Testament scholar, but added the warning that I should tread carefully: those in authority were never to be trusted. I was both delighted and amazed. There was I, yesterday's pious seminarian from provincial Hungary, trained to honour and obey the powers that be, suddenly embarking on a twofold campaign to 'reform' the church. I was to seek to convince Rome that she should correct the many distorted Christian ideas about the Jews and grant her scholars complete freedom of enquiry in the domain of biblical research!

Was this sheer arrogance on the part of a twenty-four-year-old apprentice theologian? It had all the appearances, yet I felt that my perhaps irrational zeal could be backed by rational argument. A simple backward glance at nineteen hundred years of history culminating in the Holocaust was enough to make plain the pernicious and indeed *un-Christian* nature of Christian anti-Judaism. Had I been a prophet, I could also have foreseen the great changes which were to occur in the second half of the century: the formal rejection of the anti-Jewish trends in Catholic theology and liturgical worship by the Second Vatican Council; the progressive revaluation of post-biblical Judaism in Christian thought; and the discovery (how funny this sounds now!) of the Jewishness of Jesus. In retrospect, it is hard to conceive how primitive in this respect the ideas of ordinary Catholics were half a century ago. Likewise, the lamentable state of Catholic biblical exegesis cried out for modernization which, in turn, constituted an exciting and somewhat dangerous task in the late 1940s. With unbridled enthusiasm, I threw myself into the battle.

The best part of my time during the last two years of the theological curriculum was spent on improving my knowledge of Hebrew and acquainting myself with the major problems of Old Testament interpretation. There was no time to waste; I had to choose a dissertation topic for the licence in theology which was to be submitted before the finals in 1950. I knew one thing: I did not want to get involved in some peripheral issue. So, oblivious of the consequences, I plunged into one of the 'unsolved' major problems of the Hebrew Bible, the so-called Songs of the Servant of the Lord in Deutero-Isaiah (Isaiah 40–55). In fact this was a highly unwise project. Not only did it lead me straight to the still slightly dangerous morass of the Book of Isaiah (beware Condamin!), but by choosing it I was also faced with hundreds, if not thousands, of books and articles written on the question. Years of experience have since taught me that those biblical themes which generate an inordinately large body of secondary literature, like the Servant Songs in the Old Testament and the 'Son of Man' in the New, are flawed and ill-conceived. Or, to put it flippantly, ask *one* silly question and you'll receive not one, but *a thousand* silly answers. Not unexpectedly, Lambert was slightly concerned, but could not dissuade me. So we agreed that I would limit myself to the investigation of the first of the four songs (Isaiah 42.1–4) for the licence and, if all went well, would carry on with the other three poems for the doctoral degree.

This was late 1948, and I hastened to lose myself in the philological, literary and theological complexities of four verses of the Bible (Isaiah 42.1–4). By 8 December 1949 I had completed the job, a seventy-five page typescript. In the Foreword, the Reverend Father Gustave Lambert SJ is most warmly thanked for his very valuable '*conseils savants*'. I handed over to my director of research this first fruit of scholarship with great shaking and trembling. I have just paged through the slender fascicle; its reading fills me neither with pride nor with shame. It is what one could expect in the circumstances. The opening paragraph reads well in French (better than in English translation), but the substance of the piece says little to me today.

Among the most difficult problems of the Old Testament there are subjects whose riches are unfathomable. The Songs of the Servant of the Lord belong to them and have pride of place there. The student of literature admires their poetic beauty; the historian is impressed by the elevation of the thought they express, the climax of the pre-Christian revelation; the theologian discovers in them traces of a mysterious divine plan; as for the exegete, he is carried away by the fascination of the most difficult and most alluring problem he can encounter anywhere in the Bible.

I find it highly amusing that the phrase 'Deutero-Isaiah' or 'Second Isaiah' is nowhere to be found in the thesis. Of course, I whole-heartedly subscribed to the theory that Isaiah 40–55 dated to the mid-sixth century BC, the final period of the exile of the Jews in Babylonia, and not to the age of the original Isaiah, who lived in the late eight century BC. No doubt on Lambert's advice, I simply used as a protective disguise the innocuous code word, 'The Book of the Consolation of Israel', instead of the loaded 'Deutero-Isaiah', except in quotations borrowed from 'non-Catholic' writers. In those days, by the way, bibliographies were often split into two categories: Catholic works (with ecclesiastical approval or *Imprimatur*) and the rest. I am relieved to say that the list of works consulted which is appended to my dissertation does not testify to such a dichotomy.

It is characteristic of my state of mind that almost cheekily I insinuated that the papal encyclical *Divino Afflante* of 'SS Pie XII' (His Holiness Pius XII) was the source that inspired my primarily historical – rather than theological – treatment of Scripture.

By the time the mini-thesis was finished, the final examinations began to loom on the horizon. We were in the spring of 1950, and I forced myself to revise the other less cherished subjects. Lambert exempted me from the test and gave me top marks in Old Testament. The dissertation also carried the maximum of ten points. Three days before the orals, I decided to stop work and went for long walks instead. A clear head on D-day is likely to serve me better than a little extra knowledge, I said to myself. The gamble worked, but I was also assisted by the tiredness of some of the examiners. With a name beginning with V, I came almost at the end of the list. I remember how Professor Louis Malevez, whom I esteemed highly, was nearly collapsing of exhaustion on an exceedingly hot summer day. All he could murmur was, 'Say something about a subject of your choice and in the manner you wish.' I willingly complied. He was pleased. I passed the examination with flying colours and graduated with high honours as a *licencié en théologie*. The first step towards a scholarly career was completed.

Ahead lay another two years of research culminating in a doctoral thesis. To enhance its quality, I obtained permission from my Sion superiors concurrently to register at Louvain University's *Institut Orientaliste* and study for a *licence* in oriental languages and history. Father Nicolas, Father Démann and the Paris authorities gladly consented. All seemed to be set for a smooth progress towards a doctor of theology degree to be earned by further work on the Songs of the Servant of the Lord, and towards a continuation of religious, soon to be priestly, life among the Fathers of Notre-Dame de Sion.

Everything appeared so neat; but mysterious forces interfered once more. In 1947 the Dead Sea Scrolls were discovered in distant Palestine, and also from Jerusalem at the end of 1950 came a mysterious stranger, by the name of John Bradburne. The Scrolls enticed me away from the Servant Songs and launched me on a search which is still unfinished today, and a few years later innocent John was to become indirectly and unintentionally responsible for changing the course of my life.

Providential accidents again?

8

Meeting the Dead Sea Scrolls

(1950–1952)

NB. What follows in this and in other chapters of this autobiography is an account of a life-time of personal involvement with the Scrolls. Those unfamiliar with the subject are offered an instant guide to the Qumran discoveries in the appendix attached to this chapter.

It was in Gustave Lambert's classroom some time in the autumn of 1948 that, still an undergraduate, I first properly encountered the Dead Sea Scrolls. Although the chance discovery by the young Taamire Bedouin shepherd, Muhammad edh-Dhib, of the original seven documents in Qumran Cave 1 took place in the spring of 1947, for over a year the matter largely remained secret apart from rumours which circulated in the press, where the story was usually distorted. For instance, the headline in one of the leading Brussels dailies, *La Libre Belgique*, spoke of an *eleventh* century BC biblical manuscript found on the shore of the *Black* Sea (*sic!*).[1] Then one sunny morning Lambert entered the lecture hall in Eegenhoven, visibly excited. He was waving a white sheet of paper in his hand. It was a letter he received from Jerusalem which contained the transcription of chapter 40 of the Book of Isaiah from a manuscript said to have originated in the pre-Christian era.

It is hard to imagine, half a century after the event, how extraordinary, indeed well-nigh unbelievable, this announcement sounded. It flatly contradicted the textbooks, which asserted that no biblical manuscript, indeed no Hebrew text of any sort produced in antiquity on leather or papyrus, could survive in the climatic conditions of Palestine. This axiom was founded on the experience of generations of archaeologists who for the previous one hundred years had been digging in every corner of the Holy Land, and searching every nook and cranny; the only written documents they found were inscriptions on stone or potsherds. Hence the dilemma arose: were we facing something unprecedented, indeed revolutionary, or a forgery? The ghost of Shapira haunted the academics.[2] Not surprisingly, most established scholars were reluctant to express a firm opinion on these scrolls whose provenance was witnessed only by unreliable Arab boys. I had no such hesitation. In my young bones I felt that here we were dealing with genuine stuff. I ought to declare that throughout my life my intuitions have almost always been correct, but for ages, in fact until fairly recently, I lacked the courage to act on them.

Fired by curiosity and enthusiasm, I set out to find out all I could about these mysterious manuscripts. They comprised two lots. Half of them were acquired by the Syrian Orthodox archbishop, Mar Athanasius, of St Mark's Monastery in Jerusalem, during the dying months of the British mandate in Palestine, and the other half by Eleazar Lipa Sukenik, the renowned professor of archaeology at the Hebrew University. The archbishop enlisted the services of the American School of Oriental Research in Jerusalem, whose resident staff, under the directorship of Professor Millar Burrows of Yale University, at once set out to publish them. But Sukenik moved faster, and by 1948 released a preliminary survey of his own material and also photographs, with his own decipherment and commentary, of texts which belonged to the rival camp. In later years people might have questioned the ethics of Sukenik's action, but in those halcyon days he was applauded for releasing much precious information with exemplary expediency. Both Sukenik and the leading American orientalist, archaeologist and biblical scholar of the mid-century, W. F. Albright, unhesitatingly accepted the authenticity of the Scrolls and dated them to the end of the pre-Christian era. Albright coined the phrase 'the greatest manuscript find of modern times'. His American colleague G. E. Wright outbid him with 'the most important find ever made in the field of Old Testament manuscripts'. I became more and more excited.

By early 1949 the cave from which the manuscripts had been removed was identified. The story had a Belgian angle. Captain Philippe Lippens, a bored Belgian officer of the UN Palestine Armistice Observer Corps whom I actually met a little later, decided to seek some harmless excitement by trying to identify the hiding place where the Dead Sea Scrolls had remained concealed for centuries. With the assistance of the Arab Legion of Jordan his enterprise had a successful ending, and the final proof confirming that it was the right cave came from the discovery of hundreds of manuscript fragments, some of which were detached from the known Scrolls. Muhammad edh-Dhib did not bother to collect small scraps.

At the beginning interest focussed on the complete scroll of Isaiah from which the passage triumphantly carried by Lambert was copied and which was thought to antedate our oldest previously known manuscript of this biblical book by at least a millennium! I looked for and soon found a photograph of the text, which surprisingly was almost as legible as a printed Bible. Chapter 40 was also nearly identical with the traditional version, but my eager eyes quickly noticed a difference: instead of the customary 'Who has measured *the waters* in the hollow of his hand?', the old scroll read 'Who has measured *the waters of the sea* in the hollow of his hand?' Admittedly not very significant in itself, this was nevertheless my first discovery of something previously unknown which gave a delightful feeling to an apprentice scholar who was still hesitant and unsure of himself. I knew that I should have busied myself with other matters, but the attraction of this age-old text was irresistible.

All my time was spent in libraries, and I devoured all the new periodicals which included something about the Scrolls as soon as they arrived. After a few months of intense enquiry, I screwed up courage and wrote up the story for publication. Naturally, I was in continuous contact with Professor Lambert. He not only encouraged and approved of my venture, but himself seemed to have caught the Scrolls fever from me. Overcoming his habitual reluctance to put his thoughts on paper, he suddenly turned into a prolific writer, producing one article after another in the College's monthly, the *Nouvelle Revue Théologique*. The friendly pages of the *Cahiers Sioniens*, by that time under the editorship of Paul Démann, provided an outlet for my first effort. So along came a ten-page article, seasoned with footnotes, and entitled 'Nouvelles lumières sur la Bible et sur le Judaïsme' (New Light on the Bible and Judaism). It was dated June 1949, and appeared on 1 August of the same year. This paper in fact makes me the most senior writer on the Scrolls still active today.

In retrospect, this first fruit of my pen, or rather my typewriter, was a tolerable piece: a promising start, as people remarked at the time, well-informed and reasonably informative. But it also displayed what I now see as naiveté: the fact that the individuals originally involved with the Scrolls belonged to a variety of nations was interpreted by me as the sign of an impending mutual understanding between Jews and Arabs and the rest of the world. Naturally I was over the moon realizing that my career as a writer had begun, and I was determined to carry on with the job. However, as I still had my final year of theology and the completion of my dissertation in front of me, I was not in a position to commit myself fully to Qumran studies straight away.

The new academic year which opened in September 1950 brought about important changes in my circumstances. Not only did I begin my doctoral research, supposedly on the remaining sections of the Servant of the Lord poems, but I also became a graduate student in the University of Louvain, a seat of learning founded in the fifteenth century. Its *Institut Orientaliste* covered the full spectrum of the relevant subjects, but I naturally set my heart on the study of the ancient Near East. Earlier in the century, those reading Semitica had to offer all the main Semitic languages – Hebrew, Aramaic, Syriac, Akkadian, Arabic and Ethiopic (Geez) – but by 1950 we were required to choose only three, and I opted for Hebrew, Aramaic and Akkadian (Assyrian and Babylonian). Out of interest, I also attended classes in Arabic and Egyptian.

At the *Institut*, I came into close contact with internationally renowned scholars. Gonzague Ryckmans, whose fame was mainly based on his work on pre-Islamic Arabic inscriptions, was my favourite master; he taught me Hebrew and comparative Semitic grammar. One of our Hebrew set texts for philological analysis was the Book of Isaiah. We read chapters 20–35, not from the traditional printed Bible, but from the big Isaiah manuscript found in Qumran Cave 1. This was exciting and marvellously suited my penchant. Robert De Langhe, an expert in Ugaritic, an important ancient Semitic language discovered twenty years earlier, was my professor of Aramaic and Akkadian. I found him particularly kind and he allowed me to spend hours in his library. When years later I unexpectedly ran into him in a darkish late afternoon in Tom Quad in Christ Church during a conference in Oxford, and was unsure whether he would know who I was as I was no longer wearing clerical garb and was sporting a beard, I asked whether he recognized me. 'Of course I do,' he said. 'One can never forget those eyes.' Sadly, he died not long after that meeting when he was in his early fifties. I also attended at the theology faculty the lectures of Canon (later Monsignor) Joseph Coppens, a noted and very productive Old Testament specialist with tremendous bibliographical expertise. As orientalists, we formed small groups of two or three students per subject, and the teaching was much more informal than the large classes of forty to fifty with the Jesuits.

From then on I discussed my research problems with my teachers in both camps. I felt that Father Lambert, who considered me his own 'property' and Coppens his rival, resented my dual allegiance. He should not have worried: for me Coppens came a poor third to Ryckmans and De Langhe.

I can no longer exactly remember how the change in the doctoral thesis topic came about. My total absorption with the Scrolls must quickly have extinguished my remaining sparks of interest in the Servant Songs. And although study of a fresh discovery with no firmly established results to rely on was not the most suitable terrain for a novice researcher, Father Lambert's own new-born enthusiasm for Qumran alleviated his concern about the feasibility of my project and I was formally authorized to embark on a dissertation which in the end was given the title *Le cadre historique des manuscrits de la Mer Morte* (The Historical Framework of the Dead Sea Scrolls). The only technical problem which arose from this essentially historical enquiry concerned – as will be seen – its questionable suitability for a doctorate in theology. I was amused to discover, in going through my papers, that although I was more and more caught up in non-theological matters, I was still careful to observe church rules. I applied for and obtained from Joseph Ernest Cardinal van Roey, Archbishop of Malines, permission, valid for three years, to 'read and possess prohibited books with the exception of obscene or expressly anti-religious works'. In those days, a pious Catholic was not supposed to read any publication on religious matters which was without the *imprimatur* ('let it be printed') of the ecclesiastical authority. This permit expired in 1953, but by then I had ceased to worry about such matters and did not bother to renew it.

In the summer of 1950, I was once again deeply engaged in reading, translating and interpreting new Qumran texts freshly released by Professor E. L. Sukenik in his second preliminary Hebrew publication, entitled *Hidden Scrolls from the Judaean Desert*, and others by the American School of Oriental Research earlier that year. This was *The Dead Sea Scroll of St Mark's Monastery* I [The Isaiah Manuscript and the Habakkuk Commentary] by Millar Burrows. It was followed in 1951 by *The Manual of Discipline*.[3] In fact, the September 1950 issue of the *Cahiers Sioniens* carried my first substantial research paper; this included an annotated translation of four Thanksgiving Hymns and an attempt at dating them by means of literary comparison with Jewish writings assigned to AD 70–90. When the proofs arrived, I was shaking and trembling. With hindsight, I admit that the opinion I advanced in it was mistaken, but in those early days it sounded perfectly plausible. My subsequent contacts with more senior specialists made clear that it was this paper, dated June–July 1950, which placed me on the map of Dead Sea Scrolls scholars. Indeed, it brought about the first invitation to contribute an article to a long-established periodical. It came from Professor Joseph Coppens, who was then the editor of *Ephemerides Theologicae Lovanienses*.[4]

The general atmosphere surrounding the study of the Scrolls underwent considerable changes following the identification of Cave 1 and a superficial survey of the ruins of Qumran in early 1949, and in the wake of the already mentioned publication of texts by Professor Sukenik and by Millar Burrows. Two professional archaeologists, the French Dominican Father Roland de Vaux, one of the key figures in Scroll matters for the next twenty years, and the Englishman G. Lankester Harding, head of the Jordanian Department of Antiquities, also intervened, but started off

Qumran research on the wrong foot twice over. To begin with, after a perfunctory survey they declared that the site was not connected with the manuscripts. In an article in *The Illustrated London News* (1 October 1949) Harding wrote: 'It seemed at first possible that the cave deposit might have some relation to this site, but a trial excavation showed that it dates to the third or fourth century AD, much later than the cache. It appears to be a small Roman fortress.' Next, R. de Vaux asserted in his turn that the pottery found in the cave was Hellenistic, and that in consequence all the scrolls must predate the Roman conquest of Palestine in 63 BC. Both these erroneous statements were soon abandoned in the light of fresh archaeological data furnished by the first season of excavation at Qumran at the end of 1951. As a result, Father de Vaux dramatically changed his position in a thrice repeated public *mea culpa* – 'Je me suis trompé ... Je me suis trompé ... Je me suis trompé' (I was mistaken) – confessed before the French Academy of Inscriptions on 4 April 1952.[5] But already in 1950, following the publication of a commentary on the Book of Habakkuk by Millar Burrows and his colleagues, de Vaux's Hellenistic dating of the Scrolls had come under fire. Another Qumran pioneer, André Dupont-Sommer, the renowned Semitist of the Sorbonne in Paris, deduced – correctly as it turned out – from the study of the Habakkuk Commentary that the events alluded to there took us beyond de Vaux's closing date and well into the Roman epoch (beginning in 63 BC). More sensationally, Dupont-Sommer immediately asserted not only that the Qumran sect was identical with the ancient Jewish ascetic group of the Essenes but that its founder, the Teacher of Righteousness of the Habakkuk Commentary, suffered martyrdom. Finally, the Sorbonne professor concluded, reviving the great nineteenth-century French orientalist Ernest Renan's thesis about Christianity being 'an Essenism which has largely succeeded', that the contents of the Dead Sea Scrolls place the origins of Christianity in their true perspective: 'Today, thanks to the new texts, connections appear between the Jewish New Covenant, sealed with the blood of the Teacher of Righteousness in 63 BC, and the Christian New Covenant, sealed with the blood of the Galilean Master around AD 30.'[6]

Dupont-Sommer's claims, expounded in learned articles and in a well-written book of *haute vulgarisation*, gave fresh fuel to the scholarly debate. From the perspective of the Scrolls and *not* that of Christian theology, I found fault with his thesis and considered several points crucial to his interpretation to be philologically questionable. In particular, his theory concerning the presumed deification of the Qumran Teacher of Righteousness appeared patently forced. I quickly wrote an article voicing my criticisms, at the same time supplying fresh parallel evidence from the first-century AD Jewish historian, Flavius Josephus, regarding the Roman worship of military standards or *signa* alluded to in the Habakkuk Commentary according to Dupont-Sommer. When Father Lambert read my paper, he suggested that we should jointly publish it in the Jesuits' *Nouvelle Revue Théologique* together with his 'improvements', which mainly consisted in the use of stronger language in the critical passages. I agreed, as long as he had no objection to my own version appearing in the *Cahiers Sioniens* under my name. The two articles came out more or less simultaneously in the spring of 1951, and this double presentation turned out to be a blessing in disguise. When a year or so later I first visited Dupont-Sommer, I offered him off-prints of both versions. It was left to him to identify the source of the somewhat intemperate language contained in one of them. In the meanwhile I received flattering comments on the study from senior scholars of the stature of R. de Vaux, P. Kahle and E. L. Sukenik. One of the subsequent *Cahiers* of 1951 contained another paper of mine in which the technique of Bible exegesis in the Habakkuk Commentary was subjected to a detailed analysis and compared to the handling of Scripture in the New Testament. This was the first step towards the next stage of my specialization on ancient Jewish biblical exegesis, which was to culminate in 1961 in the publication of a book, *Scripture and Tradition in Judaism.*

It was also in 1951, in the late spring I think, that Professor Sukenik visited the University of Louvain and gave an illustrated lecture on his Dead Sea Scrolls. Although my comprehension of spoken English then left much to be desired, I attended the talk with enormous anticipation and, thanks to my familiarity with the subject, could roughly follow the gist of his talk. However, the greatest impression Sukenik made on me came not from his topic, or from the slides representing manuscripts or jars, but from his reading of a section of the Book of Isaiah. Unlike my professors, for whom Hebrew was a dead foreign language, on Sukenik's lips Isaiah sounded like living poetry. I had neither the courage, nor the opportunity, to speak to him on that occasion. Nor could he receive me in the last quarter of 1952 when I first visited Jerusalem, because of ill-health. He died a few months later in the spring of 1953. I failed to make his personal acquaintance but had a thirty-year-long friendly association with his son, who started as a general and finished as a professor of archaeology, the renowned Yigael Yadin.

Amid all this elation another significant event took place quietly in the last months of 1950: in my curriculum at Notre Dame de Sion I reached the stage of priestly ordination. Monsignor L. Suenens, then auxiliary bishop, later Cardinal Archbishop of Malines and a leading figure at the Second

Vatican Council, made me first a sub-deacon and soon afterwards a deacon in Louvain, and another bishop, whose name I can no longer recall, ordained me priest in a place called Hal, not far from Brussels, on 27 December 1950. The rite was moving and I genuinely believed that when that anonymous bishop put his hands on my head, some mystical power was passed on to me which originated with the apostles of Jesus. However, unlike my co-ordinands who were surrounded by their families, being away from my home ground I had no one with me to share the emotions of the moment. My first mass on the following day in the miserable little chapel of our Louvain house was also a low-key happening. From then on, the daily mass early in the morning, attended only by one of the novices, became the regular spiritual introduction to a full-time scholarly existence. During my six years as a priest I was never entrusted with any formal pastoral duties.

Another event, unremarkable at first sight but momentous in its later consequences, is linked to the last weeks of 1950: a couple of days before Christmas a new postulant, i.e. prospective novice, arrived in Louvain. 'He seems to be a rather unusual character', Father Nicolas told me. This was surely an understatement, as the person concerned was John Randal Bradburne. John was an Englishman, then approaching thirty, three years and eight days my senior. He was the son of an Anglo-Catholic parson. During the Second World War he served as a captain in the Indian army, first with the Gurkhas in Malaya, and later with Orde Wingate's Chindits in Burma. After his return to England, in 1947 he was received into the Catholic Church by the Benedictines of Buckfast Abbey, and in 1950 a benefactor provided him with money to go on pilgrimage to Rome. There he said to himself, 'I ought to carry on from here to Jerusalem', and with next to no money but plenty of faith and initiative he somehow got as far as Cyprus, which was still a British colony. There this vagabond approached officialdom for help as he wanted to sail to Haifa. 'Who is going to guarantee that the money will be repaid?', he was asked. 'Why don't you cable my brother who is British consul in Tripoli?,' he replied. Philip Bradburne bailed out his 'crazy' brother and after arriving in the Holy Land John hitch-hiked to Jerusalem. He had nowhere to go, but he knew from his Buckfast Abbey days that the friendly Benedictines had a house in Jerusalem on Mount Zion. So he asked someone for the way to Zion and was directed (providential accident?) to the house of the Fathers of Sion (or Zion). At 'Ratisbonne', as the establishment was called, he was kindly received by a charming and aristocratic French superior, Pierre de Condé, and John at once felt convinced that his 'miraculous' arrival at the Sion convent was a divine sign of vocation. Without further ado, he expressed his wish to join the congregation which, unknown to him, was very short of fresh blood. So before he might change his mind, he was quickly shipped to Louvain, where he arrived, full of enthusiasm and *joie de vivre*, but with little understanding of what Sion was about, and equipped only with a typical English public schoolboy's French. John was truly a fish out of water. His only palpable assets were a beautiful singing voice – he was probably the most naturally musical person I have ever met – and a powerful but unbridled piety. Father Nicolas, always patient, tried his best without visible success, but my younger colleagues showed little tolerance towards this cuckoo in the nest. I was his only friend, a friendship that lasted for some years, then sank, only to surface once again in 1978, the year before he died in extraordinary circumstances in Southern Rhodesia (on its way to becoming Zimbabwe).

John Bradburne will turn up more than once in my story. At this opening stage of our relationship he was first and foremost my English tutor. A little later, he (or rather his sister) helped me to obtain an English magazine (I think it was *The Sphere*) in which the picture of an unpublished Qumran manuscript had been accidentally printed. This allowed me to score a hit in the field of Scrolls studies.

John and I spent many hours together reading. He obviously wanted to introduce me to poetry and gave me his copy of the *Oxford Book of English Verse*. It was more than I could cope with at that time. One day I brought back a little pamphlet which I had found in the Egyptology seminar room at the University, and suggested that we should read it. He was not too keen on it, because he did not think its English to be of high enough quality. It was an account, written by the wife of the renowned German orientalist and biblical scholar, Paul Kahle, of the quasi-miraculous escape of the whole Kahle family, father, mother and five sons, from Nazi Germany in 1939. They were not Jewish, but Mrs Kahle and her eldest son Wilhelm[7] had got into the Nazis' bad books for assisting a Jewish friend after the infamous *Kristallnacht* the previous November. On their way to England they passed through Belgium, and my professor of Egyptology, a graduate student in 1939, was commissioned to act as their guide and helper during their short stay in Louvain. How could John and I have suspected that Paul Kahle, by then living in Charlbury, not far from Oxford, would soon be one of the first leading foreign scholars to support and encourage me in my Scrolls work, and that six years later he would be my devoted and efficient patron when, as a stateless and jobless tourist without a work permit, I was desperately struggling to obtain a university job in England?

To return to my main story, by January 1952 two crucial dates were looming on the horizon: my university examination for the degree of *licence* in Oriental history and philology and the submission and defence of my doctoral thesis in theology. The family size of the student group at the *Institut Orientaliste* allowed for informality in examination practice. When I was ready, I asked for a date for an oral test, the only form of examination in use in Louvain. Then professor and student spent half an hour or so *tête à tête* and that was it. This routine was broken only once. Canon Ryckmans, with whom I had lengthy discussions about my work on the Scrolls, dispensed me from taking the exam. 'You know all these things,' he said rather over-generously in his quiet voice and with a gentle smile on his face. 'Let's not waste each other's time.' By contrast, Canon (later Monsignor) Coppens gave me a treatment which I found somewhat insulting. He asked me to translate and interpret a passage from the Hebrew Bible (it was from Amos or Hosea, I am no longer sure which), and when I had done so, he suddenly began to point with his pencil at words here and there in the text: 'What does this mean?' 'And this?' Accustomed to testing theology students, he was checking whether I had just learned the translation by heart like some of them did. I complied with his demand but with a dirty look on my face. The message was received and the examination came to an abrupt end.

I was confident that I would gain good marks, but I was nevertheless left pleasantly speechless when I learned that I had passed the test with the highest honours (*'avec la plus grande distinction'*). On the day when the results were published in *La Libre Belgique*, according to the local custom I also received a hand-written note of congratulation from the Rector of the University. A couple of weeks earlier all my university professors attended the public defence of my doctoral dissertation on the Scrolls at the Jesuit college.

During the last months of 1951 and in the first quarter of 1952 my thesis was making steady progress and was completed, or so I thought, by the end of March. It contained all the published and some of the unpublished information about the Scrolls. I spent some weeks in Paris before Christmas and there met the French Dominican Dominique Barthélemy, who was then engaged in editing the fragments retrieved in 1949 from the first Qumran cave. He put me fully in the picture about the new situation which arose from the first stage of the excavation of the Qumran site in November–December 1951. I learned from him that Father Roland de Vaux no longer claimed that Khirbet Qumran was a fourth-century Roman fortress but had come to recognize it as an establishment occupied from the late second century BC to the time of the first war of the Jews against Rome (AD 66–70) by the religious community to which the Scrolls belonged. I was also told that two other caves had been found with further manuscript fragments and that there was a good prospect that more would follow. In a letter which reached me early in February 1952, he assured me that the date of the deposit of the manuscripts around AD 70 was 'quasi-certain', and that consequently I should take note of this in my dissertation without spreading the news straight away.

I took all this on board and fast proceeded with the thesis. Apart from a fresh translation and analysis of the then available Qumran Hymns with their rich religious message, and the Habakkuk Commentary which gave a good insight into the sect's Bible interpretation and origins, its principal contribution was a detailed reconstruction of the historical framework of the Dead Sea Scrolls. In the light of the increased evidence, I abandoned my previous opinion that the Scrolls were composed in the second half of the first century AD, and instead adopted the 'revolutionary' conclusion that the formative stage of the Qumran sect – the struggle between the Teacher of Righteousness and his political opponent, the Wicked Priest – reflected the situation of the age of the Maccabees in the middle of the second century BC. At that time I was the only one to propound this theory, which according to my pocket diary of 1952 I first discussed with Lambert early in January.

Although my supervisor, not fully convinced, hummed and hawed, I stuck to my guns and by the end of March completed the redaction of the thesis. He was not to know that this brainwave of a research student would soon become the standard opinion among scholars; it remains so to this day.

My self-confidence was steadied by the sympathetic hearing I received from the leading British Scrolls scholar of those days, Professor H. H. Rowley of the University of Manchester. In March 1952, he read three lectures in French in Louvain which appeared later in that year in book form as *The Zadokite Fragments and the Dead Sea Scrolls*.[8] Professor Coppens, who was Rowley's host and the translator of the lectures into French, invited me to lunch with them and Rowley kindly listened to my report, in broken English, on the progress of my research. I felt encouraged and excited, yet I was also nervous. Rightly so, as it turned out, because my way of tackling the Scrolls ran into a snag. After a preliminary reading of my 260-page dissertation, which I had deposited on 28 April, the Jesuit board of examiners felt that despite its merits in the field of Hebrew studies and Jewish history, it was not sufficiently theological for a doctorate in theology. (As they were unaccustomed to conferring research degrees, which they did on behalf of the Gregorian University of Rome, they were worried that my unorthodox topic might get them into trouble.) So gently but firmly I was instructed in a letter dated 7 May 1952 to add a theologico-apologetic supplement to the original three sections of my opus.

I was shocked and annoyed, but set out at once hastily to compile a further section on the doctrinal aspects of the Dead Sea Scrolls and a criticism of André Dupont-Sommer's anti-Christian views, and three weeks later my judges were presented with an additional piece of 65 pages. I was not very pleased with the result, but luckily they were happy. In fact, when I was revising the typescript before submitting it for publication, I decided to replace the supplement, custom-made for the Jesuits, with a freshly written chapter on 'The Search for God' at Qumran which contained no anti-Dupont-Sommer polemics.

The date of the proceedings for the doctorate was fixed: Friday 27 June 1952 at 10 a.m. I was to give a lecture in Latin before the Jesuit faculty. I proposed three subjects: 'The Songs of the Servant of the Lord and the Theology of the Suffering Messiah', 'Traditions concerning the Davidic Origin of the Psalms', and 'The Doctrine of Original Sin in Jewish Theology in the Age of Jesus Christ'. The choice fell on the third title. All I remember about it is that it went off to everyone's satisfaction. At 3 p.m. came my presentation of the thesis and its defence in French. The attendance of half a dozen professors of the University put most of the non-expert Jesuits on their guard, so that I had to handle only Lambert's objections. It was not an easy task. The presence of Canon Coppens, whom he considered his arch-rival, made him extremely talkative, but he never managed to ask a question, so that I found it hard to get a word in edgeways. At the end all turned out well, and I was declared a doctor of theology, but had to wait for the actual conferment of the title until my dissertation, or at least a substantial part of it, appeared in print. Unlike in Britain, publication of a doctoral thesis was an essential requirement in those days in most countries of continental Europe.

There was celebration at Notre-Dame de Sion. After all, I was the first ever member of the congregation to gain a doctorate. (Paul Démann was registered for one, but never completed his research.) I was delighted to learn that I would be transferred to the Paris house, where the Superior General of the Fathers resided and, more important for me, where Paul Démann was publishing the *Cahiers Sioniens*. A few months later, a letter from great-aunt Gizi brought me congratulations from my surviving relations. They were delighted by the success of 'the youngest shoot of the family'.

After a short break, I left for Paris, there to spend the best part of July 1952. The day after my arrival, not without trepidation, I paid a visit to the leading Parisian Scrolls expert, Professor Dupont-Sommer. I knew from a letter of Paul Démann's collaborator, Renée Bloch, that he was rather cross with me. I learned from her that a few weeks earlier Dupont-Sommer had burst into the editorial office of the *Cahiers* to buy a copy of the issue which contained my critcism of his thesis. He tried to extract as much information as possible about me from Renée, a former pupil of his. But when she jokingly told him that I was really a 'good boy', the grand Monsieur of the Sorbonne showed no willingness to believe her, and preferred to describe me rather as a *'méchant garçon'* (a naughty boy). Renée suggested that, in order to find out which of them was right, he ought to see me. He had no objection, he said. So with a palpitating heart I crossed the Boulevard St. Michel to call on him in his home in the rue du Val de Grâce. From the fact that according to my diary I spent four and a quarter hours in his company, from 2 till 6.15 p.m., it would appear that he changed his mind about my *méchanceté*.

In the days that followed I also made preliminary arrangements with the Jesuit editor of a Paris periodical for the partial publication of my thesis as required by the Louvain regulations. A full chapter of the dissertation appeared in two instalments in 1953, and I duly received from the College St Albert a diploma certifying that I was a DTheol. I also approached a Belgian-French publishing house (Desclée & Co, Paris and Tournai) to enquire whether they might be interested in publishing my dissertation. In due course the proposal was accepted, but I felt that the thesis needed some reworking before it was turned into a book, and that it would also derive considerable profit from a visit to Jerusalem. My request for a temporary transfer to 'Ratisbonne' was gladly complied with by the Sion authorities and I was allowed to spend the last three months of 1952 in the young State of Israel before taking up my new post in Paris in January 1953.

While I was in Paris, news reached me from Louvain that John Bradburne had decided, to the great relief of the novice master, Father Nicolas, to leave the Sion order, which he found too stuffy, and that he was on his way to Paris to say farewell to me. He arrived, jolly as ever, with hardly any money and travelling extra light. Destination? Jerusalem. I helped him to obtain an Israeli tourist visa and we warmly embraced. 'This is not a goodbye,' I said. '*Au revoir* in the Holy City.'

Things did not turn out that way. John began to hitch-hike in a southerly direction. He wrote a note 'between Marseilles and Toulon', still ending with an '*à bientôt* in Israel'. 'If I can't get an "*autostop*" by aeroplane from Cannes, I'll be going on, by God's grace, to Assisi, Rome, Brindisi and Bari.' In fact, he sought help from the Pope, without success, 'begged' his 'bread shamelessly' all the way, and finally got stuck for nearly a year outside Naples where he was, in his own words, the 'very inefficient sacristan' and general factotum of a local priest. So we did not meet in Jerusalem, but our paths crossed again in 1954 in England with unforeseen and unforeseeable consequences for both of us.

I felt on top of the world. I had completed my studies with flying colours. My first book was practically done, and a trip to the Holy Land was only weeks away. Finally, fulfilment of my dreams, I was to move to Paris. Once more, I thought that life was just beginning. This was true of my scholarly career, but not of my life in a fuller sense. Indeed, the great watershed lay only four and a half years ahead.

APPENDIX: THE DEAD SEA SCROLLS IN A NUTSHELL

In the spring or summer of 1947 a young Arab shepherd accidentally discovered seven Hebrew and Aramaic scrolls in a cave not far from the northwestern corner of the Dead Sea. Two years later the cave was identified by archaeologists, and hundreds of manuscript fragments, overlooked by the first discoverer, were retrieved from it. They were housed first in the École Biblique of the French Dominicans and later in the Rockefeller Museum in Jerusalem. Three of the scrolls, an incomplete manuscript of Isaiah, a collection of hymns and a work describing the final battle between the sons of light and the sons of darkness, were acquired by the professor of archaeology of the Hebrew University, E.L. Sukenik, whose edition of them was posthumously published in 1954. The other four scrolls, purchased by a Syrian Orthodox archbishop in Jerusalem, were entrusted to scholars from the American School of Oriental Research for publication. Three of them, a complete Isaiah text, a Commentary on Habakkuk and the rule of a sect, were issued by them in 1950 and 1951, but the fourth remained unopened. All four were subsequently bought by an intermediary for the State of Israel and now they are all housed in the Shrine of the Book in Jerusalem. The best-preserved parts of the previously unopened Genesis Apocryphon were published in 1956.

Between 1951 and 1956 ten further caves with a considerable number of fragments and several further scrolls (a fragmentary Psalms manuscript, part of a Leviticus scroll, an apocryphal Temple scroll and a list of hidden treasure on copper) were discovered in the area surrounding the ruined settlement of Qumran. The archaeological excavations of the site, the final occupation of which dates to a period between the mid-second century BC and the first Jewish War against Rome (AD 66–70), was conducted in successive campaigns under the direction of Father Roland de Vaux of the École Biblique. He was also in charge of the edition of the material found in the caves and the organizer of a small international team of editors assembled in 1953–54, and commissioned to prepare the publication of the texts in a series entitled *Discoveries in the Judaean Desert* (DJD) by Oxford University Press.

After a promising start, with five volumes of DJD appearing between 1955 and 1968, the editorial process slowed down to a snail's pace, while the unproductive scholars in charge of them denied access to unpublished material to all outsiders. The situation became so intolerable that it led to a revolution by the frustrated majority and in 1991 the embargo on the scrolls was finally lifted by the authorities. Today the publication of the manuscripts is steadily proceeding under the very capable supervision of the editor-in-chief, Professor Emanuel Tov of the Hebrew University, who expects the series of thirty-eight volumes to be completed by 2002.

A more detailed account may be found in my books, *The Dead Sea Scrolls: Qumran in Perspective* (London 1994) and *The Complete Dead Sea Scrolls in English* (London 1997).

9

Jerusalem and Qumran

(September–December 1952)

It was on board an ageing former British steam ferry, renamed *Artzah* by the Israelis, that I sailed from Marseilles towards the land of my forefathers at 9 a.m. on Wednesday, 24 September 1952. I travelled inexpensively in a four-berth tourist cabin shared with three other men in the belly of the ship. I was full of anticipation, more on account of the possibility of catching a glimpse of some Dead Sea Scrolls than of the certainty of setting foot on holy places. But I was also nervous, as this was my first sea journey and I had no idea what to expect, especially as it was the week of the autumn equinox and potentially breezy. In fact the Mediterranean was as smooth as a millpond, and we sped as fast as the ancient engines could propel us, stopping in Naples only long enough to take on new passengers. The Day of Atonement fell on the following Sunday and the captain hoped to get rid of us well before the great fast began.

Most of the travellers were Israelis returning from Europe for the High Holidays. Being with them was a new experience. The young ones were bursting with enthusiasm. The state was only four years old and they all seemed to dream of a rosy future. I made no lasting contact, but an episode which I witnessed with amazement deeply impressed me. Two middle-aged men, a schoolmaster and a judge, both of them *sabras* (born in Palestine as it then was), were engaged in a kind of party game of Bible knowledge. One of them began to quote a scriptural verse in Hebrew and the other was to finish it off and start another passage from a different book. Neither of them seemed to be an Orthodox Jew, yet they knew their Book inside out and the game ended in a draw. I was soon to learn that for non-religious Israelis the Bible, the ancient literary treasure of the Jewish people, lay at the heart of the new nation's secular education. For the Orthodox, however, it was child's stuff, and came a poor second to the Talmud.

The pleasant and fast race across the blue Mediterranean, smoothly sailing along the northern coast of Crete, took us to Haifa in good time. On the last day of the voyage, I was anxiously watching for the first sighting of the Holy Land. It happened on Sunday morning, 28 September and filled me with deep emotions, but whether their source was religious or purely atavistic, I cannot tell. The superior of 'Ratisbonne', Father Pierre de Condé, was waiting for me. I was offered a delicious drink of grapefruit juice, but when, parched, I asked for a second, I was told that that would be extravagant. We boarded a coach for Tel Aviv, where we took a taxi for Jerusalem, reaching it just before everything froze to a standstill on the arrival of the awesome Yom Kippur or Day of Atonement.

'Ratisbonne', set up about a hundred years earlier by the junior founder of the Fathers of Sion, Alphonse Ratisbonne, was a large complex of buildings which in former times served as a school, but by the early 1950s simply housed a few Jewish families in addition to a handful of Fathers. At the earliest opportunity, I registered for a course of modern Hebrew. I soon met one of the senior librarians of the Hebrew University, Dr Ezra Pfeffermann. He and his wife lived in the neighbourhood and came from Hungary. He was extremely helpful and arranged for me to meet scholars whom I wanted to visit. Thus I was introduced to Jacob Licht, who was to become a Dead Sea Scrolls authority, but who in 1952 was the humble assistant of Professor Sukenik. Through Licht, I sought permission to see the then unpublished Hymns found in Cave 1, but my request was met with a blunt refusal. It was in the Licht home that I first came across one of the real characters of Qumran studies and later of the quest for the Jewish Jesus, David Flusser, a close friend of the Lichts. He also became a renowned Scrolls scholar and the first holder of a chair at the Hebrew University dealing with the origins of Christianity, previously a taboo subject. He was a great talker. The renowned American man of letters, Edmund Wilson, who interviewed him when preparing his famous articles on the Scrolls for *The New Yorker* in 1955,[1] was warned that every question addressed to Flusser would be followed by an answer lasting three hours. Flusser told Wilson that his favourite language of conversation was mediaeval Latin (which he practised with the Jesuits), but I can add that New Testament Greek came close second. When Mrs Licht gave birth to a baby in December of that year, David Flusser greeted his many acquaintances, including me, in the streets of Jerusalem with a recitation of the nativity accounts of the Greek Gospels. Ezra Pfeffermann was also the mediator in arranging another momentous meeting. I hoped to obtain a chance to visit the great religious thinker Martin Buber, whose recently published, pioneering comparative study of Christianity and Judaism, *Two Types of Faith*, was the subject of a review article in the *Cahiers Sioniens*. He promptly consented to receive me. I was advised that in order to find his home in the Talbiye district of Jerusalem, I was to ask, not for Professor

Buber, but for someone even better known than he in the neighbourhood, the grocer Rosenzweig.

I arrived in the Buber home at 3.30 p.m. as agreed and, sitting in the drawing room, I had an unexpected glimpse through a half-open door of the great man, lying on his back fast asleep and prominently displaying the profile of his protuberant well-rounded belly. The maid went in to wake him and announce my arrival. Martin Buber was seventy-four years old then, very short, but holding himself straight with a flowing white beard and shining penetrating eyes. He was to live another thirteen years until 1965, most of them spent on completing the great German translation of the Hebrew Bible which he started with his friend Franz Rosenzweig (not the grocer) in the 1920s. We conversed about *Two Types of Faith* in French, which he spoke fluently. I was deeply impressed. I was not to know that he would be part of my life for thirty years, while Pam, my future wife, would devote much of her time to a study which led to two books on Buber; and that twenty-seven years later, in 1979, I would visit her hero's grave in Jerusalem. Nor was I to know that Pam's own Westmoreland slate tombstone would carry the twenty-third verse of Psalm 73: 'I am with You always, You hold my right hand' – with both the Hebrew text and artistic lettering borrowed from Buber's Jerusalem memorial.

Another noteworthy event of the first few weeks spent in Israel was my participation in an archaeological conference held in a kibbutz on the shore of Lake Kinneret or Gennesaret in Galilee. I spent a day in Nazareth, where I much preferred the undisturbed quietness of the first-century AD ruins in the basement of the convent of the Dames of Nazareth to the 'touristy' vulgarity of the great basilica of the Annunciation. I visited Tiberias, Kefar Nahum, the Capernaum of the Gospels, but I was most deeply impressed by the ruins of another New Testament village, Korazin (or Chorozain), which lay in the wilds in those days and could be reached only by jeep. Forty years later, in 1992, when a highway was running along the ruins of Korazin's ancient synagogue, I advised a British television crew engaged on making a documentary on 'Jesus before Christ' to hold one of our discussions on the teaching of Jesus there. The episode was originally planned to take place in Capernaum. However, the Franciscan guardians of the reconstructed ruins of the Capernaum synagogue changed their minds at the last minute and refused us permission to make a non-religious film on the site where Jesus preached and healed the sick.

I also explored the archaeological sites of Israeli Jerusalem, and clearly remember my first visit to the ancient rock tomb furnished with a rolling stone like that of Jesus according to the Gospels, the monument known as the tomb of the royal family of Herod. In later years I returned twice to this tomb. First I sheltered there in the company of Pam in 1961, seeking refuge from the August midday sun. We were resting in the enjoyably cool underground air when a group of American tourists entered and were taken aback at the sight of living occupants. We reassured them that the place was not private property. Some thirty years later, in the early 1990s, we were supposed to record a discussion on the resurrection of Jesus there, but the filming was delayed for nearly an hour by a group of extremely noisy Arab boys who considered that the surrounding park was their legitimate playground and did not give a damn for inconveniencing a foreign TV crew.

The principal aim of my visit to the Holy Land, to catch a glimpse of the Dead Sea Scrolls, was still unfulfilled. Sukenik's refusal to grant me access to 'his' manuscripts kept in Jewish Jerusalem left only one alternative: an excursion to Jordanian Jerusalem and, dream of dreams, a pilgrimage to Qumran itself. The task was hazardous for a Jew, even for one wearing Catholic clerical dress, but also quasi-impossible in that by now almost forgotten age of a divided Jerusalem. As a stateless person, I would be frowned on, I was assured, by the Jordanian authorities, who would not dream of granting me a visa. But worst of all, while one-way travel for (non-Jewish) pilgrims was possible from Jordan to Israel (as long as the passport used in Jordan contained no Israeli visa; those who travelled in those parts of the world were issued with two passports, one for Israel not to be shown in Arab countries, and a second for the rest of the world), to do what I wanted, namely to cross from Israel to Jordan and back again from Jordan to Israel was impossible – unless you were a diplomat or a United Nations observer.

Embracing the Napoleonic slogan '*l'impossible n'est pas français*' (the impossible is not French), I set out to devise a stratagem. I was told that the French consulate would ignore me as I was not yet residing in Paris, so I sought Belgian help. Foreseeing well in advance that I might face problems of this sort, I had obtained a letter of recommendation from my Louvain professor, Gonzague Ryckmans. I struck lucky: he was a cousin of the Belgian consul in Jerusalem, and since the Western countries did not recognize the division of Jerusalem between Israel and Jordan, a single consul served both halves of the city. A few days after my arrival, I wrote to him and was delighted when by return I received an invitation to luncheon. Could he provide me with a *laissez-passer* and obtain an Arab visa for a short visit for me? The consul, who was a Belgian count, saw no difficulty in issuing me with the document. As for the visa, he said, one could never be sure what would happen. But since he hardly ever asked anything from the Jordanians, he added with a smile, it would be difficult for them to decline his request.

The precious 'Substitute for a Belgian passport No. 53' carries an 'emergency visa valid for a single entry' and for one month into the Hashemite Kingdom of Jordan. Meanwhile, arrangements were made from Paris with the École Biblique of the Dominicans, the shrine of Scrolls research, to offer me hospitality and assistance. The day of the crossing arrived: it was Thursday, 16 October. I turned up at the consulate, a little nervous, but full of excitement. My destination was the famous Mandelbaum Gate in Jerusalem, the only transit point between the two halves of the divided city, and indeed between Israel and the Arab world. In fact the crossing was an anticlimax. The Israeli guard simply stamped my travel document, and as I was driven by the consul himself in his diplomatic car, the soldier of the Arab Legion on duty glanced at my paper and politely waved us on.

At the École Biblique I was given a friendly reception by Father de Vaux and his colleagues. Next day, I went to the Basilica of the Holy Sepulchre, presumed to be built on Golgotha and also containing the (empty) tomb of Jesus, to celebrate mass where Christians believe that Jesus died on the cross and rose from the dead on the third day. It was not a particularly inspiring place; it was cold and ugly, and the stories about the constant in-fighting among the Greek Orthodox clergy and the Latin church mainly represented by Italian Franciscans further diminished the aura of holiness that this ancient sanctuary of Christendom should have radiated. I was also the guest of the Sisters of Sion in their Ecce Homo convent on the site of the Antonia fortress, from where the Roman troops had kept an eye on the happenings in the adjacent Jewish Temple. The Sisters were convinced that it was also the location of the Roman 'pavement' (*Lithostrotos* in John 19.13) where Pilate condemned Jesus to death, but some of the expert Dominicans disagreed, creating a feud common in those parts in the case of rival claims to holy places. One of the local jokes in Nazareth alleges that Saint Joseph was a property tycoon, because so many religious institutions claim that their church stands on a plot owned by the Holy Family.

I inspected all the antiquities worth seeing in Jerusalem and spent many hours among the remains of the old city of David, now outside the walled area; I also paid a number of visits to the Rockefeller Museum, a treasure house for students of Palestinian archaeology. Wide-eyed and sometimes open-mouthed, I stared at the many amazing relics of the Canaanite and Jewish past of the land. I also visited the site of the Temple of Jerusalem, which is now occupied by the splendid mosques of El Aksa and the Dome of the Rock, from where according to Muslim tradition Muhammad ascended to heaven. For the Bible and the rabbis of old, the Temple mount was Mount Moriah, on which Abraham sacrificed (or almost sacrificed)

Isaac. The Christians of the early centuries, innocent of modern ecumenical ideas, held that the destruction of the Temple by the Romans in AD 70 was the divinely ordained proof of the rejection of the Jews by God and their replacement by the church as the new chosen people.

A little later the Belgian consul kindly took me to Bethlehem, where we briefly stopped at the uninspiring Basilica of the Nativity, and to Hebron, the burial place of our father Abraham and his family. When we entered the great mosque of the city shoeless, I had to struggle to suppress a smile at the sight of several holes in the socks of the consul, who was a bachelor. But the site that impressed me most was neither the Christian basilica nor the Muslim mosque, but the totally abandoned and neglected ruins outside Hebron of a Jewish and Christian holy place of pilgrimage where many centuries ago pious men and women prayed, believing that it was the spot where the tent of Abraham stood next to the Oaks (or terebinths) of Mamre. Silence reigned, the Roman walls were impressive, and the well from which Abraham and Sarah may have collected water was still there, its limpid water revealing hundreds of old coins thrown in by pilgrims of ages gone by.

After these preliminaries I must now come to the heart of the matter. The chief purpose of my somewhat risky trip to Arab Jerusalem was to see Scrolls and caves and all the remains of Qumran. My hopes were not disappointed. At the École Biblique I once again met Dominique Barthélemy, who a few months earlier had acted as my friendly informer on undisclosed Qumran secrets. In 1952 work on editing the Dead Sea Scrolls was still a kind of cottage industry. The heaps of fragments which de Vaux and Harding had collected from Cave 1 in 1949 were entrusted to young Barthélemy, then aged about thirty, who recruited from Rome an equally young collaborator in the person of a very learned Polish priest, Józef Tadeusz Milik. He is *'un type très bien'* (a jolly good chap), Barthélemy told me in colloquial French. In fact, Milik soon proved to be an outstandingly gifted Scrolls scholar who fitted together, deciphered and identified more illegible and mutilated Qumran fragments than the other members of the first editorial team put together.

In those early days, the cult of secrecy, i.e. the refusal by the lucky few to share information with 'outsiders', the scourge of Qumran studies for almost four decades, had not yet been introduced. Barthélemy and Milik discussed their work in progress freely with me and showed me the unpublished fragments. In particular, I was invited to study a two-column jigsaw puzzle, put together from dozens of fragments but still with many missing bits, and to suggest ways to fill in the gaps. I was in the seventh heaven and made a number of suggestions, one of which is actually listed in the official edition of the Rule of the Congregation or Messianic Rule, published in 1955 by Oxford University Press.

We lived through exciting times at the École. By 1952, the Bedouin of the Judaean desert had become expert Scroll hunters, and nine times out of ten outwitted and beat their rivals, the professional archaeologists. They knew that after the customary Middle-Eastern bargaining, Father de Vaux would buy those old bits of dry and perishing leather or papyrus scraps, so they came along singly or in small groups carrying their loot in matchboxes. I saw several such new acquisitions during my short stay. When the sellers realized that larger fragments fetched more money, they tried to glue their bits together. These were an unbelievable sight: untouched for two millennia except by mice and rats, they still held their original secrets. (Not for much longer, once Milik managed to put his hands on them.)

All I needed after this practical initiation into Scroll work was to make my pilgrimage to the 'holy of holies' in Qumran. An opportunity soon arose to fulfil my dream. On Monday 27 October the École organized an archaeological trip to the Jordan valley which I was permitted to join. We travelled from Jerusalem eastwards along the spectacular Wadi Kelt heading towards Jericho. We passed the Herodian Jericho of the age of Jesus, and approached through the modern town the relics of the Canaanite and Israelite city. The excavated ruins were both magnificent and insalubrious because the poor inhabitants of the depressing Palestinian refugee camp of Tell es-Sultan used them as their latrines. According to the Bible, the walls of Jericho came tumbling down when 'Ole' Joshua blew the trumpets. But the famous British archaeologist, Dame Kathleen Kenyon, spoiled the story, claiming that while Jericho had seven successive fortified ramparts between 3000 and 2000 BC, it was wall-less during the late Bronze Age when the Israelite conquest of this Canaanite city occurred. Few male archaeologists or biblical scholars dared contradict this frighteningly learned cigar-smoking Amazon, as I was to find out some twenty years later in Oxford when she, by then principal of St Hugh's College, and I sat through many a heated debate at the meetings of the Board of the Faculty of Oriental Studies.

I and my fellow travellers spent the night in a cheap Arab hotel in modern Jericho, noisy and dreary, which was an experience in itself. I could hardly sleep, not just because of the lack of comfort and the unbearable heat, but also because next day our main port of call was Qumran, some eight miles to the south. On our way, we admired the breathtaking splendour of the castle of Khirbet Mefjer, a pearl of Umayyad architecture. From there our decrepit bus headed towards the Dead Sea and its savage beauty, and turned south on to an unmade road, today tarmac and furnished with signposts to Qumran. The bus finally stopped in the middle of nowhere and we were summoned to follow our leader and climb the cliff which ran parallel with the shore. Our destination was 1Q or Qumran Cave 1, the blessed hole in the rock where the whole Dead Sea Scrolls saga began. My heart was beating fast both from exertion – climbing had never been my forte – and even more from inward exhilaration: I would soon see with my own eyes the hiding place where the two scrolls of Isaiah, the Habakkuk Commentary, the Community Rule, the Hymns and the War Scroll had lain concealed for nineteen centuries until lucky Muhammad edh-Dhib had stumbled on them five years earlier.

We continued our rock-walking towards the neighbouring Cave 2 before rejoining the bus which took the party to Khirbet Qumran, the ruined settlement which according to local tradition stood on the site of the ill-fated biblical city of Gomorrah, and which was the centre of the group which owned the Scrolls. The view of the Qumran remains was very different from that which meets the visitor's eye today. It was much less spectacular because the excavations were still at an early stage. Everything was just inchoate and mysterious, and as such full of promise. Adrenalin was racing through my veins. Now I had seen the caves and the ruins. Now I would be able to turn my dry thesis into a real book.

The trip ended a couple of miles further south with a visit to Ain (or Spring of) Feshkha, the farmstead cultivated by the inhabitants of Qumran. There was nothing much to see there except the spring which made farming possible. Some of us took the opportunity to follow the stream to the Dead Sea close by and I decided to try a swim in those blue waters, so salty that apparently no one could sink in them. Vespasian, the Roman general and future emperor, sent to Judaea to quell the rebellion of the natives, heard about the characteristics of the water of the Dead Sea. Standing on the shore in AD 68, he decided to make an experiment. He ordered one of his soldiers to be tied up and used as a guinea pig. Vespasian and his entourage watched the man floating on the surface of the water with amazement. I repeated the experiment without the use of a rope to restrain my limbs, but although I tried, I could not sink. On the other hand, I discovered that the statement that no fish could live in the Dead Sea was not literally true. A yard or two from the shore where the sweet waters of Feshkha ran into the Dead Sea, I saw small fish happily swimming about. I washed off the deposit of salt from my skin in the cool stream and, exhilarated, gazed in the light of the setting sun at the mountains of Moab in Transjordan beyond the opposite shore of the Dead Sea.

My mission was accomplished: I came and I saw – *veni, vidi*. I had 'the feel' of the place, its solitary remoteness, its remote solitude. I experienced the excitement of discovery and observed wide-eyed how fragments were cleaned, assembled and deciphered. From now on I would be able to write on the Scrolls as an eye-witness, an insider. I could not foresee then that I and most of my fellow students of the Scrolls would soon be denied this 'insider' quality when in the course of the next two years Roland de Vaux established his notorious international and interconfessional (though Jew-free) editorial team which would withhold the unpublished material from all the scholars of the world who were not members of the arcane coterie of the chosen. I had to wait nearly forty years, until 1991 to be precise, before I was invited by Emanuel Tov, the first Jewish editor-in-chief of the Dead Sea Scrolls publication project to take charge of the edition of the Cave 4 fragments of the Community Rule. Though this is one of the most fundamental Qumran texts, it was merely gathering dust until then, due to the endless procrastination of the highly talented but dilatory J.T. Milik. Perhaps others would have lost interest after such a long wait, but so powerful was the impact on me of the early bond with the Scrolls that thirty-nine years after my first visit to Qumran I did not hesitate for a second and took on the task with alacrity and almost youthful enthusiasm.[2]

The rest of the archaeological tour, fascinating though it was, seemed an anticlimax after Qumran. We crossed the Jordan and advanced as far north as Pella, one of the ten Greek cities of the Decapolis where, if tradition is to be believed, some early Christians fled during the first Jewish war in the late 60s AD. The *tell* of Pella, the heap of rubble containing the remains of successive historical periods, was the tallest of the many tells I saw during that voyage. On the way back towards Jerusalem, we stopped at various sites on the biblical plain of Moab, south-east of Jericho, still in Transjordan. If someone had told me then that fifteen years later I would be the Hebrew tutor in Oxford of the Crown Prince of Jordan, I would have laughed.

A little later Joseph Milik took me to Nablus to see the remains of ancient Samaria. We visited the small group of Samaritans who still lived there in unhealthy isolation. We observed their archaic Jewish customs, and were shown the mediaeval manuscript of the Pentateuch which, they claimed, went back to the age of Moses. We stopped and had a drink at the Well of Jacob, site of the (fictional?) encounter between Jesus and the Samaritan woman in the Gospel of John, and returned to Jerusalem via Jericho.

My stay in the École was nearing its end. The last few days were spent in waiting in various offices where I had to collect a series of stamps on my phony *laissez-passer*. I picked up the final exit permit on the very day of the crossing. I had tried the day before but was firmly instructed to come back next morning. The final tally of the Arab stamps on my document for a single visit thus rose to seven. To enter Arab Jerusalem through the Mandelbaum Gate was simple; not so the return. The Belgian consul was not free, so while he kindly took charge of my luggage, he simply told me to walk across on the specified D-day, at the equally specified H-hour. I was driven to the crossing point, and made sure that I pulled the correct piece of paper out of my left pocket to show it to the Jordanian frontier guard with whom I spoke in my basic English. He looked at the unusual document and took it to the office inside a wooden hut. He stayed there for what seemed an eternity and I was getting nervous. Finally he came out and sternly asked (I swear I am not making this up): 'Did you enter on 16 October?' 'Yes, I did.' 'What is the date today?' 'Monday, 10 November 1952.' 'Hm. From 16 October to 10 November, is there more or less than one month?' (This was the length of validity of my Jordanian emergency visa.) 'Less than one month,' I replied. 'That's OK, then. Goodbye.' I moved on.

I put my 'false' document back into my left pocket and walked through the few yards of no man's land towards the Israeli checkpoint. There I pulled out my real travel document from the right pocket and handed it over to the young man on duty. Two unexpected things happened. First I was greeted in Hungarian by him, a pleasant surprise. But I was also told that I had no visa. 'How come,' I riposted, 'my visa issued in Brussels was valid for four months.' 'True,' the immigration officer admitted, 'but look, it is printed here that the visa is for a *single* entry. It was automatically cancelled when you left Israel for Jordan.' I suddenly imagined myself as a tent-dweller in no man's land, unable to enter Jewish Jerusalem or return to the Arab city. However, my Hungarian expatriate was less pessimistic. 'Sit down here. Would you like a drink while I consult my superiors?' A short telephone conversation in very fast Hebrew followed, the gist of which I guess was something like: 'What shall I do with this hopeless but harmless-looking tourist who is trying to re-enter Israel with a visa which is no longer valid?' The answer he received equalled King Solomon's judgment in wisdom: 'Issue him with another visa, but make him pay for it!' So the drama ended happily.

While I was waiting, I learned that Israel was in mourning; the first president of the state, Chaim Weizmann, had died the previous day, 9 November. It was lunchtime with relatively heavy traffic at the Mandelbaum Gate. The whole United Nations personnel seemed to be moving towards the Old City. 'They are all going there for a good meal in Arab restaurants,' my interlocutor explained. 'I wish I could join them,' he added. Unlike Israel, Jordanian Jerusalem had no food rationing.

The rest of my stay in Israel was unsensational. I had a number of

further Scrolls discussions with Drs Licht and Flusser and regularly
attended classes at the Hebrew University, which in those days were held
in the Italian Franciscan establishment called Terra Santa. The University
buildings on Mount Scopus lay in no man's land. Inaccessible to civilians,
they were guarded by an Israeli police detachment which was taken there
and back once a fortnight by a convoy of vehicles under the supervision of
the UN.

Christmas was approaching. I was invited to say midnight mass in the
chapel of the Sion Sisters in Ain Kerem, the place, close to Jerusalem,
where the pregnant Virgin Mary is believed to have visited her equally
pregnant elderly cousin Elizabeth, the future mother of John the Baptist. I
expected a quiet event, but the little church was absolutely filled with very
Jewish-looking people. 'Are there so many Christian Jews in that
neighbourhood?', I asked. They were not converts, I was told. They were
mostly nostalgia-stricken German Jews, recalling the old days before their
arrival in Palestine/Israel. They longed to hear again the tune of *Stille
Nacht, heilige Nacht* (Silent Night) and joined in the singing with gusto.

I am glad I had the chance to see the new Jewish state in its heroic days,
only four years after the 1948 War of Independence. One of its heroes, the
thirty-five year old General Yigael Yadin, of later Scrolls fame, was still
Chief of General Staff, and his photograph appeared in the newspapers
almost daily. The next year he retired and returned to his doctoral thesis,
appropriately on the Scroll of the War of the Sons of Light against the Sons
of Darkness, under the supervision of his father, Professor Sukenik. Israel
was a youthful and proud nation. One still witnessed the Tower of Babel
syndrome there. In the streets of Jerusalem one could hear every language
of the creation, even Hebrew. When I returned there nine years later in
1961, the situation was already changing in favour of Hebrew. And when in
1979, after the lapse of another eighteen years, I found myself in Tel Aviv
and Jerusalem lecturing, all the Israelis, young and old, spoke Hebrew as
though they had lived in those parts since biblical times.

The moment of departure arrived: I travelled to Haifa on 30 December
and embarked on the good old *Artzah*. I waved goodbye to the disappear-
ing Israeli coastline under blue skies on a very hot day. I imagined that the
return journey would be as smooth and pleasant as the outward voyage, but
I was in for something of a surprise. During the second day of our trip, the
blue sky disappeared and dark clouds were gathering, and when we were
steaming north of Crete on the third day, a heavy storm broke out. *Artzah*
was shaken and thrown about by the waves and for the first and, I hope, the
last time in my life I was violently seasick. Without going as far as being
shipwrecked, I shared the experience of St Paul. His boat heading towards

Rome and captivity was caught in a storm close to Crete and sank after being blown across the Mediterranean for two weeks, but miraculously he and some of his companions landed alive in Malta. Our miserable trip continued until, past Sicily, we reached the Ligurian Sea and found shelter from the north-easterly wind in the land mass of Italy. What a relief it was.

We stopped in Naples. From Israel I sent a postcard to inform John Bradburne of my coming and suggested that he should meet me. I did not see him in the port. So instead I went to visit Pompeii on 5 January 1953. It was pouring with rain, so the purpose and usefulness of the elevated stones in the middle of the streets of the old Roman city became obvious. By hopping from one stone to the next in wintry weather the inhabitants could avoid getting their feet too wet until the inferno of lava showered by Vesuvius extinguished life in Pompeii in AD 79.

The ship docked in Marseilles two days later. The south of France under deep snow was an unusual sight, but Paris beckoned, signalling the beginning of a new career. A couple of days after my arrival, I received a letter from John dated 7 January. In his execrable French he explained that he had left his presbytery at Palma to catch a bus to the port of Naples. He waited and waited (in the wrong place) but no bus came. He was extremely sorry, as he hoped that we would drink a lot of wine in an Italian bar.

Some eighteen months later John and I drank, not Italian wine but pints of Devon cider, in a pub in the splendid little town of Ottery St Mary in Devonshire, a momentous episode to which I will return presently.

10

Paris and the *Cahiers*

(1953–1955)

In January 1953 I joined the central establishment of the Fathers of Sion and thus became a proud Parisian. Geographically, the residence of the Superior General, 68 rue Notre-Dame des Champs, was situated in a small two-storey detached house in a quiet street of the central sixth *arondisse-ment*, between the Boulevard Montparnasse and the Luxembourg Gardens. The property belonged to the Sisters of Sion, whose large, grey and dull-looking mother house and much-sought-after girls school stretched out on the opposite side of the street. The Fathers performed the many religious services in the Sisters' chapel, for which they were provided with a roof over their heads and with fairly decent meals.

The place was comfortable, at least by the Louvain standards to which I was accustomed. It even had a telephone, an instrument never installed in Louvain, as the superior, Father Nicolas, who was hard of hearing, had been frightened of it. He had occasionally received messages in the students' hostel across the road, but usually sent someone else to take them. On one occasion I was called to jot down and convey to him details of his sister's funeral arrangements. The Paris telephone was in the corridor on the first floor; it lacked privacy. But the only person who could have over-heard conversations was the Superior General, who was also slightly deaf and usually kept his door closed. He constituted no great danger.

The personnel fell into two symmetrical halves. First, there was the old guard. The Superior General, Father Henri Colson, was a short, rotund and jovial man from eastern France. He was used to the traditional ways of the congregation and quite happy with them, i.e. *praying* for the Jews, but mainly serving ordinary parishes. Before the First World War he spent many years in Palestine and had unending stories about the life of Christian Arabs in the final days of the Ottoman empire. I heard, for instance, how Father Colson was pulled out of his bed on a Sunday morning when it was still dark, and told to say mass at once. There had been a razzia. The people of the neighbouring village had raided the place and all the horses, donkeys and camels had been driven away. So before setting out in hot pursuit of the rascals, his pious parishioners wanted to acquit themselves of their Christian duties. Apparently they returned in the evening, bringing back not only all the stolen animals, but also those of the offending village. Father Colson was mainly a competent administrator, and his duties entailed a great deal of travelling. His constant worry was that he might be late for his train. He always left early for the station and got there just in time to be annoyed at missing the previous one. Likewise he regularly arrived in the dining room five minutes before mealtimes and was cross with the others even when they were punctual. The novelties which we, 'the young ones', were trying to introduce filled him with unease and displeasure.

The Paris superior, Father Théomir Devaux, was of the same age as the Superior General, i.e. pushing seventy. He 'manned' the office of the Archconfraternity of Prayer for Israel, which was housed in a little extension on the ground floor. It was also 'womanned', if this is a permissible way to put it, by Mademoiselle Paulette, an ex-nun, secretary cum housekeeper, constantly accompanied by an enormously fat neutered tom cat, and assisted by Mademoiselle Georgette. Both ladies, of indeterminate age, were long-term devotees of Père Devaux. He was from Normandy, a former Superior General, quiet, industrious in his own way, pot-bellied with a long beard, and an addict of the *gros rouge*, the ordinary red table wine. Come the afternoon, he was regularly under the influence, but never really drunk. We wickedly nicknamed him Noah after the biblical 'patron saint' of wine-bibbers. One day, in such a slightly inebriated state, Père Devaux was grumbling about not having enough money for publishing his little pious bulletin. 'You must trust Providence,' I teased him with a straight face. 'Oh, yes,' he mumbled, establishing a new kind of practical theology, 'I always rely on Providence as long as the funds are there twelve months in advance.'

Against these two stalwart upholders of the ancient regime of the *Pères de Sion* stood the 'youngsters', Paul Démann and I, assisted by an admirable and delightful young woman, Renée Bloch. Not that we were babes: Paul was past forty and Renée and I were both twenty-eight (she was eighteen days older than me). The contrast between young and old was indescribable.

Paul, as I have noted earlier, was a Hungarian Jew. A brilliant student of architecture at the Technical University of Budapest, he had already started a promising career in Hungary when in the mid-1930s he converted to Catholicism and joined the Sion order in Louvain. He spent the war years in Belgium and was very active in saving Jewish children under the aegis of the Belgian resistance. He, too, studied theology at the college of the Louvain Jesuits and became an outstanding graduate researcher. He was full of promise, but alas ultimately failed to deliver. This lack of perseverance became transparent at a later stage of his career, but in 1953 it was not yet obvious. Paul was still convinced that as soon as he had sorted out a few pressing problems he would return to his thesis, which was as good as finished in his head, before proceeding to dozens of other great projects. These pressing problems were connected with people in trouble: spiritually, financially and quite often both; with religious politics in the domain of Jewish-Christian relations; and with the running of the *Cahiers Sioniens*, for which he acted as editor, chief contributor and only fundraiser.

New to Paris and to French life, and fresh out of the protective environment of the Louvain theological school, I looked to Paul for guidance and received much support from him. He had the qualities which I lacked, in particular experience and limitless self-confidence. First I admired and almost idolized him. He in turn could rely on me a hundred per cent and, without using the title, he made me an assistant editor of the *Cahiers*. As my room was just above his on the second floor we were in daily contact, and my numerous unscheduled visits further added to his difficulties in getting on with his work.

Renée Bloch was the third member of the trio of the *Cahiers*. Born in 1924 of Jewish parents in a chic suburb of Paris, she converted at the age of sixteen, and immediately fell in love with the Scriptures, Old and New Testament alike, a love which continued to grow throughout her short life. As a university student she went through the trials of the German occupation in Toulouse and after the Liberation she graduated as a *licenciée* of letters. For a time she tried religious life as a novice Benedictine nun, but the experiment misfired and the memories were so painful that despite our close bond of friendship I never really learned what went wrong. She returned to Paris after the war to study theology at the Institut Catholique, and Semitic languages and biblical exegesis at the Sorbonne and the École des Hautes Études. She met Paul Démann by chance in 1948 and came under his influence for the rest of her life. Their relationship was very close but I am sure totally 'pure'. Renée, though highly sophisticated in every other respect, struck me as completely childlike as far as men were concerned. She might have shared a room with Paul during their many journeys, but without thinking of anything but sleeping.

I believe I was first introduced to her during my stay in Paris in 1952. Anyway, we instantaneously took a liking to each other. She was not only charming and great fun to be with, but we shared a great many interests and were both workaholics. After an initial concern with the Hebrew Bible and the New Testament, which resulted in a historical survey of the terms 'Israelite, Jew, Hebrew', she turned her attention to rabbinic Bible interpretation and produced several important papers. Our research topics often coincided, for instance in connection with the Targums, ancient Aramaic paraphrases of Scripture, where I continued our joint project for years after her death. We constantly exchanged ideas and helped one another. In particular, she relied on my more thorough linguistic training in Hebrew and Aramaic and asked me to vet her articles. In turn, being a native speaker, she was to check my French and willingly did so ... when she had the time.

It was also Renée who first took me to the lectures at the École des Hautes Études of a scholar who profoundly influenced my outlook on research. He was Professor Georges Vajda, a quiet and enormously learned man, with clear views and firm convictions. As the name indicates, he also hailed from the land of the Magyars and had been a pupil of the world-famous Hungarian Jewish Theological Seminary in Budapest before settling in France in the 1930s. From him I learned not only all I know about mediaeval Judaism, his speciality – we read a substantial number of mystical (Kabbalistic) texts, many of them unpublished (Vajda was a manuscript man) – but also a methodological principle which was particularly welcome after years of theological training, namely that instead of dwelling on topics which require *élucubrations* (elaborate speculations) one should concentrate on questions for which factual evidence exists. My research students of later years greatly benefited from Vajda's advice when we were discussing whether a given subject was suitable for research. Renée and I spent many happy afternoons at the Sorbonne in Vajda's classes, in the company of other students who are today internationally respected experts in mediaeval Judaism. After the two-hour sessions we all repaired to a neighbouring patisserie for coffee, cream cakes and lively discussion lasting for another hour or two.

At the beginning those were happy days, the fulfilment of my desires. We lived through exciting times. Following the lead of Paul Démann, the little trio was enthusiastically engaged in a war to establish *the truth* in matters pertaining to Christian-Jewish relations. More often than not this meant in plain words that we wanted the Catholic Church to acknowledge nineteen hundred years of error in her attitude to Jews and to expiate all the injustice resulting from religious antisemitism. The very idea struck the older Fathers, Colson, Devaux and Co., and all the Sisters, as obnoxious. Démann and his acolytes with their confounded *Cahiers* were propagators of heresy or something very close to it. Of course, we enjoyed this tension. The internal strife had started in 1949, four years before my arrival in Paris, following Paul's favourable review of Jules Isaac's epoch-making and deeply moving indictment of Christian anti-Judaism in *Jésus et Israël*. I remember Father Colson's strong disapproval of the title of the article: 'At the *Christian* sources of Anti-Semitism'. This phrase, which is a cliché today, seemed utterly provocative to our senior colleagues and their like-minded *bien-pensant* cronies.

The first year of my stay in rue Notre-Dame des Champs witnessed two major clashes. The first was already in the making when I spent a month in Paris in the previous summer of 1952. The office of the *Cahiers*, that is Paul's room, was filled chock-a-block with textbooks of Catholic religious education intended for all ages of the school curriculum, from six to eighteen. A major survey of the treatment of the Jews in Catholic pedagogi-cal literature was in progress. Renée, a very fast reader, devoured the volumes one after the other, made notes and prepared a rough draft for Paul, who was going to turn it into a 220-page book which simultaneously served as a double number of the *Cahiers Sioniens* (nos. 3–4, 1952). Shortly after my arrival, it came out as *La Catéchèse chrétienne et le peuple de la Bible* (Christian Religious Education and the People of the Bible), by Paul Démann with the collaboration of Renée Bloch.[1] What they discovered and exposed was horrendous. With the exception of a few books mostly published after 1947, when the Nazi atrocities were still fresh in people's minds, the large majority of the textbooks actually used in Catholic schools in the early 1950s were replete with the coarsest form of anti-Judaism, and devoid of any historical perspective, so that twentieth-century Jews were regularly charged with the crimes which the authors (wrongly) attributed to the contemporaries of Jesus *en masse*.

Here are a few chosen pieces. Anonymous nuns wrote under the charm-ing title of *Silhouettes évangéliques* (Gospel Silhouettes): 'Pilate washed his hands … It was finished: the people of God ceased to exist … The Gospel indicates the precise moment of the end of the Jewish world.' Another 'Sacred History' quoting Matthew 27.25, 'His blood be on us and on our children', comments: '"His blood be on us." We know how the whole nation paid less than forty years later for this sacrilege … "And on our children," dared to add the assassins of Christ. With their wealth, their commercial spirit, and indomitable energy, the Jews who reside everywhere without ruling anywhere, who possess the gold of the earth without being able to create for themselves a country,[2] who live, go about and die despised, ill-treated, and cursed as though one could still read on their fore-head, written with the bloody letters of yesterday, the cause of their misery, "Deicides"!'

I could carry on quoting page after page. To think that these books filled with hatred, spiritual superiority, indeed triumphalism, were meant to instruct the young, to inspire piety and love in tender souls; that they were written by priests, monks and nuns who considered themselves devout ... Today, more than forty years after the appearance of this survey, I imagine this sort of stuff would leave most decent Catholics speechless. Thirty years ago the Second Vatican Council eliminated all these 'un-Christian' sentiments from official church teaching. But in 1952 we were more than ten years *before* Vatican II, and the ideas propagated by the *Cahiers* must be reckoned, directly or indirectly, as the sources of the great reform of the attitude of Rome to Judaism and the Jews. However, by the 1960s when the *Cahiers* policies became official teachings of Rome, Renée was dead and Paul and I were no longer members of the Catholic Church.

The second clash opposing the team of the *Cahiers* to the rest of the Fathers and the Sisters of Sion was connected with an 'affair' of national significance which for weeks made massive headlines in the French press. The 'Finaly affair' exploded almost immediately after my arrival in Paris.[3] Dr Fritz Finaly and his wife fled to France after Austria's *Anschluss* by Hitler in 1938 and settled in Grenoble. Two children were born there, Robert and Gérald, in 1941 and 1942. In 1944 the parents were deported and perished, but the two boys were hidden by the Sisters of Sion, who entrusted them to a Mademoiselle Antoinette Brun. This devout Catholic lady looked after the children, and although from 1945 onwards surviving close relations had sought to take care of the boys, she refused to part with them and in 1948 arranged for their baptism in the Catholic Church. Lengthy litigation started, which ended in January 1953 with a judgment in favour of the Finaly family, but in the meantime the two children had vanished. They were rediscovered on 1 February in Bayonne, close to the Spanish border, where they had been taken by the sister of the Superior of the Sisters of Sion from Grenoble and placed in a Catholic school under false identities. However, by the time the legal representative of the Finalys arrived in Bayonne a couple of days later, the two boys had been spirited away to Spain with the help of five Basque Catholic priests. The Superior of the Grenoble house of the Sisters of Sion and Mademoiselle Brun were arrested on a charge of kidnapping, and so were the priests involved, but they were soon released. A bishop and a cardinal intervened and asked for the return of the children, but their instructions were ignored. It was only after the Supreme Court of Appeals decided that one of their aunts should be the guardian of the children that Robert and Gérald Finaly were brought back from Spain and flown in secret to Israel.

It would be hard to imagine an affair of this sort today in a country like France. Nowadays children are usually kidnapped by a divorced parent who has been refused custody by the court. But in the Finaly case, the fundamental underlying motivation was religious: the Superior of the Sisters of Sion, the Basque priests and even brave, generous but misguided and obstinate Miss Brun, were motivated by a desire to save two innocent baptized souls from spiritual death, for the ungrateful Jewish aunts and uncle would surely deprive them of their Christian heritage. To protect them, male and female ecclesiastics happily broke the state law and turned a blind eye to the half-hearted appeal of the church authorities. The latter, in the person of Cardinal Gerlier, archbishop of Lyons, went so far as almost to congratulate the Basque priests on the noble motives which landed them in gaol.

Despite the deep involvement of the church, and even more closely of the Sisters of Sion, the Démann-Bloch-Vermes trio felt that we had to stand up and be counted. All the more so, since in the first weeks of the scandal the Catholic press whole-heartedly rushed to Miss Brun's support, and attacked the members of the Finaly family. In one of its leaders, the influential daily *La Croix* (The Cross) attributed the 'affair' to 'the primitive and violent reactions of some Jews, in particular among those from Central Europe', and the same paper qualified Mademoiselle Brun's attitude as 'not only natural, but also irreproachable and admirable'. So after the three of us had discussed the matter, Paul Démann wrote a letter to the editor of the most influential Paris daily, *Le Monde*, dissociating himself from the action of the Catholic participants in the affair because it harmed the children, the church, the common good and the relationship between Christians and Jews. He urged the ecclesiastical authorities to intervene and put an end to this disgrace. I acted as the messenger boy and delivered the letter to the office of *Le Monde*. A couple of hours later, the editor's secretary was on the telephone to check the genuineness of this sensational letter. It appeared on 7 February 1953. On both sides of the rue Notre-Dame des Champs, the Sisters and the male old guard considered Paul, me and 'that Mademoiselle Bloch' as disloyal so-and-so's to the church and to the Sion order. I am sure that some mutterings of 'What else can you expect from these Jews?' could be heard. We weathered the storm. In fact, the lead given by Paul's letter was soon followed by statements issued by influential Dominican and Jesuit theologians arguing in the right direction. Once more, the *Cahiers* represented the vanguard of Catholic thinking.

Our little team was also working on another more comprehensive project, the creation of a Catholic centre of research and documentation on Judaism. The idea was first mooted after I joined the Démann-Bloch duo in 1953, and a vague programme was set out in a note entitled 'Orientations' in the March 1954 issue of the *Cahiers*. Its underlying philosophy stated that improved relations between Christians and Jews depended on a correct knowledge of Judaism, and since such a knowledge was generally lacking among Catholics, a *Centre d'étude* with a specialized library and a staff to deal with enquiries would provide the answer. This was a typical Démann plan: grandiose, vague and unbudgeted. The 'orientations' also envisaged courses and conferences to be organized by the Centre. With growing aspirations to a recognized teaching post, I found this aspect of the plan particularly pleasing. Needless to say, nothing came of it, but the faint prospect of a quasi-institutional lecturing position kept me happy for a while.

The common projects did not stop me taking steps towards ensuring my future and carrying on with my own work. First of all I was looking for academic status. I was advised by my most senior Louvain professor, Gonzague Ryckmans, to seek some attachment to the great French research institution serving both sciences and humanities, the Centre National de la Recherche Scientifique (CNRS). Ryckmans, a foreign member of the French Académie des Inscriptions et Belles Lettres, thought that his support would be enough but he was over-optimistic. I duly put in an application with the study of the peculiar Hebrew of the Dead Sea Scrolls as my research topic. I was also looking for a second sponsor and imagined that no one would be a weightier referee in this field than the director of the Scrolls project in Jerusalem, Father Roland de Vaux. Since he had been so amiable during my stay at the École, I was sure that he would give me the support I solicited. But he refused. In a letter written on 17 March 1953, he told me that he would recommend only his own pupils or former pupils. This was the first, but not the last, hurt inflicted on me by de Vaux. By contrast, two leading French scholars, André Parrot, Keeper of the Oriental Antiquities at the Louvre, and Edouard Dhorme, a world famous Semitist and biblical scholar, a former Dominican priest of the École Biblique, assured me of their help. Both were members of the committee which was to consider my case, but despite their backing my application failed.

I got over the upset and pressed on with preparing my doctoral thesis for publication. I had already staked my claim for all that was new in it in an article published in the *Cahiers* early in 1953, off-prints of which had been widely distributed in advance among scholars who mattered. The text submitted to the Jesuits a year earlier was enlarged by the annotated translation of a number of additional Dead Sea Scrolls and a final chapter was appended which replaced the one I had to improvise in order to allay Jesuitical worries concerning the suitability of the dissertation for a doctorate in theology. This new presentation of the religious ideas of the Scrolls community also served as the subject of my first public lecture at the *Journées bibliques*, the yearly biblical conference held in Louvain in the autumn of 1953. In June, I was informed by the owner-director of the publishing house Desclée of their willingness to publish my work and a contract was signed to the effect that 3,000 copies would be printed in the first instance.

The manuscript had to be submitted to the office of the Archbishop of Paris for the *Imprimatur*, the church permit to print. The censor found only one phrase to quibble with. I must not state that the biblical Book of Daniel contains an error in its chronology, but he would not object to my saying that it contained a computation which resembles that of other Jewish works of that age (which I proved to be erroneous). O ecclesiastical double-talk!

The completed typescript was sent to the printers in September; the proofs came and were returned in November, and a couple of weeks before Christmas I held in my trembling hands my 'first-born', *Les manuscrits du désert de Juda* (The Manuscripts from the Judaean Desert). No other book of mine has been produced faster than that. More shaking and trembling, and two lists were compiled, one of prominent scholars and another of newspapers and periodicals for the despatching of complimentary and review copies. Nail-biting followed, but soon I could relax. The senior scholars were most kind and their praises fulsome. For example, Professor Millar Burrows of Yale, editor of the first Dead Sea Scrolls, called it 'the best book that has yet been written about the manuscripts'. Cardinal Liénart, Bishop of Lille, and the Vatican's 'Eugène Card. Tisserant, bishop of Ostia, Porto and S. Rufina' (this is how the letter is signed), added their words of approval. These were all the more precious as they were both from former professors of Scripture. I thought I was dreaming and hardly could believe my eyes. After all, five years earlier I had been a complete ignoramus in biblical studies.

Favourable personal reactions went hand in hand with similar public comments. Reviewers in learned journals kept on calling the book 'excellent' and the British monthly, *The Expository Times,* described it as 'the best general account of the Scrolls'. I was interviewed on French radio, and had friendly notices not only in the Catholic press but also in national dailies and weeklies such as *Le Figaro* (21 January 1954) and even *Paris-Match* (13–20 February 1954): 'Scholars will take rare pleasure in these pages and lay readers will approach with emotion the mystery which this young priest has succeeded in explaining in the clear and precise language of solid erudition.' A literary weekly printed a two–page account, illustrated by a picture of the author. I was sent in advance a copy of the photograph, the verso of which carried the following legend: 'Monsieur Vermes, l'auteur des *'Manuscrits de la mère morte'* (Mr Vermes, author of 'The Manuscripts of the Dead Mother' – instead of *Mer morte* = Dead Sea). Luckily I was able to warn the editor in time.

Perhaps just to remind me that I was not yet due for apotheosis, I received a letter dated 31 January 1954 which started with lukewarm praise, but was meant to put me firmly in my place. Its author was Père Roland de Vaux. Writing to thank me for sending him the complimentary copy of *Les manuscrits du désert de Juda*, although he had had no time yet to acquaint himself with it beyond a cursory glance, he nevertheless felt compelled to comment: 'I regret a little that here and there you should have made public pieces of friendly information given to you when you stayed at the École.' [What he meant was that I had divulged matters which should have been kept private, a first manifestation of the secrecy rule which he was to impose as chief editor of the Scrolls fragments during his lifetime.] 'This,' he continued, 'may give undue authority to the factual errors contained in your book for which we bear no responsibility.' He listed two examples: wrong numbering of the caves and erroneous attribution of some of the texts to a fictitious owner (namely the Palestine Archaeological Museum, the place where they were kept). This was followed by an unspecified 'etc.'

With the hindsight of over forty years, the criticism appears petty, but at the time and in my circumstances, the beginner being told off by the top man in the subject, they might have been devastating. When I recovered from the initial shock, I hastened to answer on 4 February. I pointed out that not thanking the École and de Vaux in particular for their help and kindness would have been boorish. In regard to the two 'errors', his *re*numbering of the caves, first published in October 1953, was indicated on a loose sheet inserted into my book which must have escaped his notice. As for the question of ownership, I would be only too pleased if he would enable me to correct my errors in the second edition of *Les manuscrits* ... which was already in preparation. I was also naive enough to ask him to let me see the proof of a new major paper of his announced for the April 1954 issue of the *Revue Biblique*. I did not realize then that my mention of a new edition, decided by the publishers only a month after the volume saw the light of day, was a powerful though unintentional counterblast to de Vaux's grumbling.

He replied promptly on 12 February, starting with half-hearted congratulations on 'being already obliged to think of a second edition', but his answer to my two requests was firmly in the negative. My rubric concerning ownership should be deleted and the proofs of his forthcoming paper could not be released in advance, as he might make last-minute changes. 'Please accept the expression of my religious devotion', signed, R. de Vaux OP. I managed without his assistance. If I report this exchange in such detail, it is only because it is indicative of de Vaux's high-handed behaviour towards 'outsiders'. This may help to explain his tyrannical policy during the next almost twenty years in connection with the publication of the Scrolls fragments. Denial of access to them to all but the handful of editors chosen by him was all of a piece with the spirit which inspired his attitude towards me.

The new enlarged edition of my book appeared in the summer of 1954, and in September I first set foot in England to attend an international congress of Orientalists in Cambridge. There I met several famous names with whom I had corresponded before, including W.F.Albright, the American Scrolls guru, Paul Kahle and G.R. (later Sir Godfrey) Driver from Oxford. (The last two were to play a significant role in my first and second university appointments in Britain.) I remember several immediate reactions on meeting me: 'I never thought you were so young!'

It was while queueing for one of the official receptions that I heard a conversation in Hebrew behind me. I recognized one of the speakers from the photographs I had often seen in the Israeli newspapers during my stay in Jerusalem: it was Yigael Yadin. We had a very friendly chat, at the end of which I agreed to act as his Paris letter-box for his correspondence with Father de Vaux and other Qumran scholars in Jordan. For although they lived as it were within shouting distance from one another, communication from the new city had to follow the long road to the Arab half of Jerusalem. Yadin and I regularly exchanged off-prints. One of these from the *Cahiers*, dealing with the War Scroll of Qumran which was the subject of Yadin's forthcoming doctoral thesis, elicited the following note: 'I find your article very interesting and was "sorry" to see that some of my interpretations were anticipated by you.' Again, who would have thought then that in 1982, twenty-eight years later, I would edit a *Festschrift* for Yadin's sixty-fifth birthday, or that I would be called to make his eulogy as a Qumran scholar at the memorial meeting organized by the Anglo–Israel Archaeological Society in London after his premature death in 1984.

Before the Cambridge congress I spent a few days in London in the house of the Fathers of Sion at Whetstone, a horrible little suburb almost at the end of the Northern Line of the Underground. One of the Fathers took me for a day trip to Oxford, where from 1965 onwards I would spend the most fruitful and happiest part of my life. Finally, after the congress came the non-academic episode of the trip, my meeting with John Bradburne and with destiny. However, this will have to wait until the next chapter.

Back in Paris I carried on with routine work. I continued to publish in the *Cahiers* and elsewhere not only on the Scrolls but also on ancient Jewish Bible interpretation, my second special interest, a subject which I often discussed with Renée Bloch and with Professor Georges Vajda. One of my papers, a review article entitled 'Rabbinic Literature and the New Testament', deals among other books with the second (1954) edition of *An Aramaic Approach to the Gospels and Acts* by Professor Matthew Black of St Andrews who, in collaboration with Paul Kahle, would help me in 1957 to land my first English job and would involve me in the mid-1960s in a twenty-year labour producing the 'New English Schürer', that is to say a fundamental revision and updating of Emil Schürer's three-volume classic, *The History of the Jewish People in the Age of Jesus Christ*. I will be saying more about that in due course.

On a tragi-comic note, the same paper served to debunk a standard French work, *Le Judaïsme palestinien au temps de Jésus-Christ* (1935) [Palestinian Judaism in the Time of Jesus Christ], by the Jesuit Father Joseph Bonsirven. Eighteen years after the publication of his two-volume study, he decided to issue in French translation an anthology of the rabbinic texts on which his earlier work was based.[4] When I began to read these extracts, I realized that Bonsirven's grasp of rabbinic Hebrew was wholly inadequate: the translation was full of howlers. Having demonstrated this example by example, I drew the readers' attention to Bonsirven's description of rabbinic literature as a *'fatras'* (hotch-potch) before delivering the *coup de grâce*, namely that the impression of nonsense was due to the translator rather than to the rabbinic writings themselves. Since the aged author suffered from a heart condition (which I did not know), his thoughtful Jesuit brethren concealed from him the number of the *Cahiers* which contained my piece. So I did not need to feel particularly guilty when a little later the death of Joseph Bonsirven was announced.

Outwardly everything seemed to move forward steadily and smoothly. Early in 1955 I even managed to be appointed to the Centre National de la Recherche Scientifique for a period of two years, to start the following autumn. Unlike in 1953, this time I had my local support in the person of Professor Vajda, and my research project on the history of the Jewish interpretation of the biblical book of Genesis promised to be exciting. I began with a Dead Sea Scroll, the Aramaic Genesis Apocryphon, the best-preserved parts of which Yigael Yadin and Nahman Avigad had just published.

Yet by 1955 there were also clouds on the horizon. They concerned not my future as a scholar, but the prospects of the plans associated with the *Cahiers Sioniens* and my own position in the little team. I became more and more worried about Paul Démann's *insouciance* about the finances of the journal. He always shrugged off my queries, being convinced that things would sort themselves out or, if circumstances became really tight, that someone would miraculously come along to bail us out. I also felt that I was

very much the junior partner in our trio. I was told about plans after they
had been decided by Paul and Renée, and if outside contacts were consulted, more often than not it was done in my absence. Once more with
hindsight, I am sure that Paul had no intention of excluding me, but the
two of them were so used to doing things together and had so many friends
and contacts in common that they either forgot or found it often inopportune to involve me in everything.

I was more upset than resentful, and after moments of depression I
decided to confide my feelings in Renée. We had a long talk on a bench in
the Luxembourg Gardens. Charming, amicable and full of understanding
as always, she reassured me that matters would improve. Obviously she had
had a word with Paul and they saw to it that I would no longer feel left out.
Renée also looked after me with loving care when I suddenly fell seriously
ill. It was late spring or early summer of 1955 when very early one morning
I woke with a dreadful pain in my abdomen, the wall of which was in spasm
and was as hard as stone. Appendicitis was diagnosed, and an emergency
operation was performed, but in the light of what happened in January 1956
I doubt that appendicitis was the full story.

I more or less recovered and soon reverted to my normal routine of
research and writing. The atmosphere at 68 rue Notre-Dame des Champs
was warm and friendly. It was summer with plenty of tasks ahead. Renée
was getting ready for a study trip to Israel. We spent the evening of 26 July
together, talking about her project. She was enthusiastic and I shared her
joy. Her El Al flight was scheduled late in the evening. I said goodbye to
her and she got into a taxi.

Next morning Paul telephoned the Israeli air line to find out whether
everything was all right. Apparently it was not. Chaos reigned. We were
first told that the aeroplane had had an emergency landing in Bulgaria, but
that all was well. However, bit by bit it emerged that something more
disastrous had happened. Somewhere over Yugoslavia, as it then was, the
aircraft got slightly lost and penetrated Bulgarian airspace. Two Bulgarian
fighters intercepted it and without further ado shot it down. The
passengers and crew perished, fifty-seven in all. I was devastated, speechless. I could not believe then that that delightful young woman, thirty-one
years of age, who had been so full of vitality a few hours earlier when we
were pacing up and down the quiet rue Notre-Dame des Champs talking
about the future, was no more. Our trio was reduced to two. What was
going to happen to all our glorious projects of reform and revolution? I did
not know, and would not have wished to believe, that this tragic 27 July
1955 marked the beginning of the end of the *Cahiers* and our dreams, and
indirectly of my priestly life in the Catholic Church.

11

The Turmoil of Transition

(1955–1957)

The shock caused by Renée Bloch's tragic death, coupled with the debilitating after-effects of the recent operation, forced me to take a brief rest and spend a couple of weeks in Haute-Savoie in the French Alps before returning to Paris with improved health. Paul, in turn, was completely shattered, and suffered from a resurgence of the tuberculosis which had affected him in his youth. For months he was under medical care and lost much of his apparently limitless energy. I myself felt that some further rest and relaxation were imperative, and was delighted to say a final yes to an invitation to revisit friends in England whom I had met a year earlier through John Bradburne as intermediary. To introduce them, it is necessary first to go back to that time.

After a stay of about a year as the sacristan and servant of an Italian priest, John had been summoned home on the death of his father to be with (rather than look after) his mother. They lived in a house called Fir Grove on West Hill, overlooking the Otter Valley and the charming little town of Ottery St Mary in Devonshire. I informed him of my impending visit to Cambridge for the 1954 Orientalist Congress and with his usual warmth and enthusiasm he insisted that I should come and stay in the Bradburne home. I hastened to accept the invitation, completely unsuspecting that it would mark the turning point of my life. It took me another year to realize this and another eighteen months – the turmoil of transition – for the change actually to come about.

John met me at Sidmouth Junction, and we spent the rest of the afternoon and the evening in friendly chat, filling each other in with all the happenings since the day over two years earlier when he set off in Paris on his unfinished journey to Jerusalem. I had to tell him all about Qumran, the Scrolls and especially the Commentary on Habakkuk because it reminded him of his beloved bird, the cuckoo! In the course of our conversation I learned that John did not normally stay in his mother's place; West Hill was far too genteel for him. The mother of a girl whom he used to court after the war before the religious bug bit him had introduced John to a couple who lived on the other side of Ottery, on East Hill. They had a large garden with a wooden hut in one of the corners. With their agreement John settled in this hut and turned it into a hermitage. There he lived on brown bread, apples and cider, in prayer and meditation. He wrote reams and reams of poetry (or something he called poetry) on Christ the King and his Virgin Mother, and played Bach on the recorder to entertain the birds and the angels. He insisted that I must see his hut and that his friends, although unable to put me up, hoped at least to say hello to me.

The following morning we took a bus down to Ottery, stopped in a pub for a pint of cider, and walked up to East Hill, quite a distance as I remember, to inspect the hut. At tea time, John took me to the house to meet Charles,[1] who held a chair at Exeter University, and Pam.

Charles was an Oxford graduate and had been a lecturer there before accepting a professorship at Exeter; he belonged to one of the leading families of the Victorian intellectual elite. Pam's father was an Irish doctor who married the daughter of Sydney Dark, a well-known writer and journalist, and for many years editor of the *Church Times*. The marriage broke up when Pam was four years old, but her mother would never give a divorce to her straying husband, so that he might not make – as she used to say – another woman's life as miserable as hers. The family was High Church, but Pam, aged ten, decided on her own to become a Roman Catholic. She was not allowed to go to university; her mother interpreted her desire to read medicine as a gesture of sympathy for her absentee father. Besides, 'gels' of her generation and social setting were sent to finishing school instead, to be taught languages and learn the fine details of how to be a lady. After two years in a convent school in Bruges, she spent one year in Vienna studying German. Her fluent Italian came from an Italian boy friend whom she met there; she was engaged to him, but thought better of it before it was too late. Then along came Charles and married her in no time.

I was charmingly received by both. Of course, I had no inkling of what was awaiting me immediately or in the future, nor had they. I did not need to have recourse to my shaky English; both knew French, especially Pam, who for two years had been educated by French-speaking nuns in Belgium. So I was nicely put at my ease and did not realize that in fact I was on trial.

Soon it turned out that Notre-Dame de Sion did not rate very highly in Pam's esteem, and that despite John Bradburne's enthusiastic words about me, my belonging to the Sion Fathers rendered me suspect. Pam had received the best part of her education from the Sisters of Sion in their boarding school in Worthing and had taken a distinct dislike to them and the ideas they stood for, long before she was expelled from their school at the age of fourteen or fifteen. Though not Jewish herself, she could not bear what she sensed as a superior attitude on the part of the sisters towards Judaism, an attitude which in fact was completely changed after Vatican II. In particular, already as a child she felt an intense dislike for the Latin prayer sung in a lugubrious tone by the superior or a senior nun after the elevation of the consecrated host in the middle of the mass: *Pater dimitte illis quia non sciunt quid faciunt* (Father, forgive them, for they do not know what they do). She expected an argument and was watching to see how I would react, and was pleasantly taken aback by my whole-hearted agreement with her outlook, and even more by my comment that the words of *Pater dimitte illis*, borrowed from the Gospel of Luke (23.34), did not mean that Jesus sought God's pardon for all the Jews of all times, as the Sion Sisters and like-minded Catholics believed in those days. I further added that there were serious doubts about the genuineness of the passage, which is missing from some of the most important New Testament manuscripts. I promised to send her an article by Paul Démann from the *Cahiers* devoted to this particular passage.

The ice was broken: in a single instant two fellow spirits became friends. I can no longer remember the subject of our conversation, but we went on talking for a long time, no doubt about the Dead Sea Scrolls. Finally the moment arrived when John and I had to leave. Next day, I returned to London after thanking Mrs Bradburne for her hospitality and John for sharing his hut and his splendid friends with me. 'See you soon, I trust.' I did.

Before we parted from East Hill House, both Pam and Charles expressed the hope that we should meet again. 'That would be delightful', was my instinctive reaction. Friendly correspondence followed. In the spring of 1955, I was asked by both to stay with them for a fortnight or longer if I liked. A copy of my Scrolls book lies in front of me, dedicated on 26 May 1955, 'To Pamela and Charles, in gratitude for the pleasant time we had together and as a sign of profound friendship'. At about the same time I indicated that a visit during the coming holiday period was more than unlikely. I was wrong in my forecast. After those terrible summer days in 1955 I needed some peace; so I gladly said yes to the standing invitation. As far as I can recall, the idea that my return to East Hill might imply anything more than straightforward friendship did not occur to me, except perhaps once. But I squashed the thought as a pure flight of fancy.

So it came about that in September 1955, after my rest in the French Alps, I flew from Paris to Exeter by Jersey Airlines, which was quite an adventure in itself. To begin with it was my introduction to air travel. The aircraft was tiny and was scheduled to head first for Jersey and to continue from there to Exeter. Our departure was delayed because the incoming plane had ended up with a flat tyre, and since no spare of such a small size was available in Paris, we had to wait for another one to be flown in from Jersey. In consequence, by the time we reached the island it was dark, and the second stage of the journey had to be delayed until the morning, because the primitive airport of Exeter was not equipped to handle night landings. I therefore had to spend the night in Jersey as a guest of the visibly grumpy airline. If this was a warning, I took no notice of it. An even smaller aircraft, carrying perhaps no more than six passengers, took me to Exeter on the English mainland where Pam, Charles and their two young daughters were waiting for me. Charles drove us back to Ottery, and there I met the rest of the household, a yellow and a black Labrador, and the much-beloved Vicky, then a one-year-old cross between a terrier and a foxhound, who died much lamented thirteen years later in Oxford.

The innocent joy of the reunion lasted only a day or two; then suddenly it dawned on me and on Pam that this was not just ordinary friendship: we were in love. The realization filled both of us with delight mixed with torment and fright. We did not contrive anything. Nothing was engineered. What happened just happened. It was obvious to any onlooker. Happiness and pain alternated. We did not try to hide our state of mind from Charles; it would have been futile even if we had done because the change was so obvious. In any case, Pam, being the personification of directness and honesty, would have refused to conceal anything. We were perplexed, but in theory at least we knew where our 'duties' lay. I had to find a way to work things out, I tried to reassure myself. So late that same month, after a brief visit to Oxford and the Bodleian Library, I left for Paris with a burning and bewildered heart.

68 rue Notre-Dame des Champs was not an ideal place to struggle with problems such as mine. Paul Démann was getting sicker, so I could not burden him with my dilemmas, and after Renée's death I had no one in whom I could confide. Correspondence with Pam and with Charles continued, but no miraculous solution appeared on the horizon. I did what I could at my end. I tried to get lost in work and busied myself in particular with preparing supplements for the American translation of my Scrolls book. I went (without Renée) to Georges Vajda's classes at the École des Hautes Études, and by that time I had also my CNRS research to cope with. I also hoped that the Institut Catholique, an independent university in Paris, would offer me an opening, however modest. No offer materialized; nothing came to tie me to Paris. The Sorbonne was out of the question, because without French nationality and a French degree I stood no chance there.

Meanwhile both Charles and Pam urged me to return. Problems such as ours could not be resolved, Charles told me, by pretending that they did not exist, or by correspondence: they had to be talked through. I agreed, and told the Fathers that I had to go without explaining why. Eyebrows were raised, but no questions asked. On 20 January 1956, the special Sion feast commemorating the purported apparition of the Virgin Mary to Alphonse Ratisbonne in Rome in 1842, I set off to England trembling with joy and worry. The visit was intended to last only a few days.

We decided not to launch into communal self-analysis straight away, but first to create a relaxed atmosphere. Next day a dinner party, arranged weeks earlier with another academic couple, had to be prepared, and this kept Pam busy in the kitchen most of the time. The following day we were to get hold of ourselves and confront 'the situation'. We didn't. It was not meant to be.

I woke up, as I had in Paris nine months earlier, with another excruciating abdominal pain and a high temperature. A friendly doctor was called, who did some tests and prescribed some medication, but as I showed no improvement, next day he whisked me to hospital in Exeter. There the specialists discovered that I had a perforated duodenal ulcer with, I believe, peritonitis, and an emergency operation was performed. Apparently the forecast was touch and go. So Pam, not being a relation, was bluntly told. But I got better. Pam came to visit me daily, travelling by taxi the twelve miles from Ottery to Exeter. She smilingly told me later that on the first occasion she instructed the cab driver: 'Drive in where it says *No Entry*!' Charles came fairly often, too. They suggested that I should convalesce in their house when I was discharged from the hospital after a fortnight or so.

I arrived at East Hill at the end of January with the sincere intention to do my part in the common unravelling of our entanglement, but once again something unintended (a providential accident?) intervened. Life under the same roof, unending conversations, the warmth, the care, the love ... Need I say more? As before, it hurt and gave delight; joy and pain marched hand in hand. Everything was in the open. Nothing was done underhand.

Two further factors rendered the sorting out of the conundrum well-nigh impossible. Charles felt that, despite the changed circumstances, he had to honour his prior acceptance of a fellowship in South-East Asia which had been offered him by an American research foundation and decided to take the two girls, Tina and Anna, then aged fifteen and thirteen, with him. Pam was not ready to go with them. She had never been keen on the idea. She also felt that I was still too frail to be left on my own. She might join them later, she said. So she and I were left on our own in solitary East Hill House. For a short while it seemed like heavenly bliss, which was not disturbed by John Bradburne's sudden return to his garden hut. He was too naive and simple to suspect anything, we thought, and did our best not to arouse his suspicion.

This staccato account should not give the impression that this was a quiet drift away from one's 'duties' into a state of love. No. Tension was constant, but neither of us was ready for a decision. We both wanted to discover 'the right thing' so that we might do it.

By April I felt fine again, but then the second practical difficulty arose. I knew that separation was needed if I was to confront the future objectively. But my stateless alien's travel document had expired during this extended stay in England. The French administrative machine was never famous for its speed, and it took weeks to make it accelerate, especially as I was acting from a Devon hilltop. The document arrived in late May. I parted broken-hearted but determined to work out 'the correct solution'.

Life was misery, and a month or so later we were together again in Paris and in Chartres, where despite the internal hurricane, we found time to admire the stained glass of the famous cathedral. Charles flew back from Asia for a mini-summit, and we talked and talked and sipped aperitifs in the splendid surroundings of Versailles. We agreed to carry on trying and stop communicating for a while. Charles took Pam back to England, and almost immediately left to go back to his job.

The separation was horrible. I was dazed, but attempted to re-adapt myself to my former life. An international biblical conference in Strasbourg offered a momentary escape. All the Scrolls people were present and there I met Krister Stendahl, who was to become one of the world's leading New Testament scholars and for years the influential Dean of the Harvard Divinity School, with a short escapade to his native Sweden as Bishop of Stockholm. We became lifelong friends, and years later he would visit us whenever he passed through Oxford. Another curious episode of the Strasbourg congress which has remained engraved in my memory concerns a paper read by the famous American expert, Professor W.F. Albright. His French was quite fluent, and after the lecture he answered questions with reasonable ease in French until a German professor addressed him in that language. The German discussion began smoothly, but suddenly Albright got stuck. He abandoned German, tried but did not succeed in reverting to French, and had to fall back on English. This was an experience which I myself was to repeat more than once, slipping back to English from French, and even more from my native Hungarian which, until much later, I never used in academic discourse.

Another momentary distraction was provided by the negotiations preceding the signing of the contract with Desclée, New York, on my thirty-

Wedding photograph of Terézia Riesz and Ernő Vermes (Makó 1923)

The author with his father (Makó 1926)

Lang   G.V.   Tarnay   Pfaff

First year in primary school. The author with three lifelong friends, Steve Lang, Francis Tarnay and Louis Pfaff (Gyula 1931)

School-leaving procession (Gyula 1942)

Pfaff G.V. Tarnay Lang

Reunion fifty years after leaving the gymnasium (Gyula 1992)

The author, aged nineteen, with bowler
hat (Szatmár seminary 1943)

Great-aunt Gizi (left) with a friend
(Budapest 1970)

Prof. G Lambert S.J   G.V.   Prof. J. Coppens

Biblical conference (Journées bibliques, Louvain 1951)

John Bradburne entertaining birds, angels and Italians (outside
Naples 1952)

From the left: Paul Démann, the author and Renée Bloch at a party in the library of the
Sion Fathers (Paris 1954)

The author aged twenty-nine in Paris after the publication of his first book (1953)

J. T. Milik

G.V.

J.A. Fitzmyer SJ

P. Kahle

R. de Vaux

International Old Testament Congress (Strasbourg 1956)

Pam and Geza (Ottery St Mary 1957)

Dr George Boobyer and the author (sitting) among mature students (Newcastle 1959)

Pam and Geza in America (West Baldwin, Maine 1971)

The author with his dogs, 'Irish' Kelly and 'black' Lulu in his garden (Boars Hill 1973)

Sir Isaiah Berlin (in the middle) in conversation with a fellow of Wolfson and the author
(Wolfson College, late 1980s)

The author with Emanuel Tov, editor-in-chief of the Dead Sea Scrolls (Jerusalem 1992)

The author at an Encaenia procession. Fergus Millar (capless) is on his right

After the honorary degree ceremony at Durham University, 5 July 1990.
From left to right: J. M.Young (Hon. MA). Dame Margot Fonteyn (Chancellor of the
University), Toru Takemitsu (Japanese composer, Hon. DMus.), Crown Prince Hassan of
Jordan (Hon. DCL) and the author (Hon. DD)

Margaret, Ian and Geza (Oxford 1997)

second birthday, 22 June 1956, for the American edition of *Les manuscrits du désert de Juda*. They proposed to print 8,000 hardback copies instead of the 3,000 of the first French paper-cover issue, and the volume – *Discovery in the Judean Desert* – actually appeared later that year. A substantial supplement, evaluating and partly translating newly released documents (the Thanksgiving Hymns and the War Scroll), was added to the second French edition.

Good resolutions notwithstanding, in October I was again in England. Pam and I struggled with our feelings and listened to the radio, with the 1956 Suez campaign as well as the Hungarian revolution and its brutal suppression by the Soviet army filling all the news bulletins. We agreed to separate and make a final effort, and I was back in Paris.

I knew by then that the last life-line which might keep me at Notre-Dame de Sion and in the Catholic Church was my friendship with Paul Démann. He was aware of what I was going through and had met Pam when she came to Paris a few months earlier. As usual, he was very busy. On one occasion, when I hesitantly asked whether we could talk, he was unable to fit me into his tight schedule. Could it be postponed until the following week? I did not try again. I am not blaming him, for my final decision would almost certainly have been the same.

In the meantime I heard from my relations in Budapest, unharmed by the revolution but not by the passing of years. I sent them medicines, including cortisone, the wonder drug in those days. They also received a splendid parcel from Pam. Would I thank her, aunt Gizi asked me.

The last weeks of 1956 and the beginning of 1957 were spent in self-examination amounting to self-laceration. I must admit that the priestly ideal was the least of my concerns. Faithfulness to an abstract vow of celibacy seemed secondary to the prospect of wounding a real and deeply loved person. As for the church, my loyalties were already divided. On the one hand, I felt – and still feel – a sentiment of gratitude for the help and protection I had received during the years of ordeal in the 1940s. But on the other hand, by that time I also saw the darker sides of the church, her less than exemplary behaviour towards the Jews over the centuries, and her highly objectionable attitude in more recent times towards the search for truth in biblical studies. Leaving Sion as such caused no great tribulation; I was more concerned with the future of the *Cahiers* and all that it entailed, and my dear friend Paul Démann, already sorely tried by the demise of Renée. But then I could not help sensing that the *Cahiers* was a lost cause.[2] No job that I cared for was there to hold me. There was nothing to counteract the magnetism of love.

What I feared most was that by linking our destinies, I might damage

Pam and those around her. Her husband and her children were bound to suffer, as also would Pam's mother, whom I had met and who, before becoming truly fond of me, sent me in the spring of 1957 a letter replete with bitter recriminations. What had I to offer Pam by way of prospects and expectations? Where would we live? In France, where my miserable job at the CNRS was due to expire in September 1957? Communist Hungary seemed out of the question and Israel in those days unthinkable. England? Would the British let me in and grant me a work permit? Would any university employ me on hearing my less than perfect English? And outside the academic field I had no qualifications whatever.

The practical outlook was gloomy, indeed hopeless, yet somehow subconsciously I was convinced that what I intended to do was what I was meant to do. Could I call it a leap of faith?

By the beginning of March my mind was made up. I dealt with outstanding literary commitments and a report for the CNRS. I emptied my small bank account accrued from book royalties and quarterly pittances from the CNRS, adding up to a sum just enough to live on for a few months.

My farewell to Paul was all the more a sad occasion because we both felt guilty, I for abandoning him and he for not having taken better care of me. At the end, I had to comfort him. Kurt Hruby, whom I mentioned in my Louvain account and who by that time lived with us in Paris, was his big warm-hearted self; he gave me encouragement and wished me all the blessings of the patriarchs.

On 9 March I decided that the next day would be D-day. There was a final hiccup, fortunately only momentary. I could not reach Pam on the telephone to let her know what was happening. I kept on trying without success. Had she gone? My failed attempts went on for several hours in a post office, as the home telephone standing in the corridor was not made for calls of this nature. Finally I got through; Pam had just returned from a shopping expedition in Exeter. Yes, yes, she would be at the airport next day.

On 10 March 1957, not quite thirty-three years old, with eyes closed I leaped into the dark.

FAREWELL TO JOHN BRADBURNE

After bringing Pam and me together, and even more because of it, John Bradburne bowed out of our lives for good, or almost for good. We met once more, accidentally I believe, in 1959, when Pam and I last stayed in East Hill

House before it was sold. The atmosphere was friendly but without the usual spirit of fun. He blamed himself for what happened to us. After leaving Ottery, he became sacristan in Westminster Cathedral in London and shortly before our last encounter he was made housekeeper of Cardinal Godfrey's country house in Hertfordshire. We wished him well and let him go. A few years later I learned from the woman friend called Cecil, in whose house Pam first met John, that he had left for Africa in 1962, where he met up with an old army friend who became a Jesuit missionary and was doing good works in Rhodesia. We did not hear from or about him until 1978 when Alec Burkill, head of the Department of Religion in the University College of Salisbury (as Harare was then called), for whom I acted as a referee when he applied for that job, was made a visiting fellow of what was to become my Oxford college, and with his wife spent a year at Wolfson. 'I recently had a most extraordinary experience,' he told Pam and me. 'At a dinner, I set next to fantastic chap who runs a leper colony. His name is John Bradburne and he says that he knows you both.' Sure enough this was our John, and once he had learned our whereabouts from Alec and Bella Burkill, he picked up his pen to send us warm greetings followed by some theological doggerel about the Trinity being Thought, Voice and Word, Three in One. Out of the blue the last line reads, 'Forgive me if I was ever unkind'.

We were delighted to hear from John and were not altogether surprised by his ideas. Pam, who was as fond of him as I was, decided to answer him in light-hearted verse, but could not quite conceal the hurt caused by John's prolonged silence. But the two final lines spoke her true sentiments:

'Heaven keep you safe and sound, dear John
and bless the bed you lie on!'

This last prayer was not heard in heaven. A little over a year later, on 6 September 1979, *The Guardian* carried the sad news of the murder of the 'lepers' saint' who had been taken three days earlier from the leper colony at Mtemwa by guerrillas of the Zimbabwe African National Army and shot in the back in the bush. My Hungarian benefactor, Bishop William Apor, had been murdered when he tried to protect defenceless women. Dear harmless, innocent John lost his life for not releasing the pennies with which he was meant to feed the outcast of humanity.

As I had already witnessed in the case of the heroic bishop, people are unable to accept human grandeur for what it is and try to transform an outstanding individual into a text-book saint. The same phenomenon has been repeated, but in an infinitely more embarrassing form, in connection with John. The tragedy of this 'man of love and peace who could not hurt a fly' – words of a black friend – was said to have been followed almost immediately by miracu-lous events of the hocus-pocus kind. 'Mystery of blood spots at mass', ran the headline in *The Daily Telegraph* two weeks after the murder, on 17 September. 'A large spot of fresh blood, which suddenly appeared beneath the coffin of Mr John Bradburne ... has baffled Roman Catholics in Salisbury.' Although nothing unusual was observed during the mass, conducted by the local archbishop and attended by more than seventy priests, just before the service ended one of the priests noticed a spot of *fresh* blood. The coffin was reopened but there was no mark inside. Some immediately believed that they had witnessed a supernatural happening. This was only the beginning. According to *The Times* of 3 February 1996 the Catholics of Zimbabwe are keen on having their first local saint, and the secretary of their Bishops' Conference considers John 'an ideal prospect for beatification'. A John Bradburne Memorial Society has been formed which is engaged in collecting evidence of miracles. The prospective saint's tomb has become a place of pilgrimage and he is said to have cured believers from cancer and other illnesses. Someone has offered a video recording as proof that at sunset at Mtemwa the sun takes the shape of the Virgin Mary. Others assert that swarms of local bees carry John's healing spirit.

Revolted by such fantasies, my mind's eye recalls the real John, the 'crazy old nail, but always your friend' (*un vieux clou fou, mais toujours votre ami*), as he once described himself in a letter in his inimitable French. If I had told him that one day people would endeavour to make him into a saint, what would he have said? I just can see the twinkle in his eye, hear first his laughter and then his jolly voice: 'O let's drink wine and sing a merry song, Alleluia!'

Rest, dear Hornbeam,[3] rest in peace! May the choir of the angels make you rejoice with Bach cantatas in your heavenly hermitage.[4]

Part Three: Newcastle-upon-Tyne

(1957–1965)

12

Finding my Feet in Newcastle

(1957–1958)

On 10 March 1957 a baby aeroplane deposited me on the grassy runway of Exeter airport. Pam was there with the local taxi from Ottery. The delight of the reunion was followed by a complete physical collapse on my part. The strain of the previous weeks and months showed and I slept for thirty-six hours in a single stretch. When I woke up, I did not quite know where I was. Concern about the uncertain future ran parallel with my feeling of fulfilment. A couple of Pam's friends were sympathetic, but we were surrounded by a local world which was at best withdrawn and non-committal, and quite often, especially in the Catholic sector, openly hostile and disapproving. The eyes of some of the nuns of Ottery always seemed to be focussed on the pavement just in front of them when either of us was in sight, and a pious pre-Vatican II woman friend regularly crossed over to the other side of the street when Pam was approaching.

Despite the love and support I experienced, for days and weeks I was unable to do anything productive. To engage in some potentially useful pursuit, I decided to learn to drive. A sweet little instructor used to pick me up; we drove to Exeter and practised the usual tricks: three-point turns, hill starts, reversing and parking. More than once I was warned that on the way back to the office after the test we would come to a clock tower where the traffic already going round it had the priority. Still rather unsure of my skills, I took a chance with the test and to my real surprise everything went very satisfactorily. Extremely pleased with myself, I was speeding happily towards the Ministry of Transport building but, forgetting the warnings, did not stop where I should have and nearly collided with a red post office van. Needless to say, I experienced my first and so far also my last examination failure. It did not greatly matter: we had no car nor any close prospect of acquiring one.

Of course, my most urgent task was to look for paid employment. I particularly hated the idea of staying in a house which half belonged to Charles, even though he had no objection to our living there until I was in a position to move somewhere else. I wrote letter after letter to all the senior scholars whom I knew, mostly those in Britain and in America. I informed them about my decision to relinquish my clerical status and said that I was searching for an academic post. Could they help? The majority of them answered politely that they wished me all the best, but at the moment knew of no suitable vacancy. Should something turn up, they would surely let me know. And that was the last I heard from them. However, there was one exception: Professor Paul Kahle.

I had known of him since my Budapest student days, Kahle having been a household name among users of 'Kittel-*Kahle*', the only critical edition of the Hebrew Bible. Later, in 1951, I had learned more about his story when with the help of John Bradburne I read the account of the Kahles' escape from Germany. Shortly afterwards he became one of my regular correspondents in Dead Sea Scrolls matters, thanking me for and commenting on the off-prints of publications which I sent him. I stayed with him after the Cambridge Orientalist Congress in 1954 at Ranger's Lodge outside Charlbury in Oxfordshire, where he lived in style with his house filled with scholarly guests. Kahle, instead of shrugging me off as others did, invited me sometime in May 1957 to visit him in his new home, 89 St Aldates, Oxford, a beautiful large and old house owned by Christ Church. There, too, he led an elegant and comfortable existence with three or four women looking after the house and its usually numerous occupants. I spent a number of pleasant visits there and met his four living sons: Mrs Kahle and Paul junior, the only one who followed his father's footsteps in the field of scholarship, were already dead. On Sunday mornings they all assembled in the drawing room, with the *paterfamilias*, formerly a Lutheran pastor, sitting at the harmonium, and heartily sang German hymns.

Paul Kahle, already an octogenarian, was kindness itself. He was no longer active, he explained to me, and his links with British institutions were in any case tenuous, but he would do his best to alert those who were in a position to help me. 'What a pity,' he added, 'that you did not look for a job a year ago. You would have been just the right man for the Cowley Lectureship in Post-biblical Hebrew.' The successful candidate was none other than David Patterson, who later became my colleague in Oxford for many years.

Cheered up a little, I left Kahle, who undertook to inform his British connections, especially his former student, Professor Matthew Black of St Andrews. He promised that he would let me know if something promising cropped up. Nothing happened in the immediate future apart from a surprise visit in Ottery from Willy Kahle, Paul Kahle's Catholic priest son. Since his father was offering me a helping hand, Willy felt guilty and made a last minute attempt to bring me back to what he saw as the straight and narrow path. We politely agreed to differ, but remained in touch by correspondence over the years.[1]

Back in Ottery St Mary, I tried to arrange for a British edition of my American Scrolls book in order to create some new income. Various publishers expressed interest, and Paul Elek, the ex-Hungarian director of a small publishing house in London, went so far as to invite me for a discussion with a view to signing a contract. However, the agreement floundered because of Pam. She had a very low ceiling of tolerance as far as inadequate English literary style was concerned, and insisted that she should retranslate the whole book, considering the product of the Israeli woman translator from Paris totally unacceptable. Paul Elek was of course unwilling to pay for fresh typesetting and that was that. Pam's literary collaboration had to wait for another opportunity. It presented itself quite soon.

Preoccupation with finding a livelihood did not allow me to concentrate on matters spiritual. Peace of mind is essential if one is to move to those higher spheres. I was confused, but chose the only option possible: that of personal, internal prayer and spirituality without accompanying social manifestations. This was a timid beginning, but both Pam and I became more and more attached to such an individualistic path; someone called it prayer in the upper room.

Sometime late in June a letter came from Paul Kahle. He had heard from Matthew Black that there was an opening for a temporary lectureship in divinity in the University of Newcastle with a yearly salary somewhere between £800 and £950. The closing date for applications had already passed, but Black thought that I should write all the same. I am not sure whether I knew then where Newcastle was – I think I had to look it up on the map – but I had no choice and followed his advice. I later discovered how this 'providential accident' came about. The Newcastle head of department, a New Testament specialist, who was running divinity single-handed, had obtained funding for a one-year extra position and inquired from his friend and fellow New Testament scholar Black about suitable candidates. This letter arrived by the same post as Kahle's note addressed to Black about my predicament. The information was passed on and in July I was summoned to Newcastle for an interview scheduled for the following week.

I was thrilled, but was also predictably anxious. A job interview was an unknown entity for me. Pam was pleased on my account, but secretly depressed by the idea of an eventual move from beautiful Devon to cold and ugly north-east England. For her, as for most southerners of her type, anything north of Watford was in the wilds, and any London address not within walking distance of Sloane Square and Peter Jones counted as suburban. Naturally she did not convey her forebodings to me and I set off on an apparently unending cross-country train journey to Newcastle-upon-Tyne. The solution of a minor, but psychologically significant, dilemma preceded my departure. Shortly before I learned that I had been short-listed and had to appear before an appointment committee, with Pam's approval I had decided to mark my changed status and personality by growing a beard. Apart from the mature appearance it was supposed to convey, it made mornings noticeably pleasanter by dispensing me from the daily chore of shaving. Now imagine my perplexity when with ten-day-old stubble on my face I was asked to appear before a jury on whose judgment my immediate future largely depended. Should I cut off this beginning of 'maturity'? Pam with her usual aplomb said: 'Tell them that you've just started to grow a beard.' I followed her advice, and with hindsight I guess that my outward nonchalance, hiding inward nervousness, probably made a favourable impression on the committee.

The interview took place in a red-brick building of this genuinely red-brick university. Newcastle began in the nineteenth century as Armstrong College for Engineering and developed in the twentieth into King's College, which together with the Durham Colleges formed the University of Durham. The Warden of Durham and the Rector of Newcastle held the vice-chancellorship of the university in alternate years. In the early 1960s, after an amicable 'divorce', King's College, by that time double the size of Durham, was turned into the University of Newcastle-upon-Tyne. The half-dozen or so interviewers sitting on the other side of a large table were truly awe-inspiring. The Deputy Rector of King's College presided, with the Registrar and a middle-aged, bespectacled, slightly balding man sitting next to him on either side. The latter was the head of the department, Dr G. H. Boobyer, old George as I later used to call him. I was invited to say something about myself, but the committee was discreet and no one asked me why I had opted out of the priesthood. Dr Boobyer, to whom Matthew Black had lent my *Discovery in the Judean Desert*, asked me about my interests, and I described them. Would I be willing to teach general arts students? I firmly declared that I would without quite knowing what a general arts degree (as distinct from an honours degree) meant. Meanwhile I was wondering whether they could understand my English and would consider it sufficiently good for teaching undergraduates. As a final question, partly I suppose to show his colleagues that he was well versed in Dead Sea matters, George Boobyer wanted to know my opinion on Theodore Gaster's then freshly released version of the Scrolls, *The Scriptures of the Dead Sea Sect*. 'Is it a good translation?', he asked. 'If you can call it a translation,' I replied with a gentle smile. Of course I was required to explain what I meant. 'Gaster always knew best the parts which were lost in the many lacunae of the manuscripts; reconstructions which had no textual basis were the most brilliant parts of his book,' I replied. Once more with hindsight, I believe that this apparently flippant answer made all the difference. I remember that before thanking me and letting me go, the chairman enquired whether I had any income at present. No, I said. 'Please remain in the waiting room', was the final instruction.

Exhausted, I fell into an armchair. Some twenty minutes later the smiling Registrar informed me that they were pleased to offer me the job; that my salary would be at the top of the range, £950; that the appointment would take effect from 1 September rather than the 1 October advertised; and that the University would arrange with the Home Office for my tourist visa to be converted into one which would be compatible with a work permit. Would I like to spend another night in the hotel at their expense? 'No, thank you,' I replied, still astounded by the news. I ran to the first public phone and struggled with those confusing old buttons A and B. 'Caller, press button A', the operator repeated after I had put in the requisite number of sixpences. I disclosed the good news to Pam and caught the overnight train to Exeter. I still hardly could believe it, but *I had a job.*

Hectic preparations started for our migration to distant Northumberland. I received the list of lectures I had to deliver, mostly in the field of the Old Testament and biblical history, and hastily set out to plan my various courses. Arrangements also had to be made about the Devon house. With Charles's consent we were to look after it and stay in it during the university vacations until a buyer was found for East Hill House. The animal contingent was reduced by that time from five to three, two cats and that delightful terrier *cum* foxhound cross, Vicky, who was the only one of the original three dogs to growl when she first saw me in 1955, but who became my darling for the rest of her long life. So I was despatched to Newcastle in mid-September to spy out the land and find somewhere to live, a place sufficiently discreet and secluded to keep us out of the public gaze until our situation was regularized, and rural enough for the menagerie.

In the local paper I saw an advertisement which seemed to be just the ticket: rooms in a country mansion, eight miles from Newcastle, with large gardens and a bus stop just at the gate. North Biddick Hall, Washington, County Durham (as it was before becoming Tyne and Wear) was an architectural mongrel, with surviving mediaeval bits and subsequent ramifications culminating in a large nineteenth-century Victorian wing. The estate originally belonged to the Earl of Durham, whose address to this day is Biddick Hall, Chester-le-Street. North Biddick Hall was sold in the last century to a *nouveau riche* engineering family by the name of Cook who implied that they were the descendants of Captain James Cook, the picture of whose ship decorated one of the corridors. By the late 1950s the family, Harold and his three elderly sisters, and Harold's son Joseph, who was our contemporary, had lost most of their fortune. The mansion had already been sold to the Coal Board, and the Cooks supplemented their income by *trying* to find tenants. Why *trying* is emphasized will appear presently. The rent seemed reasonable and when I asked how many rooms were included, the answer was, 'As many as you like.' And what sort of rooms were they? The kitchen, large and tall enough to accommodate a modern two-story semi-detached house, was in the oldest part of the building. It had enormously thick walls, was very warm even in the winter, and still had above the door the old contraption installed for Victorian servants indicating the room from which the bell was ringing. Our sitting room was the old morning room with monumental French windows leading to the garden. I chose two bedrooms upstairs and a bathroom with a bath the size of a small swimming pool and hot water provided with a decrepit geyser. The animals were more than welcome. I thought I had struck lucky, but overlooked one thing of some importance: the absence of electricity in the house. North Biddick Hall, which has been pulled down since, was lit with gas lamps of various sizes in authentic Victorian style.

To my surprise, Pam did not object and willingly put up with that extraordinary place, and after her 300-mile trip in the Ottery taxi, which was packed with essentials including the two cats and the dog, we spent two years in Washington (Co. Durham), shivering in the winter when the wind from the North Sea was blowing through the draughty windows, protected only by the raggy relics of curtains, and through the cracks in several walls. Joseph, the landlord's son, an old-time dancing fanatic, invited Pam to the large parlour, which had a polished parquet floor. They danced to the music of Victor Silvester played on an age-old gramophone, while I and the ugly fungi which were growing out of the old beams watched them enjoying themselves. Both cats died quite soon in the bitterly cold north-eastern winter, but Vicky was in her seventh heaven leaping high in the large cornfields in search of pheasants, and chasing hares on the distant crests of the undulating hills, sometimes until late into the night.

The beginning of my academic career could not have been more modest. The Newcastle department of divinity had a staff of two: the head, with the grade of senior lecturer, assisted by temporary me. We were located in a little terrace house in 34 Eldon Place, a street which was engulfed in the later urban development of Newcastle. We shared the house with the slightly larger department of philosophy, which had a professor and two lecturers. Next door, at no. 32, were situated the more substantial department of English and the office of one secretary who worked not only for us, but also for English and Philosophy. It was among the staff of those two departments that we made our only lasting friendship in Newcastle. Colin Strang was then lecturer in philosophy and his wife, Barbara, a lecturer in English language; both were soon promoted to professorships. Until her sudden and untimely death Barbara was a keen horsewoman and an expert on the very rich English horsy vocabulary. She was a first-rate linguist of the modern kind who would never tell you which was the right way to put something. 'The right way is the way *you* put it,' was her usual comment. Many years later, when I mentioned in conversation with the then president of the British Academy, Sir Randolph Quirk, with whom Barbara used to collaborate, that Barbara and I were close friends, he assured me that had she lived a little longer, she too would have become an FBA.

Colin was a man of many parts, equally versed in Aristotle, plumbing and car maintenance. Ballpoint pens and screwdrivers of various kinds protruded from his top pocket, and he regularly used the turn-ups of his trousers as an emergency ash-tray. (In those days smoking was still an almost universal social habit.) From Colin I learned that the modern philosopher's principal working tool was a cup from which to drink coffee, and I can still see him surrounded by students in the departmental common room, all sipping Nescafé and arguing for hours about whether the truth can be discovered. After his early retirement he succeeded his father in the peerage without changing his life-style an iota. I recently noticed that on his senior citizen's bus pass he is described as *Mr* Colin Strang. He is one of the most level-headed, charming, loving and loveable human beings I have met in my life.

My teaching did not ask for much preparation, as it had to be on the elementary level of general arts students or aimed at the even lesser requirement of school teachers, whom I taught in twice-weekly evening classes. My worries that the students might not understand me proved unfounded; I could communicate with them without any trouble. It was the other way round that problems arose: I had difficulty in understanding their sometimes broad north-country accent. By this I do not mean Geordie, the Tyneside dialect which no one spoke to me in class. That sounds like a foreign language which not even Pam could make out. She often let out hm-s and yes-es with some embarrassment when some old woman addressed her in the bus in the local lingo.

The light burden of teaching and the splendid facilities of the library of the Oriental School in Durham enabled me to press on with research and publishing. 1958 marked the start of my English period and three articles appeared in the course of that year in *Journal of Theological Studies*, *New Testament Studies* and *Vetus Testamentum*, three leading periodicals in the field. My written English was rudimentary in those days, but after Pam's expert editing the papers read quite smoothly. It is worth noting that none of them dealt with the Scrolls, though the first of the three developed and broadened a Qumran study published in a French *Festschrift* the year before. They all reflected stage two of my scholarly interest, research into ancient Jewish biblical exegesis, and pioneered the thesis that already in pre-Christian times widely known interpretative traditions existed which conditioned the popular understanding of scriptural stories among the Jews.

The secluded character of North Biddick Hall and Washington, which, oblivious of its former glory of being the fief of the family that gave the United States its first President, was an old-fashioned mining village, made it fairly easy for us not to arouse the curiosity of potential university gossips. In the atmosphere of the late 1950s, what is called partnership today counted as living in sin, not quite the thing for a lecturer in divinity in those days. While we lived there, the local pit was still working. I also remember my difficulty in persuading the corner shop grocer to stock real coffee. He had sold only bottles of Camp coffee until then.

Our life, secure and happy on the personal level (the green light had been given for divorce proceedings to be started), still had to face uncertainty and worry. My temporary appointment was only for one year, and this meant that I had to begin a search for a new situation almost at once. An opening at the University of Melbourne in Australia came to my notice and some correspondence followed, but if I remember correctly, it abruptly came to an end with the death of the professor who was considering my case. I have forgotten what other approaches I made in late 1957 or at the very beginning of 1958. Be this as it may, the period of anxiety was of relatively short duration, and in the course of the spring of 1958 my boss George Boobyer informed me that his efforts with the college authorities had borne fruit and that my temporary lectureship was to be made permanent. I would receive a triple salary increment (3 x £50), thus raising my annual income from £950 to a majestic £1,100! To me, if not to Pam, who was used to a professor's salary, £1,100 appeared genuine riches. This news, together with progress and completion of the divorce in the latter part of April, signalled the approach of a new stage in our life. This was no longer to be lived in concealment in ramshackle Cook's Hall, as North Biddick Hall was locally known, but proudly in the open. Or so I thought, but surprises were lying in wait.

Once the decree absolute was in hand, we decided to proceed with the wedding without further delay. Clearly there was no question of pomp and ceremony. In Washington we were thought to be married and in Newcastle no one knew of Pam's existence. I had no family to attend, and as for Pam, her children were in Asia and her mother, a pious Anglo-Catholic, preferred not to know. She was convinced that the whole thing was a terrible mistake and that Pam would soon be left to pay for her foolishness.

So we did the obvious, and did it in the simplest manner. I obtained a marriage licence in Durham and named the day, 14 May 1958, at 3 p.m., and the venue, the dreary registry office at Chester-le-Street, Co. Durham. We travelled by bus from Washington, borrowed the witnesses of the preceding wedding, and listened to the registrar pronouncing us husband and wife in his north-country accent. We went to a nearby cafe for a six-penny cup of tea before returning again by bus to unsuspecting North Biddick Hall. Only a pleasant dinner in a Newcastle restaurant indicated that something was out of the ordinary. In fact, that day of 14 May was the official beginning of loving co-existence and collaboration which would last for thirty-five years. We religiously remembered the anniversary throughout the years, except that due to some extraordinary aberration affecting both of us, from 1983 – i.e. our silver wedding – onwards we anticipated the anniversary on 12 May. In 1993, four weeks before Pam's death, we both completely forgot the (wrong) day. On remembering it, quite naturally we postponed the celebration to the following Sunday. Pam preferred to commemorate the day of my arrival in Ottery St Mary on 10 March 1957 rather than our 'grotty' wedding in Chester-le-Street fourteen months later.

When out of the blue I announced my marriage to Dr Boobyer, he appeared not a little surprised. However, trying to be tactful, he invited us to his home for tea. The conversation was of course rather sticky, as Pam and I resolutely abstained from talking about the obvious topics in the circumstances: the wedding, the family and friends present, etc. Still, everything seemed to go off all right and normal routine continued, with my first stint as a university examiner taking place at the beginning of June.

Then, about the middle of that month, I was abruptly summoned to the office of the head of the department. George Boobyer, in his mid-fifties, was a truly decent person who liked everything to be tidy, predictable and above board. He had started off life as a Baptist minister, but was attracted to the Quakers in the 1930s and as a member of the Society of Friends he became a pacifist. The outbreak of the war in 1939 confronted him with a personal dilemma, and after much heart-searching and struggle he decided that the duty to fight the Nazi evil outweighed his Quaker obligation not to bear arms. So he volunteered for 'Dad's Army' and spent the war years as a territorial, guarding railway lines in Somerset. Relatively late in life, in 1948 or 1949 he was appointed to a university lectureship and on the retirement of his predecessor was promoted to the headship of our miniature department just before my arrival in 1957.

He told me that, although he did not want to pry, he felt obliged to enquire into my past, and that if it contained anything previously undisclosed which he as my superior should know, I ought to tell him. I was completely nonplussed. The only matter I had kept private was the circumstances which led to my marriage with Pam. I somehow guessed that this was not what he was after, but had no idea of what was bothering him. A rather strained dialogue followed. I was invited to tell my life story from the beginning. This went on for quite a time and the session was adjourned. Like an MI 5 investigator, mild George set out to grill the truth out of me. I was beginning to become really upset. Was my job at risk? Two further sessions followed, and when he failed to find what he was looking for in my story, he turned the searchlight on Pam. At first I objected, but he insisted that genuinely this was not curiosity on his part. After the second session I was tempted to tell him to go to hell and resign, but Pam thought the best solution would be to let him know the truth about us. So I put my cards on the table. George's mouth fell open, but at the same time he realized that my obvious caginess was not meant to hide some dangerous secret.

The dark enigma he had endeavoured to clarify was purely a figment of his imagination. Apparently when the university had asked the Home Office for an extension of my visa and work permit beyond the original twelve months, they were told to reapply in September. George interpreted this as indicating that I was being investigated and that there was something suspicious about me or my newly-wed wife. So before the department and the university were compromised, he had to get to the bottom of the affair.

Having gone to such lengths, he felt unable simply to drop the matter and say, 'Sorry, my mistake.' The case was referred to the Rector of King's College and I had to appear before him. I thought that was it, but in the person of Charles Bosanquet I faced a broad-minded man of the world who, having realized what I had been put through, told me to forget it and have a nice holiday instead.

After this unfortunate hiccup my relationship with George Boobyer became very friendly. I kept in touch with him over the years after my departure from Newcastle and after his retirement in the late 1960s. In 1993 I visited him in his sheltered accommodation at Weston-super-Mare in his native Somerset. At ninety-two, he was still his old kind self, alert and 'with it' as long as we stuck to the topic of conversation chosen by him. My visit made him happy and I presented him with a copy of my latest book, *The Religion of Jesus the Jew*. He promised to read it, but I am not sure whether he was able to.

The Boobyer ordeal must have taken a great deal out of me. Photographs of that period show me emaciated and unwell, my stomach problems regularly recurring. The summer spent on East Hill in Devon, where Pam and I were busy putting the house on the market, helped to calm my nerves and restore my self-confidence, if not my health. After a year in Newcastle I finally felt that I was standing on my feet. From Ottery we went almost every day to Sidmouth, a charming seaside resort, and spent many sunny afternoons on a beach known as Jacob's Ladder. That was a good omen. From then on it was Jacob's Ladder, rising not to heaven as in the Bible, but towards the heights of the academic knowledge of Judaism, that metaphorically speaking I was going to climb.

13

Laying the Foundations

(1958–1965)

Compared to the thirty stormy months preceding the summer of 1958, the seven subsequent years which I spent in Newcastle seemed quiet and dull. Nevertheless, they played a very important part in shaping my future. At first sight, the outlook was far from rosy. On the personal level, while our marriage was perfectly happy, the circumstances surrounding it gave cause for concern.

The first shock came from Charles. He duly sent his congratulations on receiving the news of our wedding, but in his letter he remarked almost in passing that he too was on the point of remarrying. This came straight out of the blue and deeply upset Pam. She thought that the spirit of openness which had characterized her behaviour from the start would be reciprocated and, perhaps illogically, found Charles's secretiveness hurtful. He, in his turn, considered Pam's reaction wholly unreasonable and the clash triggered off a process of alienation resulting in an almost complete loss of contact between them which was to last more than a quarter of a century.[1]

Pam was fearful of the consequences of Charles's remarriage because she saw it as a potential threat to her future relationship with her two daughters, for Tina and Anna were still abroad and in their father's care. This fear turned out to be unjustified. Within a year both girls were back in England. The younger Anna soon married a ship's engineer in the Merchant Navy. Tina, the elder, not having taken A-level examinations because of her departure with Charles to Pakistan, decided to train as a nurse at St Bartholomew's Hospital and for a time lived with Pam's mother in London. Intimacy between Pam and Tina was quickly reestablished and a progressively close relationship developed between her and me, too.

After an initial upset, Pam's mother also reconciled herself to the new situation. We regularly visited her in London. I often stayed with her on my own in her very centrally situated flat close to Victoria Station when I had to go to town for meetings. 'You will be very welcome as long as you don't mind fending for yourself,' I can still hear her saying. In fact, she used to go out most evenings with a lifelong friend, Canon C.B. Mortlock, a well-known journalist and Church of England cleric, who reviewed plays, ballet and opera for various London newspapers. So Pam's worst worry that she might lose her family could be laid to rest.

Needless to say, my Budapest relations, in whose eyes I could never do anything wrong, were delighted to hear about my change of course and longed to set eyes on Pam, a wish which, alas, never materialized. By that time, great-aunts and great-uncles were in their seventies and eighties. We provided them with medicines which not even money could buy in Hungary. But unavoidably the pieces of sad news arrived one after the other. I still have beloved aunt Gizi's one-line message announcing that her husband was no more.

On the religious front the Newcastle years represented a period of groping. Formally Pam and I were both rejected by the church on account of our prohibited and sinful marriage. For a while we occasionally attended Catholic religious services in the church of the Dominicans, but this did not last long. Nor did a very superficial contact with the Quakers lead anywhere. George Boobyer, himself a Quaker, invited us to experiment with the peculiar form of religion of the Society of Friends. So we attended the Newcastle 'meeting' on a few occasions, and enjoyed the prolonged silences, but I found many of the 'testimonies' embarrassingly naive and the Quakers' 'theology' without substance, not to say precariously fragile. So we soon dropped out from there, too. Neither Pam nor I considered ourselves members of any denomination. To the end she remained detached from any religious affiliation and during the last stage of her life she liked to describe herself as a '*religious* agnostic', though one passionately involved with Jewish mysticism! I moved in a somewhat different direction, also in the framework of Judaism, as will become apparent later on.

While today no one is debarred from teaching in a department of theology just because he or she does not belong to a denomination, people were less tolerant in those days, and my 'irregular' position as a lecturer in divinity caused some eyebrows to rise. I remember, on the occasion of my first attendance at the winter gathering of the Society of Old Testament Study, meeting the elderly head of an extreme Protestant Belfast theological college who in his matter-of-fact style enquired: 'Your name?' 'Your institution?' '*Your denomination?*' Taken aback, I came out with the phrase, '*I used to be a Roman Catholic.*' The dismay on my interlocutor's face was obvious, though I am not sure whether he found 'I used to be' or 'Roman Catholic' the more outrageous.

On the home front, two events need to be recorded. Banal in themselves, they were significant to me. In 1958, I acquired my first car. It was an outwardly magnificent twenty-two year-old dark red Morris 8 with shining black top, complete with running board and starting handle (which was needed almost every morning). The car cost only £80, and was certainly not worth a penny more, but that was all I could afford. It conked out after less than a year, but during its short existence it allowed me to master the rudiments of driving so that I successfully passed the test in January 1959. Pam also became a learner driver and in the early spring we were foolhardy enough to set out on the three-hundred-mile journey from Newcastle to Devon. We left very early in the morning, driving in relays, and arrived just past midnight at East Hill House in Ottery in the pitch dark and with very inefficient headlights. A few yards before reaching the gate, I managed to drive the car into a ditch. We had to carry the luggage to the house and found a pint of milk at the door, placed there by a kind neighbour. Pam picked up the milk, entered the kitchen and, deadly exhausted after the long drive, let the bottle slip out of her fingers. It broke into thousands of pieces, and with them vanished our dream of a nice cup of tea at last. A memorable journey, our last stay on that beautiful hillside with endless horizons.[2]

Possession of a car also enabled us to explore, Sunday after Sunday, the unspoilt Northumberland countryside, with long walks on Hadrian's windy wall west of Newcastle, unending drives in the empty Cheviot Hills populated only by sheep, and the enjoyment of the sight of the miles and miles of sandy beaches north of Bamborough Castle with the Farne Islands and Holy Island looming in the mist. Our faithful bitch Vicky curiously knew when it was Sunday and began to pester us early in the morning to get on with breakfast and go for 'car walkies'. The beaches we visited were usually covered with gulls and terns, thousands of them, but within a minute of Vicky's arrival these were all airborne. It was quite a sight.

The second move towards normal British life consisted in acquiring a house, a solid Edwardian terrace house in Jesmond, one of the better residential areas of Newcastle. Looking back, I remember the pride I felt in 'owning a plot of England' at 7 Ilford Road, Newcastle-upon-Tyne 2. Pam, who was blessed with green fingers and had had a large garden in Devon, managed to turn the tiny plot in front of the house into a glorious medley of colours which passers-by stopped to admire.

Obtaining British citizenship was the third and most crucial step towards the normalization of my life. It was a rather happy-go-lucky process in those days. I was told that the five-year qualifying period would start from my appointment to Newcastle on 1 September 1957, and that since the actual naturalization process was likely to take the best part of a year, I should apply at the beginning of 1962. I duly followed the advice and posted my application on 27 January.

Since I had been used first to Hungarian and later to Belgian and French bureaucracies, the apparently lackadaisical British way truly amazed me. All I was asked to do was to formulate my plea, give my essential data, and name three referees: no documentation was required. But wait. Several months later the doorbell rang. Two detectives, a sergeant and a constable turned up unannounced. I was seeking naturalization, was I not? Yes, I was. They then invited me to produce evidence for my various statements, one after another. Fortunately I was tidier then than I am now and could satisfy their curiosity without much delay. There was only one momentary hiccup, when I could not lay my hands on my degree certificate in oriental languages. Don't worry, I was told, we'll come back when you've found it. In fact, I suddenly recalled where the diploma was and the two detectives left with the checking of the evidence complete. Or almost. They still had to ascertain that my referees existed and were prepared to vouchsafe for my worthiness. I had named the Rector of King's College, my head of department and a commander in the Royal Navy as my three sponsors. How the first two were approached, I have no idea, but I know what happened to the third, the head of the Navy's Recruitment Office in Newcastle and the husband of one of Pam's school friends. This friend reported that one afternoon the telephone rang and someone from the Newcastle police was on the line. Could they speak to the Commander? 'What has he done?', asked the anxious wife. 'Oh nothing, Madam, but he was named by a Dr Vermes as his referee. Does your husband know him?' 'Yes', they were told, 'and I have been Mrs Vermes's friend for thirty years.'

That did it. In July, two months before the completion of my qualifying period, I was granted British citizenship, and on the same day I rushed to the office of a Commissioner for Oaths to swear allegiance to the Queen and her lawful heirs. Soon I also obtained a British passport. After sixteen years of statelessness I became a citizen of the United Kingdom and Colonies (a number of which still existed in 1962). It was a moving moment for me, a feeling of providential achievement. But the climax of the new status came when for the first time in my life I was able to cast my vote in the 1964 general election. Incidentally, from then until 1997 when I helped the Liberals to capture Oxford West and Abingdon from the Tories, I have always voted for a loser and never managed to elect anyone.

In the late 1950s and early 1960s we settled down in Newcastle. We acquired a few friends in academic circles in addition to the Boobyers, with whom now and then we had tea and cucumber sandwiches, and the

Strangs, in whose home we could always expect a lively company of articulate conversationalists, occasionally including Colin's most impressive but equally modest father, an ennobled former Foreign Office mandarin. The beginning of our friendship with Norman and Vera Cohn goes back to Newcastle. They arrived there after us and left before we did. Norman was professor of French, but his real interest and worldwide fame were bound to religious history. He was already renowned as the author of *The Pursuit of the Millennium* (1957), the epoch-making study of millenarianism, which was to be followed after his move to London and the University of Sussex, by the equally highly praised study of witch-hunting in *Europe's Inner Demons* (1975). Meanwhile, closer to home as far as my interests were concerned, Norman published in 1967 *Warrant for Genocide*, the ultimate exposition of the notorious *Protocols of the Sages of Zion* as a Tsarist-Russian forgery. The Cohns provided the most civilized and charming company, first in Newcastle and later in Hampstead.

The Newcastle Liberal party was another, less predictable, source of social contact. Pam was a lifelong Liberal supporter and was soon pulled in as secretary to the local association. I followed her lead and was put on the committee, where we discovered a pleasant little group of fellow enthusiasts. I made my début in active British politics as a regular canvasser at local elections. It was quite an experience. I soon learned to record 'I will's as possibles and 'I may's as 'noes'. One tried to deal, no doubt without success, with the fear of old ladies that voting Liberal might let Labour in by reminding them that the city council already had a Labour majority, and with the new voters from the Indian subcontinent who, not wishing to offend anyone, promised to support the Liberals but also the Conservatives and Labour. On the first occasion I naively imagined that we might win. We didn't then or on any of the subsequent occasions. Jesmond was a Tory stronghold.

Another group of friends who influenced my further development was recruited from among my contacts as a lecturer in the department of Extramural Studies. To supplement my salary, I regularly volunteered to give evening classes on biblical and Jewish topics including the Dead Sea Scrolls. As they were without precedent, they were noticed among the intellectually hungry Novocastrians and, among others, a number of local Jews became first my pupils and subsequently family friends. They varied from a hospital consultant (Mannie Anderson and his wife Rita) to the owner of a watch repair shop (dear old Moshe Gottlieb) and the *hazzan* (cantor) of the local synagogue and his wife (Chaim and Nediva Haber). Moshe, Chaim and Nediva, alas all three dead now, unintentionally and invisibly paved the way towards my re-encounter with Judaism. Apart from

Mannie, fully assimilated and torn between medicine and painting (he regularly sent canvases to the Royal Academy exhibitions which, as far as I can remember, always ended up on the reject list), the other three were Orthodox Jews. On the first occasion Pam and I visited the Gottliebs' home, Pam as usual wearing a scarf around her head, the female members of the family and the women guests were somewhat disturbed, not knowing that she was not Jewish: was this woman who refused to appear in mixed company bare-headed more observant than they? Moshe, who had a good sense of humour, told me about their concern with a big smile on his round face. It was also at his invitation that to the great surprise of the rabbi I attended the first sabbath service in the synagogue since my early childhood. The rabbi knew me in another capacity: I supervised his efforts for the degree of Master of Letters. It was also in Moshe's house that I met a Lubavitch hasid. He must have heard about my odyssey and told me a tale about a pearl lost in the mud which, however, remained very precious.

Chaim and Nediva Haber came from Israel, but originated from Hungary. They spoke better Hungarian than English or Hebrew. They were a simple but a genuinely loving couple who ran an open house. People kept on dropping in unannounced and were warmly welcomed with coffee and Hungarian poppy-seed or walnut cake (both are favourites). Pam and I spent countless hours with them, feeling truly at home in their company and sharing their *joie de vivre*, which was only momentarily upset by the birth of a handicapped child. The experience was dreadful, for all the friends immediately suspected that something was wrong with the baby boy but did not have the courage to raise the matter with the parents, who had no inkling that the newborn was a Down's syndrome case. We thought it was the doctors' business to inform Chaim and Nediva, and it was only the arrival of her mother from Israel some weeks later that allowed the sad truth to surface.

The beginning of two further friendships which were to have lasting effects date to the Newcastle period. The first is that with David Daube, the Regius Professor of Roman Law in Oxford and an expert in Jewish law as well, who was invited to give a public lecture at King's College. I was familiar with his book *The New Testament and Rabbinic Judaism* (1956) and, anxious to have an opportunity to talk to him at length, offered him overnight hospitality, which he kindly accepted. He seemed to like both of us and a very warm relationship developed. I was partly instrumental in his appointment to give the 1965 series of the Riddell Memorial lectures in Newcastle. He chose as his subject *Collaboration with Tyranny in Rabbinic Law*. However, I was unable to attend. Indeed by November 1965, when he delivered his three lectures, I was no longer in Newcastle, since I had already taken up a new appointment in which, in turn, David Daube was partly instrumental.

It was also in the late 1950s that after several exchanges of offprints I came across Dr Paul Winter, a remarkable character who until his death in 1969 became a faithful and loving friend as well as a sturdy ally in a common effort to redirect Jesus research towards historical paths. I first met him on one of my visits to London, a short, bespectacled, large-headed, typically central-European-looking Jew, twenty years my senior.

Born in Moravia in 1904 when it was still part of the Austro-Hungarian empire, after the First World War he became a Czechoslovak citizen. He studied philosophy, ancient languages and law in the University of Vienna, and practised as a barrister in Prague. After the annexation of his country by Hitler in 1939, he escaped via Hungary and the Balkans to join the free Czech army in Palestine. He fought in North Africa, in France and Germany, and in 1945 became a liaison officer attached to the United States First Army in Germany. He was responsible for the repatriation of the survivors of various camps, among them Buchenwald. His own family, including his mother and sister, perished, and Paul's major work bears the dedication, 'To the dead in Auschwitz, Izbica, Majdanek, Treblinka, among whom are those who were dearest to me'. After demobilization he settled in London and for a time worked for the Overseas Service of the BBC. Then suddenly he decided to devote all his time and energy to the study of the trial of Jesus, a subject that had fascinated him since his childhood. He worked at night as a railway porter and a post office sorter, and spent the day in libraries. In 1961 his epoch-making monograph, *On the Trial of Jesus*, appeared in English from a Berlin publishing house. New Testament scholars carped at his method, but historians were deeply impressed by his illuminating analysis of the Gospel accounts of the arrest, interrogations and execution of Jesus, where he distinguished between the early layers of tradition and the later accretions. He gained international renown, but, being an outsider in every sense, never managed to land an academic post.

I tried to persuade the powers-that-be to give him a research fellowship in Newcastle and enlisted the support of Hugh Trevor-Roper (now Lord Dacre), then Regius Professor of Modern History in Oxford, who had reviewed the *Trial* enthusiastically in one of the Sunday papers. Our effort was to no avail. It would seem that dear George Boobyer, a quintessential conformist, having already been saddled with me, could not face another odd character in his department. A recommendation by Professor Trevor-Roper which I seconded obtained a research grant for Paul from an American foundation; this, combined with an indemnity received from

Germany, slightly improved his circumstances and allowed him to go on lecture tours in various American, Canadian, German and even British universities. I invited him several times to lecture at the Oriental Institute in Oxford. He was our frequent house guest, my learned guide when I first turned to the study of Jesus, and a much-loved soulmate until a heart attack, suffered in his lonely bedsitter in London, took him on 9 October 1969 at the age of sixty-five. His most influential impact on me came a few days before his death, as I will report in the next chapter.

Reasonably securely established in a loving home and in friendly surroundings, I was well placed for the furtherance of my scholarly career. The circumstances were far from ideal. Neither the department in which I worked nor my own position in it was prestigious. First I taught Old Testament in English for general arts students and gave evening classes for working teachers. A few years later, in 1963, when King's College became the University of Newcastle, divinity was elevated to honours status, and at my insistence Hebrew was made compulsory for first-year students and optional afterwards, a rather unusual feature in Britain where not even Oxford or Cambridge placed such a burden on theologians. However, the light task of the opening years suited me very well. As I was not obliged to spend much time on preparing lectures, I was free to indulge in research and writing. Luckily I did not waste that golden opportunity.

During my four years in Paris I had become more and more involved in unravelling the complexities of ancient Jewish Bible interpretation. Study of scriptural exegesis in the Dead Sea Scrolls persuaded me that a comparative historical approach to the phenomenon of interpretation was both possible and necessary, yet very little practised. Since rabbinic writings (Talmud, Midrash and Targum, i.e. the Aramaic paraphrases of the Holy Book) were redacted hundreds of years after the Scrolls or the New Testament, they were either considered irrelevant or used in an unscholarly way as tools of comparison for the study of the Gospels. I was primarily interested in the understanding of biblical stories as distinct from biblical law, and in the process of writing a series of trial essays, comparable to scientific experiments in the field of humanities, I came to realize what should have been, but was not, previously obvious to scholars. It dawned on me that in addition to a basic understanding of the text common throughout the ages, narrative Bible interpretation possessed an historical dimension. Put differently, the same passage was seen as bearing different meanings in the varying circumstances of passing centuries, and was adapted to the particular doctrinal needs of the social group for which the individual exegesis was conceived.

The concrete example that led to this insight was supplied by an explication of the biblical verse of the Book of Habakkuk (2.17) which reads: 'The violence done to Lebanon shall overwhelm you.' The announcement of punishment for the ill-treatment of 'Lebanon' is interpreted in the Commentary on Habakkuk, a Dead Sea Scroll from Qumran Cave 1, as follows: 'Interpreted, this saying concerns the Wicked Priest [i.e. the chief enemy of the Community] inasmuch as he shall be paid the reward which he himself rendered to the Poor [i.e. the members of the Community]. *For Lebanon is the Council of the Community.*'

When I first read these words, I was puzzled: why should the Council of the Community [i.e. the Qumran sect or its principal ruling body] bear the title 'Lebanon'? In search of an answer, I set out to investigate all the instances in ancient Jewish exegetical literature in which the geographical term Lebanon is used metaphorically. I noticed three symbolic values attached to Lebanon: it could mean 'king' or 'foreign nation', but most commonly 'the Temple of Jerusalem'. The latter interpretation reminded me that in the Community Rule, another Scroll from Cave 1, the Council of the Community is declared to be the sect's 'Sanctuary', where its members worshipped after they had abandoned the Jerusalem Temple, which they held to be polluted by their enemy, the Wicked Priest and his colleagues. So, when the sectarian author of the Habakkuk Commentary elliptically asserts that *Lebanon* is *the Council of the Community*, he does so on the tacit assumption that his statement demands no justification because everyone knows that *Lebanon* is a synonym for *Temple*. In syllogistic form, but with the minor proposition omitted, this amounts to:

Lebanon = Temple
[Temple = Council of the Community]
Lebanon = Council of the Community.

The primary and common exegetical tradition of a text (Lebanon = Temple in this case) was subsequently coloured by the historical and doctrinal context in which the interpretation appeared. So Lebanon could refer to the Temple, which was still functioning if the interpreter lived in, or envisaged, the situation preceding the destruction of Jerusalem in AD 70. On the other hand, the overthrow of the Sanctuary after AD 70 could be alluded to as the fall of Lebanon. By contrast, in the sectarian framework of Qumran, Lebanon pointed to the Council of the Community, i.e. to a substitute Temple. In the light of these findings, it will now also be possible to distinguish in the rabbinic sources common traditions which may be centuries old and relevant to the study of the Scrolls and the New

Testament, and later re-interpretations dating to the period between AD 200 and 500.

Apart from the exegetical symbolism of particular words, I also set out to investigate a particular trend already attested in the last two pre-Christian centuries in writings such as the Book of Jubilees and the Qumran Genesis Apocryphon, both reworking the account of the Book of Genesis, as well as the retelling, expanding and embellishing of the Bible story by the first-century AD Jewish historian Flavius Josephus in his *Jewish Antiquities*. I observed that these writers did not distinguish between Scripture and interpretative tradition. Inserting what they believed to be the correct explanation into the text, they were convinced that they were not altering its true meaning but simply bringing it out. I further argued that, contrary to the ideas then current, the Palestinian Aramaic Targums, despite the relatively late date of their present redaction, usually reflected the most primitive and no doubt chronologically the earliest traditions. The phrase 'the Rewritten Bible' which I coined to designate this type of literature has since become part of the technical vocabulary.

A final group of studies took me to the less familiar waters of the relationship between ancient Jewish Bible interpretation and the New Testament, and in two separate essays I sought to shed light on the origins of doctrines surrounding baptism and the representation of the death of Jesus as a sacrifice. The latter, linking the cross to the post-biblical account of the intended immolation or 'binding' (Aqedah) of Isaac in Genesis 22, turned into a seminal as well as controversial study, the final resolution of which was brought about by a small Dead Sea Scroll fragment twenty-five years later.[3]

The separate studies quite naturally grew into a coherent collection in which the same fundamental theme of historical exegesis attained greater and greater precision. During the summer vacation of 1958, which I had spent in Ottery St Mary, I had attended as a guest a meeting of the Old Testament Society in neighbouring Exeter and there met Professor P. A. H. de Boer, the editor-in-chief of *Studia Post-Biblica*, a monograph series published by E. J. Brill in Leiden. I had mentioned my project to him. He asked me to send him the finished product. It took intensive hard work, first by me to complete the volume, and then by Pam, who reshaped my English, clarified my thought and typed out the manuscript. By the summer of 1959, *Scripture and Tradition in Judaism* was ready and I handed it over to de Boer at the Oxford International Old Testament Congress held at Christ Church. In the course of this large gathering of specialists, I made the acquaintance of some further Dead Sea Scrolls experts, among them F. M. Cross and John Strugnell, who will figure prominently in the chapter describing the battle over the Scrolls. I can still see young Strugnell emerging from one of the old buildings, carrying his baby daughter in his arms.

Scripture and Tradition, which appeared in 1961, was my memorial to Renée Bloch, with whom I had shared a number of the book's leading ideas. It was already at the proof stage (and how horrible those proofs were, teeming with printer's errors) when it suddenly struck me that Brill had not offered me a contract. I suppose many young scholars were so pleased to learn that their works would appear in print that they did not dare enquire about legal formalities. I did not expect much financial return either – the total print was only 1,000 copies – but hoped at least to be able to claim expenses from the tax man. So I timidly requested an agreement. Leiden did not bat an eyelid and a letter came, offering me 10% of royalties after the publishers had recouped their original investment. As a matter of fact, the accounts department of Brill must have forgotten about this clause and I was paid my dues without any delay.

To my delight, *Scripture and Tradition*, despite its relatively high price and restricted circulation, reached all the right people, most of whom considered its main contentions proven. The anonymous reviewer of *The Times Literary Supplement* (as I soon learned, none other than Professor H.H. Rowley, whom I had known since Louvain days) nearly made me blush when he referred to the outstanding learning and subtlety of the young author. But above all I treasured the praises mingled with criticism which my revered master from Paris, George Vajda, formulated in the *Revue des Études Juives*: 'Mr Vermes does not fail to conduct these delicate investigations with great erudition and with sagacity joined to prudence. Without any doubt his method is fertile, although the details of the results are not always certain.'[4] Another unexpected but highly appreciated friendly reaction to my first substantial incursion into Judaica outside the field of Qumran was an eleven-page review article by Professor Joseph Heinemann of the Hebrew University in *Tarbiz*, the house journal of Jerusalem's Institute of Jewish Studies. 'Comparative midrash', as my new historical approach to haggadic Bible interpretation became known, entered the textbooks and generated further scholarship, continuing and improving on the prototype.

The same year, 1961, also saw the appearance of *The Essene Writings from Qumran*, my translation (if this is the correct way to put it) of André Dupont-Sommer's *Les écrits esséniens découverts près de la Mer Morte*. At the author's suggestion the Oxford publishers B. H. Blackwell had approached me in 1959 with the proposition that I should turn the French work into English. I hesitated, as I had plenty on my plate, but Pam volunteered to do the job as long as I was there to check the technicalities. Dupont-Sommer expressed his gratitude in flattering words in the preface, but most of the praise should have gone to the real translator. When I half-jokingly told Dupont-Sommer that the main reason for accepting the commission was that we needed money to pay for our recently purchased house, with good humour he remarked that he was delighted to learn that his book fulfilled at least one useful purpose.

Still on the publishing front, I can no longer remember who gave me the idea to contact Penguin Books about a translation of the Dead Sea Scrolls. This anonymous adviser was a genius. I wrote to Penguin shortly after Brill had agreed to publish *Scripture and Tradition in Judaism*. The offer was promptly accepted on 17 March 1960, and a contract was signed by Allen Lane himself, the founder of Penguin Books, on 28 July 1960. Having just been sent my copy of a new agreement with Penguin for a different book, *The Changing Faces of Jesus*, an agreement which runs into thirteen pages, I note with amazement that in 1960 the same job was done on a page and a half, but of course in those faraway days no one bothered about 'single-voice broadcast reading rights', or 'electronic volume form publication rights'.[5] I dare say today's advance payment is an improvement on the £200 I was to receive in two equal instalments on signature (in 1960) and on publication (two years later).

The book duly appeared in July 1962. I opened the parcel containing the advance copies trembling with excitement, but my mouth fell open when I saw the front page reproducing a column of a Hebrew manuscript on a green background. I was totally dumbfounded and could not believe my eyes. Penguin had not shown me the cover design in advance ... and they had printed the photograph upside down! I did not know then that unless stringent preventive measures are taken, nine times out of ten printers are likely to put a Hebrew text, which is justified at the right margin, upside down, as they strive to produce the expected left-hand justification. I feared I would be the laughing stock of the world. Fortunately my worry proved unfounded: only a few reviewers remarked on the front cover, and no one blamed me for the mishap. When I later complained to one of the senior directors of Penguin, I was told that – if I really insisted – at the first reprint they would turn the picture round, but that I ought to realize that from the artistic point of view the present arrangement was *unquestionably* preferable.

The Dead Sea Scrolls in English received a unanimously warm acclaim both from the mass media and from the learned journals. Several reviewers remarked on the quality of the translation, coming straight, as they thought, from someone whose mother tongue was not English. Of course this was the work of Pam, who found herself truly in her element in turning my rendering of the Hebrew, especially of Hebrew verse, into something approaching a work of literature. The publishers of my two books expressed full satisfaction with the commercial performance of their respective ventures. Brill were delighted with the first year's sales of 200 copies of *Scripture and Tradition*, and Penguin with 10,000 orders received from bookshops by publication day.

With the hindsight of thirty-five years and four further editions, and 300,000 copies later, it is easier to grasp why this little volume[6] was an instant success. It fulfilled a genuine need in giving a succinct answer to all the questions which preoccupied specialists and interested lay people in those days. It was also easily affordable: the 1962 edition was sold at 4s 6d (the sum needed to buy a packet of cigarettes in those smoking times; theoretically 22.5p in present day currency) compared with the 1995 issue priced £8.99. In short, the Penguin steadily established itself as the leading Qumran translation in English, quickly superseding Theodor Gaster's competing volume, *The Scriptures of the Dead Sea Sect* (1957), and remaining unchallenged for more than thirty years. Originally it was intended mainly for the general reader, but soon it also became the standard text book on the Dead Sea Scrolls, used by teachers and students in colleges and universities in the English-speaking world, above all in the United States.[7]

This 'popular' paperback, combined with *Scripture and Tradition* and a number of learned papers in periodicals, assured a respectable place for me in the hierarchy of scholars in the so-called inter-testamental (i.e. 200 BC–AD 100) Jewish field, and contributed a good deal to my future academic advancement. But this advancement was neither spontaneous nor rapid. First came an approach in 1961 from the editor of the series which had provided a home for *Scripture and Tradition*. Professor P. A. H. de Boer of the University of Leiden offered me a research post financed by the Dutch state, a post to be attached to his Old Testament department. The ancient university of Leiden, famous for centuries of Semitic learning, was of course more attractive than Newcastle, but I was far from convinced that it was the right step for me. I did not consider a migration from England to Holland an upward move, or fancy the prospect of learning Dutch when I had just begun to feel at home in English. So I took refuge in my impending application for British nationality, which required continued residence in England for at least another year. And that was that.

A year or so later the headship of the Department of Semitic Studies was advertised at the University of Leeds. I was short-listed in the company of Ben Isserlin, a lecturer in the department, and John Allegro of Dead Sea

Scrolls notoriety, from Manchester. I felt that I performed pitifully during the interview, not knowing how to answer the 'searching' question: 'Now, Dr Vermes, what would you say is the difference between the role of a lecturer and that of a head of department?' In short, Ben Isserlin got the job.

Finally, in 1964 I tried for the newly created chair of theology in Bristol, obviously unsuccessfully, but the whole episode completely vanished from my memory, and only the re-reading of an old diary reminded me that I asked my Oxford friend, David Daube, to referee for me. That was the beginning and the end of the Bristol professorship as far as I was concerned.

While busy with attempts to get away from Newcastle, I kept one iron in the local fire too. A Jewish public-relations friend, whom I met in the open house of Chaim and Nediva Haber, urged me to *do* something. 'You must create an opportunity for yourself and not wait for the apple to drop into your lap. If you are after a chair in Jewish studies, find a Jew to fund it!' This was not my style at all, but obediently I set out to discover a Jewish Maecenas in Newcastle. Naturally, I had to clear the matter with my head of department, and dear George, true to his decent, puritanical self, ponderously told me that although he was only a senior lecturer, he would not dream of standing in my way towards a professorship. Dr Mannie Anderson, another Haber friend, introduced me to a mogul in the clothing business who kindly listened to my proposal. He said that he found it interesting, but that he had to discuss the matter with the Vice-Chancellor of the university. As it turned out, the VC also had his eye on the mogul for help with a view to landing a bigger fish than a Jewish studies chair. So that was the end of that story.

It therefore seemed that I was destined to stay put in Newcastle. Bearing in mind that Pam and I were happy and I was able to pursue a productive professional life there, this was a perfectly tolerable prospect. It further improved in 1964 with my promotion to a senior lectureship. I therefore decided to bide my time.

Meanwhile Pam also discovered a new task to which she was to devote the best part of her remaining years: the work of Martin Buber. Some ten years earlier she had received from a friend a copy of *I and Thou* in Ronald Gregor Smith's English translation. The book made a deep impression on her, yet she felt that she could not grasp the true meaning of Buber's message. So when, browsing in the philosophy section of the University library, one day I stumbled on the first volume of Buber's collected works in the original German, I obeyed my instinct and brought the book home. Pam revived her dormant German which she had learned in Vienna and Berlin before the last war, and read *Ich und Du*. This turned out to be a revelation for her. 'Now I can understand it!', she exclaimed. Until then Ronald Gregor Smith's translation had stood between her and the meaning of that master. Pam began to turn the book into English just to make sense of it, and this hobby, as will appear later, completely transformed her life and gave a new purpose to it.

To complete the picture of the Newcastle years, three holidays and a few personal encounters need to be mentioned. Each in its own way, these contacts had their impact on the future course of my destiny.

In the summer of 1961 I planned to attend the World Congress of Jewish Studies in Jerusalem. I hoped to take Pam with me for her first (and last) visit to Israel, but we were rather short of money. Financial stringency was overcome thanks to the sympathy and understanding of the Rector of King's College, Charles Bosanquet, who tacitly authorized me to use the sum granted to me by the university for air travel to buy, with a little supplementation, two cheaper fares by rail and sea. The journey was memorable. The incoming Greek ferry was late and we enjoyed twenty-four unexpected hours in Venice. A stop in Piraeus allowed a quick visit to Athens and the Acropolis, and we also spent a few hours on the beautiful island of Rhodes before landing in Haifa.

From Tel Aviv a friend drove us to Jerusalem (and was booked for speeding on the way), and deposited us at the flat of his son, where we camped during our stay. We visited the still-divided city and travelled north to Galilee. The trip to Tiberias and the Lake was mainly memorable for the unbearable August heat. At the Dome of the Annunciation in Nazareth Pam was so disgusted by the vulgar antics of a group of American pilgrims that we ran out of the church without exploring it. To redeem this fiasco and find some spiritual relief, she decided to walk next day to the top of Mt Tabor, where according to the Gospels Jesus prayed and was 'transfigured'. I warned her that in August we had to start very early if we were to reach the summit without melting. Not unexpectedly we missed the early bus, and it was already 10 o'clock when we began our uphill task. It did not last long. Although at the beginning she bravely turned down several offers of a lift from cars driving by, after half an hour of struggle we shamefacedly climbed on to a jeep. The view from the top was magnificent and moving. It was an invitation to silent prayer and meditation amid the ruins of a mediaeval church.

By then it was past noon and, hungry and thirsty, we entered a hostelry for pilgrims run by Italian Franciscans. There we could quench our thirst with expensive beer, but no money, love nor prayer could obtain food for us from the heirs of the holy man of Assisi. This was all the more depressing as glorious kitchen smells pervaded the place. The meal was reserved for a jolly and noisy group of Italian priests, who arrived while we were still there.

So grumbling and shaking the dust of the place off our feet, we began our downward journey. What a different experience was awaiting us! Half-way down, at the Muslim village of Daburiyye (a name which still contains a faint echo of the biblical Tabor), we were first accosted by a group of Arab children. Their dirty little hands were full of figs. With big smiles on their faces, they offered us the fruit, which they had probably stolen from an orchard. Then we met an Arab woman dressed in black, who gave us a large bunch of grapes and firmly refused money for it. Finally, at a bus stop at the foot of the mountain, teenage Arab boys, returning from school in Nazareth, invited us to share their large watermelon. They did not want money either, but were interested in us and our plans. The contrast with the lack of humanity encountered higher up could not have been more striking.

The World Congress of Jewish Studies, which was the purpose of my trip, a monumental jamboree with countless deadly short papers, was an anticlimax, and I have never attended another to this day. However, three episodes stuck in my mind. At the opening ceremony Pam and I saw Martin Buber sitting on the platform among the dignitaries. I also met for the first and last time Dr Cecil Roth, then Reader in Jewish Studies at Oxford. We had a brief and stiff conversation. He had funny ideas about the Dead Sea Scrolls and considered me and all scholars with whom he disagreed – i.e. practically everybody – his enemies. After the appearance of *The Dead Sea Scrolls in English* in 1962, I had a letter from him in which he blamed his failure to publish a book on Qumran on me. My crime consisted in not listing an earlier monograph of his in the bibliography of the Penguin. Finally, during the interval between papers, I was approached by an enthusiastic young American who congratulated me on my work on ancient Jewish Bible interpretation. This was my first encounter with Jacob Neusner, with whom I would have much to do in the 1970s and early 1980s.

The second holiday took us to the south of France in the late summer of 1963. It was on the way home, after a delightful fortnight on the peninsula of Hyères not far from Toulon, that I last saw my old Sion friend, Paul Démann. By then he, too, had severed his links with the Fathers and was living with Ida, a charming Jewish woman, whom he was soon to marry. They later had a son and seemed to live happily, but Paul's career as a scholar and especially as a leading figure in the Jewish-Christian dialogue sadly came to an abrupt end. We continued to correspond until the late 1960s before losing touch. I am told that he is still alive. He is now in his mid-eighties and a widower.

Our 1964 holiday was spent in a villa in the Tuscan countryside, between Pisa and Livorno, in a tiny village splendidly named Nugola Vecchia. It would have been delightful had it not been marred by my deteriorating health. The old stomach trouble resurfaced and I was sick every evening. An operation performed later that year in Newcastle seems to have cured me of that complaint; I have never had any further trouble. The return journey was a real nightmare: the suspension of my first and last Mini collapsed in northern Italy and two tyres were also ruined. I managed to creep to Milan, centre of the Italian car industry, but it took three days and a lot of argument to get us on the road again. As a result, our money ran out and we had to count the pennies, which were just enough for one night in the cheapest possible hotel in France. What a relief it was to reach the safe haven of England and Pam's mother's comfortable flat in Warwick Square, SW1!

Mention of the ill-fated car brings me to a crucial question: what was I doing on 22 November 1963, the day of President Kennedy's murder? I was driving our newly-acquired second-hand Austin Mini to Durham, where the famous G. R. Driver, Professor of Semitic Philology at Oxford, was to give a lecture in the evening on the Dead Sea Scrolls. It was during the dinner accompanying the talk that the news of the assassination was announced. A Semitist of the highest repute, Godfrey Driver was a kind of maverick in Qumran matters and I was keen to find out what he would come up with this time. True to himself, he delivered a talk, brilliant in appearance, but strictly unconvincing, on Qumran history, arguing that the Scrolls were documents produced by the Zealots, the Jewish rebels against Rome, in the sixties of the first century AD. I politely questioned his theories and we had a good-humoured clash, neither party persuading the other. Nevertheless, this first personal contact with the leading Hebraist of Britain, who subsequently reviewed my Penguin favourably in the *Journal of Theological Studies*, had a providentially accidental impact sixteen months later.

By the beginning of 1965, cured of years of ill-health and appreciative of the friendly gesture of my university in giving me a first promotion and tacitly implying that more might follow on the approaching retirement of George Boobyer, I was ready to settle down once more to teaching, research and publishing in the by then respectable Honours School of Divinity in the independent University of Newcastle-upon-Tyne. I was also thrilled by an invitation received from the University of Freiburg im Breisgau to preside over the 'Habilitation' procedure of the rabbinic scholar Dr Arnold Goldberg.[8] Normally such a function was entrusted to a German academic, but I was told by the authorities that in the Germany of the 1960s there was only one person capable of acting as an expert judge in that area of learning, and they were determined not to have him because he and the candidate, Dr Goldberg, did not see eye to eye. So would I do them the favour?

It was while busy reading a monumental dissertation on the various representations of the divine presence or *Shekhinah* in Talmud and Midrash that, sleepily glancing through the university vacancies column of *The Times* one cold February morning in 1965, I suddenly woke up. I noticed an advertisement in very small print which invited applications for the Readership in Jewish Studies at Oxford, vacated by Cecil Roth, whom I mentioned earlier in this chapter. I knew that he was a specialist in mediaeval and Renaissance Jewry and had written a history of the Jews in England, and naturally imagined that Oxford would be looking for a replacement in those areas which were far distant from my field of competence. Still, I said to myself that since such an opportunity probably arises only once in a lifetime, I owed it to myself to make some enquiries and sent a note to Professor Driver. With my specialization being what it was, would it be a waste of time to make myself a candidate? Back came a postcard by return: 'As I am a member of the electoral board, it would be improper for me to say much except that if you submit your papers, they will be seriously considered.' I was still not convinced that an application was worthwhile, and with my trip to Germany due later that month, I concentrated on my imminent concerns and left for Freiburg on 25 February. My German experience was eye-opening: academic administration was hopeless; the members of the faculty of arts were at each other's throats; and the Bavarians never stopped eating and drinking. The examination started at 9 p.m. and finished at 11, followed by toasts with sparkling wine and a very large meal after midnight. And on the morning of my departure, at 8 a.m. I was summoned to a champagne breakfast from which I managed to tear myself away just in time for my flight to London.

After recovering from this pleasant ordeal, I finally decided to mail an application for the Oxford job. Our dear friend David Daube, Fellow of All Souls College, kindly volunteered to act as one of my referees. The letter was sent off on 9 March and arrived at the registry on the closing day for applications. I am telling the truth when I say that I actually put the whole matter out of my mind and for the next two weeks quietly got on with my job in Newcastle.

On 23 March my peaceful Northumbrian routine came to an end for good.

Part Four: The Golden Years of Oxford

(1965–1993)

14

The Wonderland of Oxford

In the late morning of 23 March 1965 I had a telephone call from Pam. 'Are you busy?', she asked. 'Not particularly,' I replied, as I had just finished my classes. 'In that case, you'd better come home at once. Something has come that you ought to see.' She refused to say more, and I had no idea what the mystery was about. So I drove home to find a grey envelope with an Oxford postmark on it. It had been opened by Pam. I was logical enough to deduce that it was not an 'I very much regret' letter and jumped to the conclusion that I was short-listed for the post. Instead I learned that the Deputy Registrar of the University was delighted to inform me that at its meeting on March 22 the electoral board for the Statutory Readership in Jewish Studies had decided to offer me the job. If I were to accept the offer, the matter would still have to be approved by the General Board, but that would be just a formality. I did not know what had hit me. I had never heard of an academic appointment, and a senior one at that, being made without an interview. But then, thirty-one years ago, I was a total stranger to Oxford. I replied at once and accepted the offer. Next day a one-line note in long-hand, signed G.R.D. (Godfrey Rolls Driver), simply wished me 'Welcome to Oxford'. The formal offer by the General Board reached me eight days later: my initial annual stipend was set at £3,175, just one yearly increment below the top of the Reader's scale (£3,250). On April Fool's Day 1965, I re-accepted the dream post.

Meanwhile the news began to spread via the grapevine. David Daube's telegram, cabled from Berkeley on 30 March, read: 'CONGRATULA-TIONS TO OXFORD HAPPINESS TO YOU BOTH – DAVID.' Locally, George Boobyer and the Vice-Chancellor were genuinely pleased. Charles Bosanquet flattered me by saying that he knew that I was 'too good to stay in Newcastle', while down-to-earth George, who was the first person I told, solemnly advised me not to tender my resignation from my present post until the Oxford offer was made formal. With the announcement of the appointment in *The Times* on 7 April[1] congratulatory notes came from far and wide, from two further members of the electoral board as well as friends and colleagues. Pam reported the good news to her mother and daughters, and I wrote to great-aunt Gizi for her to pass it on to the rest of the family. Not knowing whether they were aware of the standing of Oxford in Academe, I must have said something to this effect. Back came loving messages. Of course they knew that Oxford was the greatest university in the world, the only one fit for the cleverest member of the family! After all, they were Central European Jews.

However, not everybody shared their joy, as I was soon to discover. After the university registry had released my name to the press, I had a telephone call from a reporter of the *Jewish Chronicle* and immediately sensed that I was facing a hostile interview. Being naive enough to assume that the Oxford Readership was an academic appointment, I was startled when, totally impervious to my scholarly achievements, the journalist was interested only in my relationship to Anglo-Jewry. Of course, I told him that I was a Jew but obviously made an egregious mistake when I also declared myself unaffiliated to any religious denomination, and even claimed that such an affiliation was not a necessary requirement for holding a university position. So a fair but unenthusiastic, indeed unfriendly report appeared in the next issue of the *JC*. It was echoed by one of the Sunday papers which, not quite sure what was newsworthy about my appointment, produced the headline, 'Ex-priest to lecture on Jews'.

What I did not know was that since part of the original endowment for the Readership had been provided by Jewish benefactions, some members of the community considered the post itself 'Jewish'. Added to this, although Cecil Roth, the only previous holder of the Readership for a quarter of a century, had made very little impact on the university *qua* teacher (he was a respectable scholar and author of a number of books), he had played as it were the role of chaplain to Jewish undergraduates, who from now on would become 'fatherless'. I also learned later, from a well-placed Jewish informant, that the then Chief Rabbi had assumed that he would be consulted as of right before Oxford filled the 'Jewish' vacancy. We lived in a different world thirty years ago, and I wonder whether his being ignored or the actual appointment annoyed him more.

Furthermore, what I forgot to take into account in my elation was the disappointment of the other four very respectable, but unsuccessful, Jewish candidates and their sponsors, especially when it became rumoured, according to the *Sunday Express* of 11 April, that 'the appointment ... was unanimous'. Some of them thought that it was improper for me to apply. A sponsor, a brilliant Oxford Orientalist long since deceased, Samuel Miklós Stern of Hungarian descent, was so incensed that for years he crossed the street when he saw me coming in his direction.[2] He even pulled strings and got on to the electoral board which was to consider my reappointment after the initial five-year period. Oxford being Oxford, they let him become an elector, but at the same time my referee, David Daube, was also put on the same board with the knowledge that, as Regius Professor of Civil Law, he would see to it that no mischief occurred. Since the other members of the board stood behind me, David did not need to have recourse to his lawyer's skills.

The next complication arose from the rather peculiar definition of the Readership in Jewish Studies. At Oxford this was linked to *four* faculties: Modern History (which among the dreaming spires begins in AD 285), Oriental Studies (the home of Hebrew), Literae Humaniores or Classics and Ancient History, and of course Theology. Since my predecessor had been a historian – though after quarrelling with his colleagues he took refuge among the Orientalists – the post was officially classified as primarily belonging to Modern History. The members of that faculty, who were quite happy with the former Reader's defection to the Oriental faculty, suddenly decided to reclaim the post and insisted that I should lecture for them. So when I came to Oxford in the middle of May to spy out the lay of the land, I received a warm welcome among my fellow Orientalists, who hastened to provide me with an office in the Oriental Institute. On the other hand, the leaders of the History faculty were urbane, but less forthcoming, and insisted that my primary allegiance should go to them. Poor me. But fortunately my mentor David Daube helped me to understand and handle Oxford. 'In the end you will make of your post what you wish. That will be the best for all concerned,' he wrote on 14 May. 'Listen politely to every-body, but do only what you really fancy. *Nobody has the right to direct you, and you have the duty to follow your own bent.*' These were words of wisdom which in due course paid off. For the first five years I was listed among the modern historians and offered them occasional, not very well attended, lectures, as I could deal only with the earliest epoch of general history, which was taken only by a handful of undergraduates. After 1970, my bond with that faculty slackened and I was officially allowed to display my true identity as a student of Hebrew and Aramaic literature and Jewish history and religion.

As the final hurdle before completing the migration from industrial Newcastle to the architectural glory of mediaeval and early modern Oxford – and how magnificent is the Broad or Tom Quad in Christ Church in the late evening sunshine of a summer day – Pam and I had to look for a new home. This was quite a problem. House prices in Oxford were double those in Newcastle, and since we had no capital to fall back on, the nicer areas of residential Oxford were beyond our reach. To my inquiry about possible help from the University – Newcastle had an arrangement for second mortgages – the Deputy Registrar looked nonplussed in a typical Oxford way, but promised to look into the matter. What he found out surprised him as much as it surprised me. One of the regional building societies was willing, against a guarantee given by 'the Chancellor, Masters and Scholars of the University of Oxford', to grant a mortgage to us, but only if the sum borrowed corresponded to the whole value of the property, all 100%! 'If I had known this,' exclaimed the Deputy Registrar, 'I wouldn't have been obliged to sell my country cottage when I moved to Oxford!' So we both discovered, I the newcomer more quickly than one of the chief administrators, that in Oxford nothing is easy to find, as nothing is written down; but if one starts digging around, sooner or later someone will turn up who has the answer.

Pam and I travelled a couple of times to Oxford for house-hunting, but discovered nothing suitable, so finally it was left to me to solve the problem. Our first home was a brand new semi-detached house in a recently completed small development in the southern suburb of Littlemore, locally known for its large mental hospital and among the more sophisticated as the place where John Henry Newman spent his last years within the Church of England before going over to Rome in 1845. The accommodation was fairly comfortable (unlike North Biddick Hall in Washington, also chosen by me, this one had not just electricity but also central heating). But it was too noisy for Pam, and although she set out at once to create a new garden, we knew that we would not stay there any longer than we could help. We devoted many a weekend idly and without real hope (as we hardly could afford anything more expensive) looking for our dream house. As will soon appear, we found it by coincidence two years later, and thanks to another rather tiresome providential accident migrated to glorious Boars Hill in 1968.

One further Oxford mystery needed to be confronted before I could settle down to my new job. Unknown to me, the University had been wrestling during the years preceding my election with the predicament of having a large number of teachers, some of them with considerable seniority and reputation, who, though holding university teaching posts, were without college fellowships. A high-powered committee chaired by Sir Oliver (later Lord) Franks, Provost of Worcester College, decided that this state of affairs was intolerable and that from 1965 onwards every University reader would be automatically entitled to a fellowship, and every lecturer within five years from his or her first appointment. But since the old colleges were unwilling to open their gates to large numbers of teachers in minority subjects not in demand among undergraduates, two new colleges were created to serve the dual purpose of providing such fellowships and catering for the increasing postgraduate population in the student body. So I did not quite know how to deal with a letter which I received soon after arrival from Mr A. L. P. (later Sir Arthur) Norrington (known as Tom), President of Trinity College, informing me that I was at liberty to choose between St Cross College and Iffley College – except, he quietly added, the former was already full.

Of the two fledgling foundations, St Cross initially had a double advantage: it had a head and, more important, it had usable premises in the form of a large prefabricated hut close to the Law Library at the edge of central Oxford. Iffley College lacked both these assets. It was so to speak headless – the renowned scientist to whom the leadership was offered turned it down – and Court House in Iffley behind the church was out in the wilds by the Oxford standards prevailing in the 1960s (I suppose it was about two miles from the centre) and required much alteration before it could be the seat of a college. After some weeks of inquiry and reflection I opted for Iffley, not because the St Cross list was already closed – with some insistence it might have been reopened – but for three seemingly good reasons. Court House, Iffley, was conveniently situated half-way between the Oriental Institute and my home in Littlemore. It had a charming location close to the Isis (the Oxford designation of the Thames) and adjacent to a beautiful twelfth-century Norman church. Thirdly, there was also a diplomatic consideration: St Cross had one of the other competitors for the Readership in Jewish Studies among its fellows. My reasons turned out to be specious, but I made the right choice. In less than a year shadowy Iffley College metamorphosed into Wolfson College, soon to become the largest postgraduate institution in Britain. In joining this budding confraternity, I unwittingly acquired a unique qualification. Devoid of any Oxford pedigree, I needed to be matriculated before the MA degree could be conferred on me by decree, and I was so registered through Iffley College. None of the other fellows required such a 'birth certificate', and by the time we admitted our first students, Iffley did not exist any longer. So I am, and will for ever remain, the only child born to Oxford by the scarcely remembered Iffley College.[3]

Furnished with a new identity – Geza Vermes *MA* – what was it like starting a fresh career in the holy of holies of Academe? First of all, I had to acquire my uniform, a black gown, which was still worn at lectures in those days.[4] Undergraduates were also expected to be begowned at both lectures and tutorials. I was not told what I was to lecture on. The choice was up to me. So after some heart-searching and some friendly consultation I offered a Hebrew text class on one of the tractates of the earliest rabbinic law code, the Mishnah (2 hours), an introductory course to rabbinic Bible interpretation (1 hour), another to the Dead Sea Scrolls (2 hours), an introduction to post-biblical Jewish history and literature (1 hour) and, to please the Modern History faculty, a course on Jewish life in the early Middle Ages (1 hour). This would have counted as a fairly light load in Newcastle. But in Oxford fifty-six lectures in one term amounted to 150% of my *annual* teaching obligation, since according to my letter of appointment I was to give 'not less than thirty-six lectures or classes in each year'.[5] I did not stick to the statutory limit even when I knew the ropes better, but at least two of my Orientalist colleagues did. One of them expected to be paid extra for anything offered beyond the obligatory minimum.

I was very nervous at the beginning because, apart from my upgraded Scrolls lectures, all my courses were new and had to be created from scratch. The text classes turned out to be the least demanding, as they were attended only by a handful of undergraduates, but the history and literature lectures attracted an audience of between ten and twenty, not only from among the Hebraists of the Oriental Institute, but also from Theology and Ancient History. I clearly remember a young don wearing his MA gown at my first performance. 'That was my Ancient History tutor from Queens,' one of my students told me. It was there that I first saw Fergus Millar, who was to become one of my closest friends and a faithful collaborator in perhaps the most demanding task which I had to shoulder in my life as a scholar, the remaking of Emil Schürer's classic, *The History of the Jewish People in the Age of Jesus Christ*. This, as will be seen, occupied my first twenty years in Oxford.

The undergraduates were incomparably better than those I was used to. They were more literate, and their weekly one-to-one tutorial contact with dons taught them the art of reasoning and debating skills. The talented ones were excellent, and I had the good fortune to number four students among my pupils in my first few years in Oxford who are internationally renowned scholars today. I enormously enjoyed their company, and did my best to stretch them intellectually. But I was recently told by one of them that I was an awe-inspiring teacher because I kept on asking apparently rhetorical questions which turned out not to be rhetorical at all.

My first graduate student arrived in October 1966 from Hebrew Union College, Cincinnati, USA: he was Japanese *and* a rabbi. Alas, we did not see eye to eye and he left Oxford without a degree. When I later enquired of his American sponsors why he was sent here, they sheepishly admitted that they chose Oxford because it was considerably cheaper than Cincinnati. In the same year, the then Regius Professor of Hebrew and Student of Christ Church suggested that I should become the tutor in biblical and rabbinic Hebrew of one of the rather special undergraduates of 'the House' (i.e.

Christ Church, from the Latin *Aedes* Christi). The said undergraduate, who used to come to our home for his tutorials in an open Mercedes sports car, and sat his final examinations bravely and successfully the following June, during the Six-Day War of 1967, is the present Crown Prince of the Hashemite Kingdom of Jordan.

A continuous source of marvel and pleasure was provided by the almost daily encounter with the *crème de la crème* of the scholarly world. Professor G.R. Driver, Sir Godfrey Driver after the completion of the *New English Bible,* though already Emeritus, still dominated the Oriental Institute which he brought into existence in 1961. Rumour had it that when the University declared itself unable to supply the finance, Driver, a former pupil of Winchester, went to see his Wykehamist friend, Arnold Toynbee, chairman of the Universities Grants Committee and, in the spirit of the old boys' network, the deal was concluded over the dinner table. A workaholic if ever there was one, this admirable, tall, lean old man sat at his desk all day long in Room 101, the choicest office in the Institute, which I was to inherit from him. One watched him apprehensively on his numerous visits to the library of the Oriental Institute and that of the Griffith Institute in the neighbouring Ashmolean Museum where, even after his first stroke, he was climbing to the top of unsteady library ladders in search of an elusive book. The day after he lost the use of his right hand, he began to practise writing with his left. At the first opportunity he summoned me to his bedside in the Acland Nursing Home to obtain from me, then chairman of the Curators of the Institute, the promise that he would be allowed to keep his room. Then I was told to act as his scribe and correct the proofs of an article at his dictation and under his strict supervision. Even after another stroke, from which in fact he did not recover, he arrived in the Acland with his briefcase filled with unfinished work. He was one of the last legendary Oxford characters whom I had the good fortune to know. 'My father and I taught in Oxford for ninety years,' he once told me. Born in Christ Church, he was the son of the famous Canon S.R. Driver, Regius Professor of Hebrew, and his first memory went back to the day in 1897 when his mother, accompanied by Lewis Carroll of *Alice in Wonderland* fame, took him to the top of Tom Tower to watch the future Edward VII inaugurating the new town hall. He was the prototype of scholarly enthusiasm, a childlike and mischievous octogenarian, an inspiration for us all.[6]

Henry Chadwick, still Regius Professor of Divinity when I first appeared on the scene before he was made Dean of Christ Church, invited me to join his high-powered weekly senior seminar on New Testament topics. I regularly attended for a couple of years and read one or two papers to it. It was the model of genuine academic collaboration, the common pursuit and advancement of knowledge.

The third, and in many respects the most remarkable, Oxford figure who made a profound impact on me was Sir Isaiah Berlin, then Chichele Professor of Political Theory and Fellow of All Souls. His name brings me back to Iffley College. Without a roof over our head, without a master and without junior members, and consequently with no practical issues to debate, the thirty-seven founding fellows could only speculate about the future – which we did weekly in borrowed accommodation. We dreamed about becoming the great postgraduate research institution of the land. Then some of the more worldly-wise came up with the splendid idea that Isaiah Berlin should be invited to lead us towards the promised land. He came to meet the fellows in January 1966 and expressed interest, but declared that since he was unwilling to spend the rest of his active days in fund-raising, he would accept only if he joined us with as it were a dowry. And that's that, I thought, ignorant of Isaiah's power of persuasion. Within a couple of months, over the dinner table in New York or Washington, he obtained from his friend McGeorge Bundy, the President of the Ford Foundation, a very substantial matching grant for the sum total of all moneys he could raise in the UK.[7] Another couple of months, and the Wolfson Foundation undertook to pay for the construction and furnishing of a large college by the Cherwell in North Oxford. By May 1966 the deed was done: Wolfson College was born.

From close quarters, Isaiah Berlin has revealed himself to be not just the profound and powerful thinker that he is, and the most amusing and amazing conversationalist, but above all, the kindest human being one can imagine. During all the years he held the reins of the college, he was loved by all. Miracle of miracles in an academic society, I cannot recall anyone ever questioning his judgment, let alone contradicting him, at governing body meetings. My hero figure also proved a true and sympathetic friend in a most moving letter of condolence after Pam's death. Since then he has publicly revealed his preoccupation with the idea of dying in an interview which he gave to *The Times* on 16 July 1996, on the occasion of his eighty-seventh birthday. During the ten years of his presidency, he acted as a magnet, attracting to Wolfson the great and the good, such as Niko Tinbergen, the Nobel Laureate animal behaviourist, and the grand old man of Roman history, Sir Ronald Syme, an OM like Isaiah himself. Surrounded by brilliant minds, by outstanding expertise in any subject one could think of, and with the unparalleled riches of the Bodleian Library at arm's length, I found in Oxford Paradise revealed.

The Oriental Institute was my academic home where I taught and worked. Soon I was elected to the faculty board, responsible for all academic matters, and was also made a member of the board of Curators who looked after the fabric and the library of the Institute. As the new boy among the Curators, I was landed with the worst possible job: I became the Institute's negotiator on an inter-departmental committee which also included representatives from the neighbouring Ashmolean Museum, the Taylorian Institution, and the Institutes of Archaeology and the History of Art. We had to address the vexatious question of how to share a car park the size of which was wholly disproportionate to the needs of the various constituent bodies. I was totally inexperienced in such matters, but I met with luck and managed to gain two extra parking spaces for our Institute. My fame grew, and on the next occasion I was promoted from car park plenipotentiary to chairman of the Curators. So I was not a little perplexed when, perhaps a couple of years later, one of the caretakers entered the lecture room where I was teaching to inform me that the elderly wife of a colleague, Richard Walzer, wanted to see me *very urgently*. Imagining that the matter was serious, I interrupted the class. Downstairs I was instructed by an impatient Sophie Walzer to get her car out of the car park. 'I can drive forward,' she told me, 'but I don't know how to reverse.' The idea that I was the car park attendant remained stuck in her mind. Some years later, she summoned me to her home. Would I drive her to London to visit an exhibition of Islamic art? I politely declined, but since I was friendly with her cat, I was forgiven. Meantime I had a last chance before she died to admire the dozens of canvases of French impressionists, Manet, Monet, Renoir, van Gogh, Gauguin, etc., which her father had bought from the artists when they were still going cheap.

On the research and publishing front matters were quiet, partly because I had to spend a fair amount of time writing new lecture courses, and partly because the big enterprise concerning the updating of Jewish history from 175 BC to AD 135 (the Schürer project), which I joined in 1965, took eight years to produce the first of its four volumes. I was also busy with another more modest topic which I wanted to try out before putting the finishing touches to it. This was a philological analysis of the Aramaic expression 'son of man', a frequent phrase in the Greek Gospels which was believed to be crucial. I had been working on it for years. New Testament experts were divided over its interpretation. All seemed to agree that the expression represented an important title linked to the mysterious figure designated as 'one like a son of man' in Daniel 7. 14, but some argued that it corresponded to Jesus' own self-understanding, while others were convinced that Jesus' allusion to a 'Son of Man still to come' pointed to a heavenly figure distinct from himself.

I started with five preliminary observations. 1. The phrase 'son of man' is nowhere attested as a title in Jewish Aramaic writings of the relevant period. 2. The Greek expression is not original, but covers a Semitic, almost certainly Aramaic, idiom. 3. In the Synoptic Gospels it is always placed on the lips of Jesus: no third person describes or addresses him as son of man. 4. The expression is not mysterious: no one enquires about its meaning. 5. Nor does it have any objectionable connotations, as no complaint is registered about its use.

I soon realized that only a search for the Aramaic meaning or meanings of the expression could resolve the mystery. So I set out to discover precisely that in the Galilean Aramaic sections of rabbinic literature which in some way echo the language spoken by Jesus. What a task this investigation turned out to be in those pre-computer database and even pre-concordance times! I had to glance through the whole of the Palestinian Talmud and the Midrash called Genesis Rabba, as well as the Palestinian Targums or Aramaic paraphrases of the Pentateuch, looking for those two words. I discovered that in addition to the well known meanings, 'a human being' or 'someone' (i.e. the indefinite pronoun), neither of which is relevant to the Gospel usage, there are a limited number of examples in contexts of monologues or dialogues where the phrase is a circumlocutional reference to the speaker himself. When an Aramaic speaker wanted to avoid a taboo subject (e.g. I shall die) or did not wish to sound boastful (e.g. I shall become king), he substituted the slightly equivocal son of man for 'I'. Such an interpretation, I suggested, might supply a generally satisfactory explanation of the New Testament usage. Indeed, it seems that the Gospels themselves allow a glimpse into such an equivocation when for example Matthew 16. 13, 'Who do men say the *son of man* is?' is compared to Mark 8. 27, 'Who do men say that *I* am?'.

An international New Testament congress held in Oxford a few days after my arrival in September 1965 provided a suitable forum to air my views. The lecture made a splash the reverberations of which continue thirty years on, although many New Testament scholars have never managed to replace their unending speculations which fill a whole library with an explanation of such apparent simplicity.[8]

The big work project which accompanied me to Oxford concerned the revision of 'Schürer', that is to say the monumental handbook on Jewish history produced between 1874 and 1909 by the renowned German New Testament scholar/ancient historian Emil Schürer (1844–1910). An admirably comprehensive and authoritative work, it covered the political, institutional, religious and literary history of the Jews from the time of the Maccabees in the early second century BC to the second Jewish uprising against Rome in the 130s AD. It almost immediately became *the* handbook on the subject and reigned unchallenged for two generations. An English translation made from the second German edition was published in Edinburgh by T. & T. Clark in 1885–1890 and continued to be sold over the years until it went out of print around the time of the Second World War. In the 1950s, Professor H. H. Rowley of Manchester advised the publishers to re-issue this modern classic in a revised version and suggested that Professor Matthew Black be asked to see to its updating. He agreed, and set the work in motion in 1964. A small team, mostly Matthew Black's former students, was assembled to prepare a new translation from the last German edition of 1901–1909. Black himself proposed to bring the work up-to-date in a separate supplementary volume. By 1965, he realized that the task was too big for him and proposed that I should join him as co-editor. Not knowing what lay ahead, I gave my provisional consent. But when I began to perceive the real scale of the enterprise, I made my agreement subject to two conditions: 1. that the revision should be made in the text itself and not in a supplementary volume; and 2. that we needed a further expert in Roman history. My stipulations were accepted. Matthew hurriedly upgraded his team of translators into 'translators/revisers' and I was to recruit in Oxford an ancient historian interested in the Jews in the Roman empire. That was easy: the star pupil of Sir Ronald Syme, Fergus Millar, then tutorial fellow of Queens College, was obviously the man for the job. I learned to admire him soon after my arrival in Oxford and we became regular collaborators. The two of us set out to re-read Schürer and survey the more recent developments in the subject while waiting for Matthew's 'translators/revisers' to produce the manuscripts which were to serve as the basis for our editorial work. They began to arrive. The first was typed single-spaced on flimsy paper; the translation was horrible, and the revision consisted in introducing fundamentalist Christian views into Schürer. I insisted on rejecting it, and after a fight with Matthew and the publishers succeeded. But when I proposed the same course of action after reading the second submission, I was firmly outvoted by Matthew and the Clarks. A compromise was needed, and in the end it turned out to be a blessing. We were to secure the help of a literary editor to ensure the reliability and stylistic unity of the translation. Pam volunteered, and the Oxford trio quietly pressed on for the next twenty years with what seemed to be a superhuman assignment. We coped, and when the first volume appeared in 1973, it was to be hailed as 'one of the few indispensable books' (*Journal of Theological Studies*).

Living in Oxford made access to London easy, and this in turn helped me to raise my profile nationally. I was one of the invited guests at the opening of the Jordanian Dead Sea Scrolls exhibition held in the British Museum in December 1965, and was one of the main speakers in Edinburgh in April 1966 when the same touring exhibition reached the National Library of Scotland. It was a bitterly cold evening, yet so many enthusiasts turned up that a second room with closed-circuit television was needed in addition to the large amphitheatre where I lectured. During question time, which continued for nearly an hour, the Scottish National Librarian himself acted as messenger boy, bringing to the main hall queries from the overflow auditorium. Just a few days earlier, an article of mine on the Scrolls had occupied half of the middle page of the *Daily Telegraph*. Later in 1966, on the occasion of an exhibition showing the Masada excavations, the Sunday paper, *The Observer*, organized a day-long symposium on the Dead Sea Scrolls chaired by one of its staff writers, Colin Cross, who came to be briefed by me some days earlier, as he was expected to present a full-page report the following week. Yigael Yadin and I were the principal invited participants. I thought that the recorded conversation was highly successful, but the paper's editorial board decided otherwise, and the article ended up in the wastepaper basket. Nevertheless, it bore fruit later on. The tape recording was lent to the great American man of letters, Edmund Wilson, who made full use of it in the revised edition of his best-seller, *The Dead Sea Scrolls 1947–1969*. But even sooner, Colin Cross, feeling embarrassed and guilty about his earlier fiasco following the symposium, published an interview with me on the Jewish historical interpretation of the Christmas story in the colour magazine of *The Observer* on 24 December 1967. It was the seed which six years later produced *Jesus the Jew*.

1968 also saw my first return to Hungary after an absence of twenty-two years. The experience was moving and perplexing, as everything seemed the same (except older and shabbier) yet at the same time altogether different. I longed to see my ageing relations, a few family friends and one or two of my childhood companions. My visit was officially arranged by the British Council, on whose behalf I was to deliver a lecture on the Scrolls in English at the British embassy. The family turned up in full strength, but so too did the whole of Budapest's intelligentsia. When I expressed my amazement at such a manifestation of freedom, I was told that no academic entered a Western embassy without first obtaining a special permit. I was lucky in that my performance coincided with a visit of our Prime Minister Harold Wilson to Moscow. Hence generally favourable treatment was given to those applying to attend a talk in a British institution. The organizers sprang a surprise on me and requested an improvised Hungarian summary at the end. I somehow managed, though the audience had to come to my rescue once or twice when the appropriate Hungarian word escaped me. Those who cannot believe that a mother tongue can be forgotten are very mistaken, as I discovered then and have done more than once since. I paid a second private visit to Budapest two years later in the summer of 1970. The depleted family was delighted. This was the last time that I stayed with my adorable great aunt Gizi who was so kind and loving when I was a child and a young man. She died in 1972, in her ninetieth year.

On the more cheerful side, Pam's elder daughter Tina, having first qualified as a nurse, finally listened to family advice, went to a crammer, gained the requisite number of A-levels, and entered the medical school of the University of London at St Bartholomew's Hospital. Staying with her father at Harvard, she met Peter, a young Jewish psychiatrist who came to London to complete his studies and be near Tina. They spent weekends and holidays with us and finally decided to marry, which they did in private in California before settling for some years in Cambridge, Mass. There Tina continued pharmacological research and gained a London PhD in 1973. She arrived for her viva with a six-month-old daughter.

Also in 1968, by one of those customary accidents, Pam and I found our dream home. One day in the spring of 1967, our weekly searches led us to a house on Boars Hill. We drove along a narrow lane bordered with tall hedges, took an instant dislike to the house which was advertised, and turned round ready to leave, when suddenly Pam ordered me to stop. There in the sunshine, surrounded with daffodils under an enormous larch tree, stood a most attractive cottage. 'Isn't this heavenly?', Pam asked. Indeed it was. So we allowed our eyes to gorge on the sight before driving on. Later that year Pam's mother came into some money, and offered to help us to get away from Littlemore. So we began in earnest to look for a property. Reading through the houses for sale section of the *Oxford Times* in January 1968, Pam let out a scream, 'Isn't this the house we admired on Boars Hill?' It was indeed. It cost £13,750, a very high price in those days, but cutting a long and very tiresome story short – mother-in-law's offer of financial help was one thing, the actual provision of cash was another – on 5 July 1968 we moved into West Wood Cottage and its substantial grounds, backed by the gigantic oaks of the 600 acres of ancient Bagley Wood. There was plenty of scope for Pam to practise her gardening skills, which she did in the company of Tom, a countryman the likes of whom are no longer born, the only helper Pam ever had whose knowledge of plants and flowers exceeded hers.[9]

We literally had to pay a price for our good fortune in acquiring this haven of peace, quietness and beauty. I suggested that my mother-in-law, who supplied half of the capital, should become part-owner. She liked the idea, as she always lived in rented flats in London. 'Don't worry, darling,' she told Pam. 'I'll leave you my share in West Wood Cottage.' She forgot to do so, although she loved adding codicils to her will, and the best part of her bequest to Pam had to be used to repurchase half of the house from the estate of Mrs E. S. Hobson deceased.

Pam's mother died on 21 September 1969. Less than three weeks later, on 9 October, my dear friend Paul Winter, too, was found dead in his room in Kilburn. We buried him six days later in the Liberal Jewish Synagogue's cemetery in London. A short letter which he wrote me six days before he fell victim to a heart attack had profound repercussions on my life. To appreciate this impact fully, I must first sketch the evolution of my thoughts and feelings towards Judaism during my first five Oxford years.

On arriving in the city of dreaming spires, I had wanted to be known not only as a student of Judaism, but also as a (non-observant) Jew. I also intended to do all that was within my powers to promote Jewish studies and be intellectually of assistance to all those interested in Judaism. The cool reception of my appointment by the *Jewish Chronicle* did not unduly disappoint me, especially as it was offset by a very friendly and courteous letter from the President of the Oxford University Jewish Society, 'most warmly' congratulating me and welcoming me 'to this ancient seat of learning'. Would I be the guest of the Society when I next visited Oxford so that we might 'get to know each other as soon as possible'. The signatory was a certain Nicholas de Lange, Christ Church. I met him a couple of weeks later in David Daube's room in All Souls and we began a friendship in the course of which I first taught him, then examined his doctoral thesis, and a little later was one of his referees when he successfully applied for the Cambridge lectureship in Rabbinics. As a result of Nicholas's cordial gesture, I soon established close links with the Jewish and the Israel Societies, and addressed them on a number of occasions.

No doubt the rumour spread that whatever I was, I was not a stranger or an enemy of the Jewish cause. After a short while, two of the chief representatives of Anglo-Jewry's public opinion, the chairman of the board of the *Jewish Chronicle*, David Kessler, and the then editor of the weekly, William Frankel, gently tried to involve me more and more in Jewish matters. In 1968 and 1969, I gained two further influential sponsors. On my first return to Hungary I met the great Judaica scholar Alexander Scheiber, director of the famous Jewish Theological Seminary of Budapest, and an instant close friendship developed which lasted for as long as he lived. He was in touch with the whole Jewish world, and I learned from various sources that he was regularly singing my praises in the right quarters. Then early in 1969, I made the acquaintance of Samuel Sandmel. He was provost of Hebrew Union College, Cincinnati, and was spending a year in London to help to set Leo Baeck College, the rabbinic seminary of British progressive Judaism, on academically and financially solid foundations. He invited me to a discussion in the course of which I suggested that both Leo Baeck and Hebrew studies at my Institute would gain if the College were transferred to Oxford. Sam was taken by the idea: fund-raising would flourish if its aim were to be to establish a Jewish theological seminary next to one of the great ancient universities. However, he did not reckon with the resistance of the students, many of whom preferred an academically less demanding curriculum, and of some of the existing teachers, who were also congregational rabbis in London and its suburbs. So our great project came to nothing, but the Sandmels (Sam and Frances) and the Vermeses became lifelong friends. In short, as a result of these personal contacts, I found myself more and more immersed in Jewish society and very much at home in it.

The occasion that led to my formal Jewish self-identification came in 1969. The *Journal of Jewish Studies* (or *JJS*), an academic quarterly owned and financed by the *Jewish Chronicle*, suddenly and tragically lost its editor when Professor Joseph Weiss of University College, London, took his own life at the beginning of September 1969. He was a brilliant scholar, an expert on Hasidism, and a kind and civilized person with whom Sam Sandmel and I had had a business lunch in a kosher restaurant in London a few months before the sad event occurred. His unforeseen demise left the already ailing periodical in a critical situation. That was when dear Paul Winter had appended to one of his regular short notes the question: 'Why don't YOU make a take-over bid for the *Journal of Jewish Studies*?' The letter was dated 3 October, and Paul died less than a week later, before I had the opportunity to comment. This was his last wish addressed to me.

If I had had time to answer him, I would probably have treated the suggestion as a joke. However, in the circumstances I felt that I had better do something about it and conveyed Paul's daydream to David Kessler, the chairman of Jewish Chronicle Publications, the owners of *JJS*. 'I don't imagine that the matter needs further discussion,' I wrote to David, 'but if I am mistaken, you know how to find me.' Back came a reply: Yes, he wanted to talk. We met, met again, and in practically no time I was put in charge of the *Journal*, the appointment to take effect from January 1971. Like my father before me, I too became an editor.

The row that followed David Kessler's decision belongs to the next chapter, but another sequel to it needs to be reported here. Though no one made this a condition of my appointment, I felt that I had to clarify my self-definition in regard to Judaism. I knew where I stood, but what about a public gesture? Of course, there was no question of a 'conversion'. I did not deliberately move from A to B, from Christianity to Judaism. By this time Christianity, with its fundamental tenets of the Trinity, the divinity of Jesus, etc., was already behind me. I did not leave it, but imperceptibly grew out of it. Nor was I inclined to embrace Judaism in its conventional form. Organized religion of any description with set rites and customs no longer suited me at all. My religion had become that of the 'still small voice' which those who listen can hear, as did the prophet Elijah (I Kings 19.12), the voice of an existential God, acting in and through people, who stood behind all the providential accidents of my life.

Those who expected something dramatic, a story of 'conversion', will no doubt be disappointed, but alas I cannot oblige, as there is nothing to report. What happened on 7 October 1970 was simply a 'regularization' of my position for the outside world. On that day, I became a member of the Liberal Jewish Synagogue of London. From then on it was easy to discover where my public persona belonged. It figured in the Who's Who section of the *Jewish Year Book* or on the register of the Union of the Progressive Synagogues of Great Britain.

15

The *Journal* and the New English Schürer

After joining the Liberal Synagogue, I progressively found myself more and more involved in Jewish activities. I addressed various London congregations, and in 1974 I was asked to deliver the Claude Goldsmid Montefiore Lecture. It was quite a big occasion, and the subject, 'Jesus the Jew', attracted a large audience. I sat on the editorial board of Liberal Judaism's now defunct periodical *Pointer*, and years later on that of *Jewish-Christian Relations*, financed by the World Jewish Congress, a board also regularly attended by the former chief rabbi, Lord Jakobovits. In addition, I was made a member of the Academic Committee of Leo Baeck College, the rabbinic seminary of progressive Judaism, when Professor J.B. Segal became its principal. I also regularly reviewed books on the literary page of the *Jewish Chronicle* and, it goes without saying, continued to support the Jewish and Israel Societies of Oxford University.

My 'Jewish credentials' were thus firmly established and recognized publicly to such a degree that in May 1974 I was invited to be the principal lecturer at the Jewish retreat of the US Army in Germany. The letter signed by the rabbi who was the senior chaplain specified that the meeting would take place in Berchtesgaden, which used to be Hitler's Alpine hideout.[1] When I enquired whether the choice of the place had some secret mystical significance, no one seemed to see the point, and I received the unexciting answer that the Jews, like all the other denominations, always convened there twice a year. I learned from the participants that the winter retreat was the one sought after because of Berchtesgaden's excellent ski-ing facilities. My lectures on ancient Jewish Bible interpretation were followed with interest, and that on Jesus the Jew with some excitement.

In Oxford, apart from lecturing and supervising an increasing number of graduates, I had to face up to three major publishing commitments. The first two were the editorship of the *Journal of Jewish Studies* and the continuation of the Schürer project, which entailed the rewriting of the Jewish history of the inter-testamental era (175 BC–AD 135). The third topic, the search for the historical Jesus, requires separate treatment.

However, in the final months of 1970 my attention was distracted from all these literary preoccupations by the exciting prospect of a trip to the United States. Neither Pam nor I had crossed the Atlantic until then, and an invitation to act for a semester as a visiting professor of Judaic Studies in the department of religion at Brown University, Providence, Rhode Island, with the then 'fabulous' semester salary of $7,000 plus expenses was attractive not only in itself, but also because it offered plenty of opportunity to be with Pam's daughter Tina and her husband Peter, who lived only an hour's drive away in Cambridge, Massachusetts.

The invitation to Brown came from Jacob Neusner, whom I briefly met in Jerusalem in 1961; he was taking a semester's leave and I was to replace him. In 1971 Jack was in his late thirties, controversial, talented, and author of a reasonable number of books. Today, twenty-five years later, his toll of books must be approaching 600. We became close friends and collaborators for the best part of fifteen years and I returned to Brown University on several occasions in the 1970s. Jack and his wife Suzanne stayed with us in Oxford a number of times and he once referred to West Wood Cottage as his 'second home'. Even following occasional clashes in more recent years on the academic battlefield, where his pugnacity is notorious, we always converse easily when we happen to meet, as though nothing had disturbed our former friendship.

The journey to Boston, our first long air trip, in a Boeing 707 began ominously, since only a few miles out of Heathrow we lost an engine and had to return to the airport. During the last stages of the descent, we watched fire engines and emergency vehicles racing towards the runway on which we were expected to land, which we did without mishap. I enjoyed the four months in the States, where Pam and I gained a good many friends, young and old. Several graduate students whom I had to teach at Brown have since made names for themselves, among them David Goodblatt, now at the University of California, San Diego; Bill Green, at the University of Rochester, New York; and Gary Porton, at the University of Illinois at Champaign. I visited them subsequently on different occasions and lectured or taught in their institutions in later years. I also learned the ropes of American academic customs. When I applied the Oxford yardstick in grading graduates, and considered a B a good mark, I was warned that unless I changed my Bs to As, my students would forfeit their scholarships. I hastened to re-grade them according to the rules of the place. When in Rome ...

Pam and I discovered other facets of the American way of life. We spent many weekends with my stepdaughter and her husband either in Cambridge or in their country house in the snowy wilds of Maine. Having a country hide-out seemed to be a must in their circles. When we returned from our first expedition, we were shocked to discover that someone had broken into our apartment in Providence. In addition to our freshly acquired television set, two passports and two return air tickets were missing. The intruder curiously left Pam's jewels untouched, but collected all our English small change. Contact with the American police was also quite an experience. First came the good news that someone had immediately found and handed in our passports; they were lying in the street. Surprisingly, one of them still contained two English banknotes worth considerably more than all the shillings and pennies taken away by the thief. Then along came a typical red-haired Irish cop who collected all our personal details and promptly released them to the local press. 'Guest professor's home burglarized' was the headline in next day's paper. A few minutes later a seven-foot tall sergeant turned up to investigate. 'You'd better ask the landlord to fix a new lock on your back door. I can open this with a matchstick,' he said with the superiority of an expert, and left, not without reassuring me that a detective would be in touch shortly. The phone call came two days later. 'I gather you've had some trouble. What's missing?' 'Our new television set,' I complained. 'Who wants to watch TV?,' he exclaimed and put down the receiver. That was the last I heard from him.

The stay in Providence, made warm and friendly by the kindness of Jack Neusner and family, did not consist only of teaching at Brown or guest lecturing at Harvard; at Columbia in New York; Duke in Durham, North Carolina; Hebrew Union College, Cincinnati; and the University of Louisiana in New Orleans.[2] Both Pam and I had other serious business to attend to.

She began to work in earnest on a book on Martin Buber, having failed to persuade British publishers to produce his collected writings in English to match the German *Werke*. She whole-heartedly threw herself into an examination and reconstruction of Buber's religious thought and was so taken by it that for her it became not just a hobby or a job, but literally a mission. Its first fruit was linked to my most pressing task, the preparation in an atmosphere of partial hostility in Britain and in Israel of my first issue of the *Journal of Jewish Studies*.

The news of my appointment to the editorship of the *Journal* and the simultaneous decision by its proprietor to dissolve the high-powered, but purely nominal, editorial advisory board created a great deal of bad feeling in certain quarters. To begin with, during the four years preceding his death in 1969, Joseph Weiss, though the sole editor actually appointed by the owner, had no longer been in sole charge of *JJS*, as he had been from 1959 until 1965. In 1966 he became part of a troika, with two other colleagues from the Hebrew Department of University College, London sharing the editorial functions. The survivors assumed that Weiss's departure did not affect their position and were determined to carry on as before. When they, and some of their influential friends – the great Gershom Scholem, the king of Jewish Studies at the Hebrew University and a member of the *Journal*'s disbanded advisory board, among them – realized that they were mistaken, quite naturally they were hurt and, to put it mildly, displeased. So the transfer of powers was not peaceful – in fact there was no communication between the outgoing editors and myself. An influential Jerusalem friend warned me that I'd better not count on any kind of collaboration from Israeli academics. According to the grapevine, Scholem would not tolerate any sympathetic gesture towards the usurper. I had a fight on my hands.

I planned to start modestly with a single slim issue, designated as Volume XXII, nos. 1–4: it numbered exactly 100 pages. (The most recent half-yearly issue, Autumn 1997, is more than twice as long.) This was in line with the previous five years' output, but I was determined to ensure that in future *JJS* would be a bi-annual *periodical*, appearing on time in the spring and in the autumn. This policy was successfully implemented, and the *Journal* soon acquired the reputation of running like clockwork. Jack Neusner supplied the leading article for this first issue on rabbinic traditions about the Pharisees, the subject of his forthcoming three-volume study, but what I needed most were contributors whose names would meet with general approval even among hostile observers. My angelic friend – may he rest in peace – Alexander (Sanyi) Scheiber of Budapest rushed to my rescue, and an article by Joseph Heinemann, the sympathetic reviewer some years earlier of *Scripture and Tradition*, secured the presence of a professor at the Hebrew University of Jerusalem, thus straightaway giving the lie to the forecast that no Israeli would dare to appear in the *Journal* as long as I was its editor. Another characteristic of this very first number of *JJS* revealed one of the basic policies of my stewardship: the privileged treatment of fresh talent. The table of contents lists an article by N. R. M. de Lange, who as an undergraduate welcomed me to Jewish Oxford. In 1971 he was a graduate student studying the relationship between the third-century Alexandrian church father Origen and the Jews. Nicholas was soon to be appointed to a lectureship in Cambridge. The same *JJS* number also includes two book reviews by P. S. Alexander, the first student to gain an Oxford DPhil. under my supervision and a dear friend ever since. The next issue carried his first article, and almost immediately he left Oxford for a lectureship in Manchester. As Professor of Post-Biblical Jewish Literature, he is there again, after a short intermediary stint as President of the Oxford

Centre for Hebrew and Jewish Studies. Finally, the fascicle ended with 'Martin Buber: A New Appraisal' by Pamela Vermes, a well-thought-out and beautifully-written first paper, auguring well for the future. Few suspected that the only 'higher education' she had had, apart from one year of a German language course at the University of Vienna, was fifteen years of life shared with me. Pam pressed on with her research and writing, and simultaneously became both a regular contributor to *JJS* with articles on Buber and book reviews, often witty and mordant, and also its (unofficial and unpaid) literary editor for five years before receiving the title and a nominal honorarium between 1976 and her death in 1993.

Planning, perseverance and hard work on the editorial side, devoted collaborators, and last but not least the proprietor's, David Kessler's, friendship and trust, coupled for a time with highly competent administrative assistance supplied by the publishers, helped the *Journal* to take off and double its circulation from 250 to 500.[3] There was a turbulent period just before the mid-1970s when the administration was handed over, not to me, as I requested – I was not a professional! – but to a small publishing firm in the Home Counties. This almost ruined our previous efforts and once again lost us half the subscribers. The person charged with administering the *Journal* never managed to send out renewal invoices or answer letters from readers who wanted to pay. Finally, on my insistence, I was put in charge of the whole operation, with both editorial and administrative activity centred in Oxford and with a small budget supplied by the *Jewish Chronicle*. I was fortunate in finding a most capable young woman assistant almost at once. Within six months our lost subscribers were all back in the fold, and we were in business once more. Indeed, during the next twenty years or more, the self-supporting *JJS* purred on smoothly and I never again had an anxious moment.[4]

In 1976, I persuaded Jewish Chronicle Publications, the owners of the *Journal*, to hand it over to the fledgling Oxford Centre for Postgraduate Hebrew Studies (as it was first called) and convinced my fellow governors on the Centre's board that it was in their interest to take on this established scholarly journal. The former proprietors were only too keen to hand over what they considered as an irredeemable loss-maker and the Centre's rulers were wise enough to give me the benefit of the doubt when I promised that I would make the publication financially viable. I kept my promise and turned the *Journal* into one of the few unsubsidized academic periodicals.

Mention of the transfer of the ownership of *JJS* to the Hebrew Centre gives me an opportunity to sketch my connection with this then newly born institution. The creation of a research establishment devoted to Hebrew studies in general and to Hebrew literature in the pre-modern and modern periods in particular was the dream of David Patterson, the Cowley Lecturer in Post-Biblical Hebrew at Oxford since 1956, a dream soon to come true far beyond his or anyone else's expectations.[5] The proposal was received with favour by the Board of the Oriental faculty, but needed the approval of the University's General Board. As it was intended to be associated with St Cross College, of which David Patterson was a fellow, two representatives of St Cross, of whom David was one, and representatives of the Oriental Board, the chairman and myself, had to appear before one of the top committees of the General Board. Our task was to convince them that the setting up of a Centre under the aegis, but outside the financial responsibility, of the University would be both worthwhile and feasible. We did our best, but left the meeting with the clear impression of utter failure. The same evening I met the chairman of the 'unfriendly' committee at a party. 'You gave us a hard time this morning,' I grumbled. 'Did you really get that impression?', he asked me, pretending to be perplexed. 'In that case, you'll be pleased to hear that we've given your plan our unanimous blessing.' In 1972, the Hebrew Centre was born, with two governors, David Patterson and Alan Jones, then Vice-Master of St Cross, named by the College, and three, myself being one, appointed by the University. We were to co-opt further governors not representing the University. They were to form the majority. We did so, and I, as the governor appointed by the the Oriental Studies Board, continued to take an active part in the affairs of the governing body of the Centre for the next twenty years. Apart from my role from 1991 as director of its Forum for Qumran Research, I think that the first of my two most significant contributions to the Centre was that in 1972, in my capacity of chairman of the Curators of the Oriental Institute, I arranged for a roof to be put above the head of the newborn establishment. Before it moved to Yarnton Manor, the office of the Centre had been housed in a room on the first floor of the Oriental Institute. It was occupied by an extremely capable eighteen-year-old, Stella, who was in full control and ran everything, including the Principal (as the Director was first called before he asked for his title to be changed to President).[6] My second and most significant long-term benefaction to the Centre consisted in arranging the transfer to it of *JJS* in 1976.

My efforts to relaunch the ailing *Journal of Jewish Studies* went hand in hand with the labour entailed in rejuvenating, re-editing and rewriting *The History of the Jewish People in the Age of Jesus Christ*. The revision of Schürer proved a bigger task than was ever imagined, and Fergus Millar and I soon discovered that we both were novices at this game. We had to find out how to pour half a century of discovery and research into the old skin of the the three volumes of the final German edition (published between 1901 and 1909), which also had to be cleansed of its nineteenth-century antisemitic overtones. Furthermore we had to hope and pray that Pam, the literary editor, would succeed in turning the rehashed mixture, often sounding double dutch, into a smooth and readable text. We were not greatly helped in our editorial work by the 'translators/revisers', most of whom did precious little revising. They were not instructed to leave enough blank on the pages to allow for corrections and additions, and some of the typescripts were not even double-spaced. When I suggested that the publishers might Xerox the text on A-3 size sheets and thus create room for our annotations, the answer came from Edinburgh that (a) their photo-copier had broken down and (b) this was in any case editorial business, for which the editors were expected to pay! Bearing in mind that we had already spent years on the project and had heeded Matthew Black's plea that the publishers should be helped by our acceptance of a royalty of 5% instead of the usual 10%, which was to be divided into three parts (Vermes and Millar 2% each and Black 1%), not surprisingly we refused. As a result, we sent very messy copy to T.& T.Clark and advised them to retype it. Our suggestion was ignored and the almost illegible sheets were sent to the printers. The proofs were a disaster. Not only were they full of errors due to misreading, but they also revealed that what we imagined to be our final version left much to be desired. So all three of us had to revise the entire volume on the proofs ourselves, to the outrage and stupefaction of the publishers creating an additional printer's bill of £3,000 (of 1972 vintage).[7] We managed to raise half this sum from three separate Oxford benefactions, leaving the other half for the Clarks to cope with. They did so without further complaint and also learned their lesson. We had their full financial co-operation in preparing the remaining volumes of the new English Schürer.

Before reaching the stage of the final proofs, Fergus and I had a major 'political' battle to face over the title page, which indicated the various responsibilities of the editors. Pam was not involved, as her title of literary editor was uncontroversial. Nor was the role of the two Oxford editors questionable. But how to describe Matthew Black who set the venture into motion, but did no actual editing himself? We came up with the unortho-dox formula of 'organizing editor', which though entirely correct, did not meet with his approval. He insisted on having the more impressive title of 'general editor'. Our conventional Edinburgh publishers, for whom a pro-fessor came next to God, were utterly dismayed when the disrespectful Oxford 'youngsters' issued an ultimatum: unless their design of the title page was accepted, they would go on strike, and if downing tools was not enough, they would resign. A meeting was called, and we flew to Scotland to confront our irate elders. We stuck to our guns and won the battle over Volume I, but conceded that if Matthew would share the burden of the following volumes, he would be entitled to appear as an editor as well as 'organizing editor'. Thus friendly relations were restored.

For Volume II, Matthew Black volunteered to take charge of the section on Messianism as he always wanted to handle the messianic evidence of the Scrolls in the form of an appendix, and also chose the chapter on the Essenes. The latter he soon bequeathed to me, since I had worked recently in the field, and when I was sent his draft of the messianic chapter for 'editing', I had politely to remind him that he had forgotten to deal with Qumran. Matthew took my comment with good humour and quickly supplied the missing appendix. By the time of the third volume, matters were clear. Martin Goodman, who did his Oxford doctorate on *State and Society in Roman Galilee* (1983) under the joint supervision of Fergus and myself, joined the editorial team proper. Indeed, his contribution to the chapters on Jewish literature in Greek is one of the best parts of the work.

All three of us did our apprenticeship in Jewish historiography through revising and rewriting the old Schürer, but so too did a number of our advanced graduate students, who first learned their skills in assisting Fergus and myself. In addition to Martin Goodman, who is by now a world authority on Jewish history in the Graeco-Roman age and my successor as Professor of Jewish Studies in Oxford, I must name Philip Alexander, Professor of Post-Biblical Jewish Literature in Manchester, equally expert in rabbinics and in the Dead Sea Scrolls, who contributed to all three volumes, and Tessa Rajak, now head of the Classics department at the University of Reading, whose preparatory work on the Josephus section of Volume I was a first step towards international fame. Since the publication of *Josephus: The Historian and His Society* (1983), she has been counted among the leading Josephus experts in Britain and in the world. Finally, Robert Hayward, now Reader in Theology at Durham, supplied the appendix on '*Sicarii* and Zealots' to Volume II.

I was often asked whether it would not have been better to write a new version of the history of the Jews in the Graeco-Roman age from scratch rather than attempt to rejuvenate the old Schürer which, excellent though it was in the first decade of the twentieth century, was out of date in every respect sixty years later. My unhesitating answer has always been, yes, it would have been better, but also, no, because it would never have been completed. What Fergus, Martin and I endeavoured to do was to cut out the old wood, factually update the work and achieve this as well as we could in the spirit of late twentieth-century scholarship. Judging from the reactions to our labours, on the whole we must have succeeded. In particular, we have injected into the work the entire contribution of archaeology and epigraphy since 1910, the year of Schürer's death; taken notice of all the major products of contemporary research on older topics as well as on subjects unknown to Schürer; and in particular incorporated into the body of the book the novelty of the Dead Sea Scrolls. Qumran figures prominently in the third volume in particular, which deals with Jewish literature in Hebrew and Aramaic, and the principle distinguishing among Qumran texts between writings produced by members of the Dead Sea sect and those which originated before its existence or outside it represented innovative thinking in the first half of the 1980s.

How much is new in the *new* English Schürer? The late Professor Menahem Stern of the Hebrew University, one of the leading experts in this field, who was murdered by an Arab extremist while out on his customary morning jogging in Jerusalem, one day gave his summary assessment of our opus in a single sentence: 'The large print is close to the old edition; the small print is mostly new but the small print is double the amount of the large print.' Another question I had to face again and again was this: 'Since you have done a well-nigh total recasting of the entire work, why is it still called Schürer? Your names should appear on top of the title page.' The answer was simple. Enough has remained of the old author for any removal of his name to seem unethical. Besides, this twenty years of slave labour was not for self-advancement: we intended to perform an act of public service.

Demanding though they were, these and other publishing undertakings (the account of the Jesus trilogy is left for the next chapter) did not occupy me fully. For a while I was also involved in a project similar in content to Schürer, if less technical, the famous Dutch venture *Compendia Rerum Iudaicarum ad Novum Testamentum* (A Compendium of Jewish Matters Relating to the New Testament). Samuel Sandmel enticed me to join in, and I attended a couple of meetings in Holland, but when Sam pulled out, I soon followed him, pleading a heavy workload; to this was tacitly added my lack of enthusiasm for denominationally orientated scholarship where a strict Jewish/Christian dichotomy and balance were to be observed in all matters. The *Compendia* were scheduled to include five sections, with several volumes in each. About half a dozen hefty tomes actually appeared between 1974 and 1996: some good, others less so. They all belong to the first two sections; hence the likelihood that the gigantic programme will one day be completed is by now somewhat remote.

An episode, academic in nature, but with heavy comic overtones, is linked to the launching in the spring of 1971 of the sixteen-volume *Encyclopaedia Judaica*, published in English in Israel under the general editorship of my Oxford predecessor, Cecil Roth. I was invited to London to attend the press conference called on publication day. At the party I was introduced to the sales director of the publishing house and, wearing my hat of editor of *JJS*, I timidly inquired whether review copies would be available. 'Oh no,' I was told. 'We have given away only three complimentary sets. One was sent to Queen Elizabeth, one to President Nixon, and the third to the Pope.' In that august company I surely stood no chance. So when a few days later the organizer of the press conference, the sister of the former Foreign Minister of Israel, Abba Eban, informed me on the telephone that the *Jerusalem Post* would appreciate a review of the *Encyclopaedia*, I told her that however much I would love to oblige, I was unable to accept the invitation. Why? Because no one had given me the volumes to review. She expressed surprise and promised that she would do something about it. Next, I received a letter from the publishers offering me the work at half price, in view of my willingness to review it. No, I replied, it is against my religion to pay for review copies, not even 50% of the cover price. A few days later, in the footsteps of the Queen, the President and the Pope, I proudly became the fourth person to own a complimentary set of the *Judaica*. I spent two weeks browsing over the sixteen volumes and produced my piece, which was deliberately shorter than the word limit given to me. I did not want them to cut my review. Of course they did, all the same. Furthermore they turned my English into 'Israeli English', and also purged the text of the word Palestine even where there was no possible political implication.[8] Finally the article appeared on 11 August 1972 under the headline, 'From the Very Excellent to the Poor', and I thought that the story was finished. However, to my pleasant surprise not only did I have the sixteen volumes gratis, but a few weeks later I also received £12 for my efforts. The cheque was issued by Hambros Bank in London on behalf of the Jerusalem Main Branch of the Union Bank of Israel, but I could hardly believe my eyes when I saw the name of the holder of the account: *The PALESTINE Post Ltd*, POB 81, Jerusalem. *Palestine Post* was the title of the *Jerusalem Post* back in the days of the British Mandate, prior to the creation of the State of Israel, and the administrators of the paper had never bothered to report the change of title to their bank!

Academic life in Oxford continued quietly to absorb me more and more. Close and precious friendships developed with the Millars, Fergus and Susanna, with Edward and Dina Ullendorff, and with Sebastian and Helen Brock. It was our good fortune that one day Edward Ullendorff decided that commuting to the London School of Oriental and African Studies from Oxford was preferable to commuting from Wimbledon.[9] He and Dina became our very dear friends, and Edward, the most erudite and precise of scholars, gave me constant support and provided me with his wise advice whenever I asked him. In the person of Alan Jones, now Professor of Classical Arabic at the Oriental Institute, I gained an experienced and trustworthy friend and counsellor. As for Sebastian Brock, I was instrumental in enticing him from Cambridge to take up the lectureship in Aramaic and Syriac in Oxford, causing a certain amount of annoyance to our Cambridge colleagues. I have always found Sebastian Brock a blessing and the most valuable asset to the Oriental Institute of Oxford. His extraordinary learning is exceeded only by his kindness and modesty. Among the many foreign visitors who were to become lifelong friends, I would like to single out Peter Schäfer, first of Cologne and later of the Free University of Berlin, a budding Judaica expert in the 1970s who grew into a world leader, and Emanuel Tov of the Hebrew University of Jerusalem, who was to rise to the chief editorship of the Dead Sea Scrolls.

I had also a devoted group of young friends, among them Philip Alexander and Tessa Rajak, whom I have often mentioned already; Bernard Jackson, a Daube pupil, and now one of the foremost specialists in Jewish law; and Michael Wadsworth, who first introduced me to Fergus and whom I helped, after his DPhil., to obtain a lectureship in the University of Sussex.[10] In the 1970s they were joined by the Canadian Larry Frizzell, who became professor at Seton Hall University in New Jersey; Robert Hayward, now Reader in Theology in Durham; and Martin Goodman, the easiest graduate student I have ever had. I always had to try hard to find something to criticize in the draft chapters of his dissertation. 'Hasn't so-and-so written something on this topic? You ought to look at his paper.' There were two standard replies. 'Yes, I know but he's not worth mentioning for such and such reason', or, 'Sorry, I've missed that.' He would return the following week. 'Thank you for drawing my attention to that.' After admitting that the paper was really important, Martin would point out something significant in it that I had not noticed before.

In the late 1970s, James Chukwume Okoye joined the company. James was a Nigerian priest, a member of a Catholic religious order and a delightful and loving Ibo, who returned home after his doctorate and set up a Catholic Theological Institute for the English-speaking countries of West Africa in Port Harcourt before being made Provincial Superior of his order. At his invitation I paid my first (and so far only) visit to Africa in 1984, soon after one of the many political coups. He took me to his home village in the bush. Seeing him in his childhood surroundings made me even more amazed at his achievement. His late father, whom he described as an unsuccessful little merchant, saw to it that his children received the best possible education. Three of them are university graduates: James's elder sister administers a large modern hospital, his younger brother is a university librarian at Nsukka, and James is an Oxford DPhil. I was happy to give him my backing when he applied (successfully) in 1995 for a professorship at the Catholic Theological Union at the University of Chicago.

For years, Pam and I regularly lunched at Wolfson College on Fridays, surrounded by this happy crowd of young faces. Their friendship and their advancement are a teacher's true reward. I cannot name all those who worked with me in later years, but they are held in equal affection.

Three Oxford events deserve to be singled out. The first was the official opening of Wolfson College on 12 November 1974. It was Oxford at its ceremonial best. The fellows of Wolfson, headed by the President, Sir Isaiah Berlin OM, were all present in the large new hall together with the students in their hundreds. Along came the 'Founder Fellow', Sir Isaac Wolfson Bt, and all the grandees of the University from the Vice Chancellor downwards. But above them all stood the frail but charismatic figure of the Chancellor, the former Prime Minister Harold Macmillan, performing at his best. One of the great orators of the century, he movingly contrasted the light-hearted *joie de vivre* of his Edwardian youth with the horror of the trenches of the Great War. The audience was made to laugh one moment, only to be almost reduced to tears the next. But Macmillan was also a great actor with infallible timing. 'This College was born out of the magnificent vision of Sir Isaiah Berlin and out of the limitless generosity of Sir I ... I ... I ... ,' and he went on seemingly trying to remember the name of the donor. Having stretched our nerves to the extreme, and just a fraction of a second before someone attempted to help him, he restarted fluently, 'and of the limitless generosity of Sir Isaac Wolfson'. Simultaneous sigh of relief and exhilaration followed.

The second memorable event is linked to my one and only active and positive participation in a public debate in Congregation, the dons' parliament.[11] If I recount the story in more detail, this is because it reveals how, despite the tortuous workings of Oxford and the scales weighted in favour of the powers that be, a small number of dedicated individuals ready to spend time and energy on their cause can change the course of events.

In the mid-1970s the Board of the Faculty of Theology decided to reshape its teaching programme from top to toe. The principal underlying aim was to remove the compulsory New Testament Greek from the syllabus, thus making optional the previously statutory obligation placed on all candidates to present themselves for examination in the four Gospels from the Greek text. Though a member of the Theology faculty, I was not involved in the preliminary discussions because I was on sabbatical leave for two terms in the 1974/5 academic year. So by the time I returned to my job in the late spring of 1975, matters had already reached what the proposers thought would be an easy run in the final straight, since the Theology Board, the General Board and Council had already placed their seal of approval on the new theology course. But they did not reckon with twelve mostly young theologians who, under the leadership of the Principal of Pusey House, the late Canon Cheslyn Jones, tabled a last-minute resolution requesting Congregation, the ultimate democratic authority, to instruct Council to annul its own decree concerning the establishment of a new Honours School of Theology. As a result of their opposition, the matter had to be debated in public before the members of Congregation.

As the holder of a senior academic post I was invited to give a hand to those who wished to keep New Testament Greek compulsory, and I gladly agreed to be the official seconder of the resolution. The meeting was convened for 3 June and was preceded by the usual skirmishes in the form of fly-sheets. The last appeals to voters were distributed by the more junior opponents of the decree, among them the present Oriel Professor of the Interpretation of Holy Scripture, a young lecturer in those days. All the voting members of the Faculty of Theology turned up, the majority of them favouring the proposed change, but along came also the rebel theologians, as well as a good many orientalists and classicists, and a medley of dons representing both arts and sciences, 135 in all.

The Principal of Pusey House proposed the resolution opposing the change, and did so eloquently on traditional grounds. Then it was my turn to rise, take the speaker's place and, a bit nervously, as it was my maiden speech, address the House. I carried under my arm a large volume bound in black cloth. People realized that it was not the Bible and wondered what it might be. As will soon appear, it was a volume of Karl Barth's *Church Dogmatics*, not my usual bedside reading, but a most apposite if unexpected weapon in my arsenal.[12]

After making a number of points I concluded:

'As they stand at present, the new decree and regulations open the door to a course of Theology-in-Translation, trimmed to suit a new type of candidate to whom not only the sources themselves, but also advanced scholarly literature on the sources will be barred. In this respect I am not thinking merely of learned biblical commentaries, but also of books such as Karl Barth's *Church Dogmatics*, the first of the new set texts in Paper 7. ... When I open this volume, what do I see? An enormous amount of small print – full of Greek and Latin ... without translation. Hence my dilemma: either candidates, excused from Greek and Latin in regard to the New Testament and the Church Fathers, will have to learn these languages in order to read Karl Barth; or the reading of the Barth text will be restricted, in the case of the classically illiterate, to the large print only: that is to say they will be dispensed from studying the evidence adduced by Barth to back his statements. Either alternative seems absurd ...

Furthermore, at the end, they will be totally unqualified for original research: for I am not prepared to concede that genuine and creative scholarship can be initiated on any topic ... without the full grasp of the prehistory of that topic.

On all these grounds I urge this House to revoke the decree ...'

The grandees of the Theology Board, among them the Regius Professor of Divinity, the Dean of Christ Church and the Warden of Keble, some of them visibly nervous, tried their best to defend the new decree, but one sensed that Congregation was against them. We won by 86 to 49. A few days later more than fifty members sympathetic to the losing side asked for a postal ballot of all those entitled to vote. The text of the debate appeared verbatim in the *Oxford University Gazette* on June 11 for the benefit of those who missed the real thing. This time 621 votes were recorded, but the Theology Board lost again, having mustered only 283 votes against our 338. I became very unpopular in certain quarters, but received many letters of congratulation from colleagues up and down the country, who were keen on maintaining standards and deeply worried by the prospect of Oxford letting them down.

My further positive and in a sense *avant-garde* contribution to a historically and philologically sound study of the New Testament followed with the successful introduction in 1977 of a two-year graduate course for the degree of Master of Philosophy (MPhil) in Jewish Studies in the Graeco-Roman Period, which was meant to cater for prospective New Testament specialists among others. In 1983 a one-year programme of Master of Studies (MSt) was also approved by the University.

The third significant event of my involvement with the official and public activity of Oxford happened when in 1978 I was elected chairman of the board of the Faculty of Oriental Studies. My two years in office were not particularly creative, as I had to spend most of my time trying to deal with a difficult colleague. In the end, he had to appear before the awesome-sounding Visitatorial Board, consisting of the Vice-Chancellor, the Proctors, the Assessor, various heads of colleges and other elected members, but characteristically he was merely admonished.

Still within the academic field, but beyond the confines of Oxford, I was instrumental in the creation of two new associations for the furtherance of Jewish studies, one national and one international. Attendance at a meeting of the Association for Jewish Studies (AJS) during one of my visits to the United States gave me the idea of setting up a similar organization in the UK. The British Association for Jewish Studies (BAJS) was born on 1 January 1975 with me as its first president. Responding to a need, the venture has proved successful and BAJS is still flourishing today.

The European Association for Jewish Studies (EAJS) was originally the brainchild of Jack Neusner, but the preparatory work and all the meetings took place in Oxford in 1981, ending with my nomination to the presidency, which I held for three years. The price I had to pay for this honour was the burden of organizing two international conferences in 1982 and 1984 at Hertford College, Oxford. Further conferences followed at three-yearly intervals and after some organizational difficulties EAJS is now firmly based, thanks to Martin Goodman's persuasive advocacy, on a permanent Oxford secretariat at the Hebrew Centre at Yarnton.

On the home front everything was happy and harmonious. Variety to our peaceful existence was provided by visits to Tina and her growing family of three daughters, the last two twins, and a regular yearly escapade to Ardnagashel on Bantry Bay in south-west Cork in Ireland, not far from the city of Bantry, where Pam and I and our dogs were treated as honorary citizens.

The mention of the dogs gives me an opportunity to sketch our 'menagerie' over the years. Darling Vicky, often mentioned in earlier chapters, died much lamented in 1968. We replaced her with the most lively border collie, Daisy, who was killed when one of my house- and dog-sitting graduate students allowed her to slip her lead on a busy road. In 1971 we picked up a young half-abandoned collie bitch, Irish Kelly, on the main road to Bantry, and acquired an English companion for her, the half-Alsatian, half-Collie big Lulu. Then in 1974, an elderly lady friend begged us to do something about her two tiny kittens whose mother had been run over by a car. I collected them; they were only three weeks old, too young to survive in normal circumstances. However, motherly Kelly decided to adopt them and, although not pregnant, manufactured milk and suckled them until they grew into healthy and lively creatures. The sight of a dog lying on the floor and feeding two cats was quite extraordinary. One day I showed them to Professor Alexander Scheiber, who could not believe his eyes and was convinced that the messianic age was dawning with, figuratively speaking, the lion and the lamb lying together. The nine-year old Kelly (sixty-three in human terms) conceived by mistake[13] and gave birth to Peg, the most spoiled of all our four-legged creatures, the darling of all those who knew her. She died aged fifteen and a half in 1995, always happy and full of years. Her place has since been taken by Poppy, the liveliest and most mischievous of black-and-white border collies I have ever seen.

To complete the picture, I must confess that I regularly feed the foxes which visit the garden nightly from neighbouring Bagley Wood. Friends dining with us were often entertained by what to them was the uncommon view of friendly foxes. One of the foxes became so tame that it took food very gently from my fingers. The latest beautiful but unwelcome intruders for the last five or six years have been various kinds of deer which keep on ravaging all the new shoots and flower buds in the garden. A recently erected fence around the whole property has finally put an end to this nuisance.

To conclude this chapter, I must report on Pam's work on Buber. Her book was steadily progressing and in 1979 it reached completion. Jack Neusner kindly offered to publish it in Brown Judaic Studies, and his offer was accepted when Macmillan, also willing to publish the volume, demanded a cut of 35,000 words to make it fit one of their series with a word limit of 80,000. *Buber on God and the Perfect Man* appeared in 1981[14] and was followed in 1988 by a smaller study, *Buber* (Pam used to refer to it as the 'little' Buber) in the series 'Jewish Thinkers', published by Peter Halban. This in turn was translated into French and Italian, and a German version is now in the making.

The last stages of the 'big' Buber coincided with the first signs of Pam's serious health problems. In December 1977, she went down with bad pneumonia and spent three weeks in the Churchill Hospital. She stopped smoking. She had been a fairly heavy cigarette smoker until she switched on medical advice (!) to a pipe. She recovered, but her lungs were gravely damaged.

Her days in hospital were not made easier by the circumstances which affected my professional future just at that time. In November 1977, I was approached by a very senior professor in Manchester asking me to allow my name to be put forward for the vacant Rylands chair of Biblical Criticism. I agreed, on the express understanding that I was not an *applicant* competing for the job. The matter went to sleep for a while, but in the meanwhile the usual channels were busy with the filling of the Regius Professorship of Hebrew in Oxford. The usual channels follow a rather contorted procedure. Oxford Regius Professors, unlike those in Cambridge, are appointed, not by the University, but directly by the Crown through the Prime Minister. The extensive search for the lucky incumbent is conducted by the Prime Minister's Patronage Secretary. The relevant faculty boards, Oriental Studies and Theology in the case of the Hebrew chair, are naturally consulted, and I knew that most of my Orientalist colleagues were backing me, but the front runner was the Oriel Professor of Exegesis of Holy Scripture, James Barr. Not surprisingly, the front runner won, which depressed Pam. As for going to Manchester, the idea did not make her happy either. She preferred Oxford, our company of friends ... and her garden.

Her ordeal did not last long. The first thing I heard from Manchester was a note from an assistant registrar informing me that I was one of the 'applicants' who were requested to present themselves for an interview. I told her that she was mistaken: that I had made clear from the beginning that I was not an applicant, and that attending an interview in the company of those short-listed would mean that I was competing for the chair. Would she report to her superiors that I was not; I had simply allowed my name to be put forward. This was obviously above the head of the young assistant registrar. At the next round, I graduated from her to the Vice-Chancellor, but he still insisted that I should be interviewed with the other candidates. I consulted a trusted friend, who a year or two earlier had been approached by the same university in connection with a different chair. He told me that he was invited by the previous Vice-Chancellor to lunch with him and a few of his colleagues and talk the matter over. So without hesitation I refused to attend a formal interview.

Pam was relieved and so was I. Another seven years were to elapse before the *big* temptation to leave Oxford came my way.

16

The Battle over the Scrolls: A Personal Account

The quarter of a century (1962–1987) that followed the publication of *The Dead Sea Scrolls in English* constituted the lean years in Qumran studies. In the 1960s the editorial enthusiasm characteristic of the previous decade was steadily dying down. From the late 1960s to the 1980s it was replaced by a general slumber, only occasionally interrupted by the publication of an odd volume of the official series *Discoveries in the Judaean Desert,* lavishly and unhurriedly produced by Oxford University Press. My interest – as I have already indicated – also wandered from the Scrolls and focussed first on ancient Jewish Bible interpretation, then on inter-testamental Jewish history, and finally on the historical Jesus. Nevertheless, I never completely turned my back on the Scrolls, even for a short time; as I once put it, I have always remained faithful to my first academic love.

The cheap paperback Penguin – a Pelican Book as it was then called – soon graduated to the elevated status of a luxury art publication. In 1966 it became one of the monthly issues of the Limited Editions Club, a book club with a maximum of 1,500 members and with a single printing of 1,500 copies on exquisite paper and in sumptuous binding. Even I could obtain only a single copy. The Israeli painter Shraga Weil, another ex-Hungarian, was commissioned to illustrate it. A slightly less elegant version was distributed to the 30,000 members of the Heritage Club. I was invited by the American publishers to a press party in London, attended by writers and artists who had contributed to the series. I felt completely lost in that company. An elderly man standing next to me introduced himself as Edward Ardizzone, but I had no idea that he was a very famous book illustrator. A white-haired lady, called Stella Gibbons, with typical British modesty, simply told me that in her younger days she had written a fairly successful novel which was also on the Limited Editions Club's list. She was of course referring to *Cold Comfort Farm*, which was the rage in the 1930s.

Even had I wanted to forget about the Scrolls, the demand for the

Penguin volume, which was reprinted almost yearly, would have obliged me to keep an eye on the Qumran field. Twice I used the opportunity to insert minor supplements, and by 1975 there was enough fresh material from Cave 4 texts to justify a second edition. But even then, the additions to the 255 pages of the 1962 edition amounted only to a mere twenty-six pages.

The log-jam created by the mass of fragments disgorged by Cave 4 in 1952 was further aggravated by the political consequences of the Israeli victory in the June 1967 war. Roland de Vaux, the editor-in-chief, and several members of his small team, were known to be pro-Arab and anti-Jewish, and most of them resented the *de facto* succession of the Israel Department of Antiquities to the corresponding Jordanian authority, even though the Israelis, mistakenly as it turned out, abstained from interfering with de Vaux's happy-go-lucky Scrolls administration. He in fact sulkingly withdrew to his tent, and as long as he lived matters relating to publishing the Scrolls remained stationary. I last met the French Dominican with the long, tobacco-stained beard in Oxford when he gave some lectures at Regent's Park College in 1970. Our brief encounter was courteous rather than friendly. The following year he died, aged sixty-eight, leaving the full report of his excavations of Qumran unwritten.

Roland de Vaux exercised a kind of patriarchal authority over all matters pertaining to the publication of the Scrolls. He was not subject to any higher supervisory body. So there were no provisions for his replacement, and the small self-governing editorial team had to find a successor. They chose the most senior member of the group, Father Pierre Benoit, another French Dominican priest attached to the École Biblique in Jerusalem. He was not a Hebraist but a New Testament scholar, whose only contribution to the publication of manuscripts came in *Discoveries in the Judaean Desert*, Volume II, in which he took charge of the second-century AD Greek and Latin texts discovered in the caves of Wadi Murabba'at, texts which had no connection with the Qumran finds. Matters were slightly complicated by the fact that the new appointment needed the approval of the Israeli archaeological authorities. The granting of this approval took some time, but rumours about it were circulating through the grapevine.

The impending accession of a new Scrolls supremo to de Vaux's empty throne gave me the first opportunity to intervene and try to influence the editorial process. I proposed to act, not through Benoit, who was unlikely to pay much attention to my urging, but through the only established body which I imagined had some muscle, Oxford University Press, the publishers of *Discoveries in the Judaean Desert* (*DJD*). In accordance with age-old tradition, this publishing colossus was headed, not by a businessman, but by a scholar, C. H. Roberts, probably the greatest Greek (and New Testament) papyrologist of the century. Some weeks previously, he and I had joined forces, arguing in the correspondence column of *The Times* against the far-fetched theory of a Spanish Jesuit, José O'Callaghan, who claimed that some minute Greek papyrus fragments found in Qumran Cave 7 represented New Testament passages. I contested the claim and Colin Roberts lent the authority of his papyrological expertise in support of my argument.

Considering him a natural ally, I wrote to him and sought his help to get the publishing activity of the Dead Sea Scrolls on the move again. OUP was, I erroneously thought, the only institution capable of wielding power over the tardy editors and – here I took a bit of a risk – I implied that it had a responsibility towards the scholarly world, which was anxiously and hungrily waiting for the thousands of manuscript fragments to enter the public domain. If Roberts felt sympathy towards these ideas, could we have a discussion?

We met on 15 May 1972 in the office of the Secretary to the Delegates, the old-fashioned title of the head of the Oxford publishing empire. (C. H. Roberts's present-day successor is known also as 'Chief Executive' and is a Master in Business Administration, MBA.) We were joined by the senior editor in charge of *DJD*. Straight away, Colin Roberts agreed that the Press had a duty towards the world of scholarship and would do its utmost to expedite the publication of the whole Qumran corpus. 'How best could this be achieved?', I was asked.

I tried to be sensible and down-to-earth. I suggested that the new editor-in-chief be asked to report on the present state of the work and, after consulting his collaborators, propose a firm time-table by which they all would be obliged to abide. Roberts and his colleague nodded their agreement and assured me that they would proceed accordingly. The Senior Editor intended to move quickly and to contact the procrastinating editors personally. His telephone call a few days later disclosed the degree of chaos and lack of co-ordination between de Vaux and OUP. Could I supply the Press, I was asked, with the names and addresses of the people involved in the editorial work, as no such list was available in the office? I did, and in my 'youthful' naiveté looked forward optimistically to seeing prompt results.

A short note from OUP reported in June 1972 on quick replies received from the English-speaking half of the editors, who were all full of optimism in forecasting early dates for the completion of their assignments. They all promised to send to Benoit their finished manuscripts between 1973 and 1976. Apparently the three scholars forming the French contingent never reacted. But in the light of the answers, which all referred to plans to be sanctioned by the editor-in-chief, the Press official realized with a shock that he had forgotten to put Benoit in the picture. 'It was perhaps rather off-hand of me,' he added. 'Would you perhaps be kind enough to give me his address if you know it?'

So OUP contacted Pierre Benoit, who on 11 August 1972 was formally appointed as chief editor by Abraham Biran, Director of the Israel Department of Antiquities. His colleagues accepted the change of *nominal* oversight, although Mgr Patrick Skehan of the Catholic University of America in Washington refused to use his own name in publications of the Israeli Shrine of the Book, so that it might not be tainted by some Israeli association, but consented to allow his work to appear anonymously! Benoit in turn informed OUP in August 1972 that he could deliver the typescript of volume VI of *DJD immediately*. In fact, for reasons to which I am not privy, the slim book, 93 pages of text compiled by J. T. Milik, did not see the light of day until five years later in 1977, being one of the *two* tomes to be produced under the fifteen years of Pierre Benoit's well-intentioned but inefficient stewardship. Needless to say, the other volumes in preparation by the three English-speaking editors, which were supposed to be ready between 1973 and 1976, all failed to materialize. Mgr Skehan's determination to prefer anonymity to a publication with his name under Israeli sponsorship was never put to the test: the work which he promised to send to the Press by 1 June 1975 was still unfinished when he died in 1980. It took another twelve years for it to appear in volume IX of *DJD* in 1992.

Without knowing what precisely lay ahead,[1] by 1976 I fully understood that without a major shake-up of the editorial process, my generation of scholars would be denied access to the totality of the manuscripts found in the Qumran caves. At the speed prevailing in those days, the completion of the project would stretch well into the second half of the twenty-first century. I also knew that the help from OUP would not be, to put it politely, as powerful as I expected. Not satisfied with the compromise negotiated by Benoit and the Israel Department of Antiquities, the Senior Editor at the Press reactivated the question of the Jordanian rights in publishing the Scrolls. He asked me to advise him on 'whether our nervousness about the Jordanian reaction is justified', and was visibly unhappy with my suggestion to let sleeping dogs lie. Thus, in my view, he gave the game away: Benoit and his team did not need to fear pressure from OUP. The only real hope seemed to lie in the mobilization of public opinion.

Already at the time of Benoit's succession, on 9 August 1972 one of the editorials of the *New York Times* urged him to expedite the publication of the texts to avoid *public outrage*. As a result, the editor-in-chief piously exhorted his troops to get on with their job and leave people no ground to complain about long delays. So when in 1976 I set out to compose my Margaret Harris Lectures in Religion to be delivered in April 1977 on the thirtieth anniversary of the first Scroll find at the University of Dundee in Scotland, I decided to end my opening address with a bang.

'On this thirtieth anniversary of their coming to light the world is entitled to ask the authorities responsible for the publication of the Qumran Scrolls ... what they intend to do about this lamentable state of affairs. For unless drastic measures are taken at once, the greatest and most valuable of all Hebrew and Aramaic manuscript discoveries is likely to become the academic scandal *par excellence* of the twentieth century.'[2] This outcry did not pass unnoticed, and during the war over the Scrolls from the mid-1980s onwards 'the academic scandal of the century', a sound-bite before the term was invented, regularly appeared as the opening quotation in newspapers and magazines on both sides of the Atlantic.

Not surprisingly, this warning made little impact on the dilatory editors, but there is evidence that Benoit, whose good intentions were matched only by his inefficiency, was kept aware of the growing dissatisfaction felt far and wide in the academic world. Reacting to a charge of 'doubts on scholarly integrity' levelled against the editorial team by John Allegro in a letter to *The Times* (17 April 1982), the editor-in-chief appended an apologia for his team to a book review written on 28 October 1982 (*Revue Biblique* 90, 1983, 99–100).

'However, beside malicious and dishonest criticisms, I perceive in the scholarly world, among decent people who do not suspect anything sinister, astonishment and regret provoked by the slowness of the publication of the large "definitive" volumes of *DJD*, a slowness by which I am the first to be upset. I wish to give a clear explanation and offer rays of hope.

... The political events which have shaken up the Near East have damaged the good continuation of *DJD*. After its nationalization by Jordan in the autumn of 1966, in 1967 the Rockefeller Museum came under the authority of another government (*sic*) ... When I undertook to relaunch the publication, I found full understanding with both the Jordanian and Israeli governments. The latter have entirely respected the editorial rights granted to the members of the team... These should therefore get on with the work. And they are doing. But less quickly than one would wish. [He explains the delay by the difficulty of the task and, with a snide allusion, by the lack of speed of OUP! Finally along comes the usual soft music.] ... One cannot promise miracles, but every effort will be deployed to advance the publication as fast as possible.'

Promises came. Promises were forgotten. No new *DJD* volumes appeared and years passed. In 1986 Abbé Jean Starcky, to whom most of the Aramaic texts from Qumran Cave 4 had been assigned, left the land of the living without having acquitted himself of his duties to scholarship. The ailing Benoit himself resigned and died the following year.[3]

In 1986, I was offered an unexpected opportunity to bring the scandal of the delays into the open. Dr (now Professor) Mark Geller, director of the Institute of Jewish Studies at University College, London, paid a visit to Oxford to consult Fergus Millar and me. He had received a relatively large grant to organize a conference or symposium and wondered what would be a good academic subject that would also attract the attention of the general public. We easily agreed that the fortieth anniversary of Qumran in 1987 would fulfil all the requirements. So I proposed to invite all the editors still owing us their manuscripts to attend a meeting in June 1987 and give a first-hand explanation of their plans. For me the date was particularly welcome, as in 1986–87 the final third volume of the 'Schürer' project containing the literary introductions to the Dead Sea Scrolls appeared in two parts, and in the autumn of that year the substantially enlarged third edition of *The Dead Sea Scrolls in English* was scheduled to be published by Penguin. The principal changes consisted in the replacement of the original introductory sections by chapters borrowed from *The Dead Sea Scrolls: Qumran in Perspective* (1977), which I suitably updated, and the addition of a number of new texts, including such large documents as the Temple Scroll, the Apocryphal Psalms and the Songs of the Sabbath Sacrifice.

Invitations to participate were duly issued to all the surviving editors, F. M. Cross, J. T. Milik and J. Strugnell, already editor-in-chief elect but not yet confirmed, as well as to the younger scholars more recently recruited to the team, among them Emile Puech, Elisha Qimron, Emanuel Tov and Eugene Ulrich. With the exception of Milik, who never replied, all declared their readiness to come. So also did Jonas Greenfield of the Hebrew University, who had inherited from Yadin (who died in 1984) the Semitic documents dating to the Bar Kokhba period in the early second century AD.

Academic interest was considerable, and the general public was also made aware of the event by a centre-page report in *The Times* a few days earlier (6 June). In this article, with the telling title, 'After 2000 years, a call for action', I am quoted as stating, 'Ten years ago I said that unless something drastic was done this would be the academic scandal of the century.

There has been no great progress since. We're not looking for scapegoats. What we want is to *get on with the job*.'

Unknown to the organizers at the time of choosing the date of the symposium, the opening meeting on Thursday, 11 June coincided with the 1987 general election in the United Kingdom. I remember arriving at my local polling station at 7 a.m. and rushing from Oxford to the Warburg Institute in London to deliver my 'Introductory Remarks'. They were meant to set the tone of the encounter, indicating that the time for pious platitudes was over and that the incoming chief editor and his crew were under observation. After a few welcoming words, I turned to the substance of the meeting.

'I feel I must screw up my courage and grasp the nettle of the delay in publishing the remainder of the Qumran material. My intention is not polemical, but constructive. Since the ultimate responsibility is always the captain's, that for the present unhappy situation lies with the late Père de Vaux and Père Benoit. But their deeds and failings belong to the past and are no longer our concern.

By contrast, the task that remains with us, the living, is to ensure that academic work in the field of the Dead Sea Scrolls and cognate areas is no longer hampered by further procrastination ...

We are all aware that a new régime is in sight regarding the publication of the Scrolls. A new prospective editor, Professor John Strugnell, is to inherit the mantle fallen from de Vaux's and Benoit's shoulders. ... Oxford University Press ... may (I hope, will) demonstrate an active interest in the future of this crucial project. Thirdly, it would seem that the Israeli archaeological authorities, the guardians of the Scrolls, are showing themselves less aloof than they used to be during the past twenty years, and appear more ready to be concerned with the fate of the unpublished fragments.

Is it not apposite therefore to ask whether the time has come for a rethinking and revision of the original editorial policy so that the publication of the remaining volumes can really be speeded up ... In the end I would opt for a genuinely radical instant solution ... I would print straight away the photographs of all the fragments as assembled by their editors, giving them full credit for their labours. That is to say, the plates would come first, followed as soon as possible by the introductions and the rest of the editorial material. If needed, I am certain funding could be obtained without much difficulty to support such an altruistic venture, enabling genuine progress in Qumran and related research. At the same time, the charge of weakness or procrastination on the part of the editor-in-chief would be lifted from his shoulders, and the other editors also would escape being accused of displaying a kind of proprietary attitude towards an immense cultural treasure whose trustees they are, but which in fact belongs to us all.'4

This clarion call seemed to please the audience, with the exception of those whom it addressed. There was no immediate come-back, and when later in the afternoon, at the end of the panel discussion, the same suggestion of publishing the photographs at once was advanced by a member of the audience and seconded by me, it met with 'violent' disagreement from John Strugnell. To an instantaneous 'Why?' coming from all corners of the auditorium (I still have the BBC recording to prove it), the forced routine justification of the *status quo* consisted in declaring that without a full commentary photographs of fragmentary texts were useless. Besides, in Strugnell's opinion, compared with the pace of the publication of the only similar corpus of fragments, viz. the Greek Oxyrhynchus papyri from Egypt, the edition of the Qumran texts had appeared rather speedily!

My plea, which echoed that of most scholars and of the general public, fell on deaf ears. We were placated by the promise of a new publishing schedule drawn up by Strugnell, the beginning of the implementation of which still had to await the confirmation of his appointment as chief editor by the Israel Department of Antiquities. However, on the whole I do not think that our London symposium was a flop. General awareness of the scandalous procrastinations increased, and by the late 1980s vociferous recriminations were heard from the United States, where opposition to the Strugnell regime and its Jerusalem backers, the Israeli archaeological authorities, was orchestrated by the Washington lawyer become amateur archaeologist and magazine editor, Hershel Shanks.

I was not prepared to lie down and acknowledge defeat, or at least to accept that victory had escaped us, when the London conference was declared closed. We learned from John Strugnell's own lips at the panel discussion that he still needed official Israeli approval and was seeking to raise funds to support the editorial activities. I knew (or imagined I did) how to proceed regarding the former; as for the latter, an opening with far-reaching consequences was provided by one of those by now familiar providential accidents.

The overall strategy I advocated was to attach stringent conditions to the approval of Strugnell as editor-in-chief which would prevent further dilatoriness in the publication of the Scrolls. I was advised by a wise and trusted friend that I should go to the top and approach the Israeli Minister of Education (I. Navon), who was ultimately responsible for the archaeological and museum authorities. On 18 June 1987, I despatched a letter to him with the request that he should not 'confirm John Strugnell's steward-ship over one of the greatest cultural treasures in the field of biblical and Jewish studies except on the binding condition that a facsimile edition of the unpublished fragments is issued by him at once, under the strict super-vision of the Israel Department of Antiquities'.

At first sight, my intervention sank without a trace. Neither the minister nor any of his officials so much as acknowledged it. But either the ministry or one of those highly placed persons in Israel who received copies of my letter allowed the news of my move to spread. Strugnell knew of it, and another senior editor strongly reproached me for my interference. So this attempt, too, seemed a fiasco, although I am told that it had its impact three years later when the Strugnell administration was brought to an end.

My association with the funding of the editorial work, and the connec-tion between this work and the Oxford Centre for Postgraduate Hebrew Studies (later Oxford Centre for Hebrew and Jewish Studies), came about in the most unpredictable manner and almost resembles a fairy story.

At the end of the London symposium on 12 June 1987, while I was walk-ing in the company of one of my graduate students in Gower Street, I was accosted by a lay participant of the conference whom I knew by sight. He was a London solicitor who had an important question to put to me. Being a leading trustee of a charitable foundation, he had been approached by John Strugnell for financial support. Should he consider the request favourably and, if the answer was positive, should he supply the funds through a British institution or through one in Israel?

I was not exactly used to being faced with questions of this importance in a busy London street but, obeying both instinct and reason, I advised my interlocutor to consider favourably the provision of a subsidy as long as very frequent and strict means of control could be devised and applied. As for the channelling of funds, I thought that it could be appropriately done in Britain by a British institution enjoying charitable status, and that in that case the Oxford Centre would be ideally suited for the job. The con-sequences of this chance encounter, out of which the so-called 'Qumran Project' of the Centre developed, made me occasionally happy, quite often exasperated, and generally busy for the next four years and more.

David Patterson, the Centre's President, warmly welcomed the idea. He saw it not only as a worthy academic connection, but also as a prestige operation and a potential fund-raising opportunity. However, as he was soon due to leave for a sabbatical year in the United States, the immediate practical handling of the matter was passed to Professor Alan Crown, of Sydney, who was imported from the antipodes to act as his trusted locum.

At the start, my dealings with the anonymous donor seemed highly promising. The first few exchanges between mid-June and mid-August 1987 ended in the donor's acceptance of my basic proposals, namely that a facsimile of all the unpublished texts should be issued not later than 1990, in advance of the full editions with commentary, and that a watch-dog committee of three or four Fellows of the British Academy should keep an eye on the progress of the work by Strugnell and his colleagues.

But from August 1987 onwards clouds started to appear on the horizon. To begin with, John Strugnell, in possession of the leaked news of my approach to the Israeli Minister of Education, complained to the donor that I was trying to stop his *de facto* appointment. I had no difficulty in showing to both parties that this was a distorted version of my plea for a *confirmation* under specified conditions. But the donor yielded to Strugnell's strongly expressed opposition to a separate facsimile edition and declared that he had no intention of interfering. Besides, Strugnell argued that since a supervisory committee had just been set up in Jerusalem, the trust did not need another in Britain. Cleverly he surmised, I imagine, that he would be able to handle Israeli academics more easily than his eventual British controllers.

So it was left to Alan Crown, in constant liaison with David Patterson, to try to chart a middle course. It was proposed that David and I should serve as advisers to the trust, and another *anonymous* committee, of which I would be a member, would do the assessing of the editors' performance. But in the meanwhile the donor came to the conclusion that Strugnell and I were incompatible. Therefore the oversight of the project and the annual assessment of the performance of the editor-in-chief were entrusted to David Patterson and Alan Crown, neither of whom claimed expert knowledge in Scrolls matters or had a full grasp of their 'political' implications. My protest went unheeded, but in due course I was vindicated by events.

The so-called 'Qumran Project' consisted of two potentially valuable constitutents. 1. The donor's trust was to channel through the Centre funds for subsidizing editorial work necessary for the preparation of the OUP series *Discoveries in the Judaean Desert*, and thereby expediting the publication of the Qumran texts. 2. With the consent of the Israeli authorities, a complete photographic archive of the Dead Sea Scrolls would be deposited at the Centre. I imagined that the presence of such an archive at Yarnton would provide us with a chance of gaining access to the hitherto forbidden treasure, the *unpublished* manuscripts. Alas, in the first instance at least, things did not work out that way.

Unknown to me until some months later, an agreement was signed on 23 August 1989 between David Patterson and Alan Crown, representing the

Oxford Centre, John Strugnell, chief editor, and General Amir Drori, Director of the Israel Department of Antiquities, whereby Yarnton would be granted a full set of Scrolls photographs on condition that those not yet edited would be kept strictly under lock and key. I protested in vain. I can still see the notice glaring at us from the 'Qumran Room' door in the library: 'Unpublished material may not be consulted without the written permission of Professor John Strugnell.' Several of my graduate students applied for such authorization, but as far as I know none was issued.

The news of the photographs coming to Yarnton was released to the press in 1990: 'Oxford fillip for Scrolls study' was the announcement of *The Times* on 3 May. Since the arrangement did not enhance access for scholars in a meaningful way, it was hardly a fillip!

The era of the Strugnell editorship, however, was fast coming to its predictable end. It was foreseeable to all except the blind or the blinkered. Journalists both in America and in Israel were after him. Under the title, 'The Dead Sea Scrolls: Will their editors perish before publishing?', in 1989 a columnist of *Scientific American* turned his fire on Strugnell's assertion that his editorial policy did not interfere with research by other specialists. Any 'competent' scholar, Strugnell claimed, could ask for and was granted access to unpublished material. 'What about Vermes?,' interjected the journalist. 'Geza is incompetent,' was the instant reply. Realizing that he had overstepped the mark, Strugnell tried to rescue himself, only to sink deeper into his self-made hole: 'He is competent in other things, but he doesn't have the necessary technical skills. I respect him for his other skills and if he came here, I would consider his request.' I was advised to sue him, but preferred to ignore the silly remark. Hostile articles appeared in issue after issue of *Biblical Archaeology Review* (*BAR*). Exasperated, John Strugnell referred to his critics on one occasion as 'a bunch of fleas who are in the business of annoying us'. *BAR* was delighted to name and print quotations from the 'fleas', starting with the customary 'academic scandal of the century' (Vol. XVI, March–April 1990, p. 24).

The pressure on Strugnell grew visibly too great; he was close to the brink. On the next occasion, interviewed by a Tel Aviv daily, he self-destructed, declaring Judaism to be a 'horrible religion' which should long since have disappeared. This was too much even for his friends and colleagues on the editorial team, who persuaded him to step down. In December 1990 the Israeli authorities politely relieved him from his duties on health grounds.

The dismissal of Strugnell resulted in a dramatic reorganization of the editorial team. The greatest innovation lay in the appointment of a Jew to head the group: Emanuel Tov, an academically highly capable and diplo-

matically gifted Israeli scholar. He had all the strategically right credentials
for being the Professor of Biblical Studies at the Hebrew University, with
a PhD. from Harvard under F. M. Cross and J. Strugnell, a hard worker
who had already a volume of *DJD* to his credit.[5] He inherited the American
and French survivors of the team, but was also subjected to a heavyweight
supervisory committee of senior Israeli scholars. The big unknown element
in the affair was the attitude of the Israel Antiquities Authority (IAA, as the
Department of Antiquities was renamed) to access to unpublished material.
Would the de Vaux – Benoit – Strugnell 'closed shop' continue? I discussed
this issue with Hershel Shanks, the editor of *BAR*, a few months earlier
when he visited me in Oxford, and our views and fears coincided. So
Shanks urged the archaeological masters of Jerusalem to 'end this scandal
and throw the doors open'.[6]

How did the change affect the situation at the Oxford Hebrew Centre?
Emanuel Tov's succession brought with it a ray of hope, but I was much
more doubtful about the IAA. Prior to the Strugnell storm, I asked David
Patterson, President of the Centre, to approach the director of the
Authority and obtain access for me to all the Scrolls photographs held at
Yarnton for teaching and seminar purposes. I had just been appointed by
the Governors of the Centre to the directorship of the Oxford Forum for
Qumran Research, an office which was to start a year later on my retirement
as Professor of Jewish Studies on 1 October 1991. On 13 November 1990,
David wrote to this effect to Amir Drori. In the midst of the Strugnell
upheaval back came Drori's faxed reply, dated 10 December 1990, which
tersely stated:

> 'Your request to grant Prof. Vermes permission to study unpublished
> Qumran material deposited in your photo collection contradicts our
> recent joint agreement which guarantees that such material is merely
> safeguarded at your institution. Please reaffirm our provision that this
> material is *strictly beyond the reach of scholars* save those who were
> allotted material personally by us.'

This blunt refusal clearly indicated that no wind of change, not even a
gentle breeze, could be expected from the leaders of the IAA stronghold in
Jerusalem. It is hard to believe, but they simply embraced the secrecy
policy of the discredited former regime. So I quickly put together a discussion paper suggesting that the changed circumstances provided a fresh
opening for renegotiation. Furthermore, unless something were done
quickly about the embargo, the academic reputation of the Centre was
bound to be seriously jeopardized.

After issuing this warning, I hastened to assist Emanuel Tov, who hoped to obtain the funding granted to Strugnell for his team. The transfer of the grant was agreed and – this must be clearly stated – did provide valuable support towards Tov's Dead Sea Scrolls Publication Project.

Emanuel came to visit me at home and expressed his hope that I might take on the editing of a major Qumran text. He was negotiating with J. T. Milik in Paris about redistributing the bulk of Milik's unfinished assignment among new collaborators. I expressed a preference for the remains of the ten Cave 4 manuscripts of the Community Rule, perhaps the most important of all sectarian documents, on which Milik had been sitting for the past thirty-eight years. Emanuel, a born diplomat, managed to extract an agreement from Milik. On Tov's recommendation the IAA, after the usual administrative to-ing and fro-ing, appointed me editor of the Community Rule fragments (4QS) on 23 June 1991.

The real emotion-filled moment came about a month earlier, on 14 May precisely, when another old friend, Professor Shemaryahu Talmon, a member of the Scrolls supervisory committee of the IAA, handed over to me a set of photographs of 4QS when he was passing through Oxford. At last, I was holding in my hands the texts for which I and the whole Scrolls confraternity had been anxiously waiting for so long.

Qumran photographs were reaching Yarnton in weekly batches and the Centre's Dead Sea Scrolls collection was approaching completion. Preparations were afoot for the much publicized opening of the Qumran Room on 1 July 1991. A week before it, another media event occurred. The director of the Shrine of the Book, Magen Broshi, another friend of many years' standing, invited me to announce the results of the radiocarbon dating of fourteen documents from the Judaean Desert, performed by the Institut für Mittelenergiephysik in Zurich. On the whole, nuclear physics confirmed the dates previously arrived at by palaeographical means. A feature article appeared in *The Times* on 24 June, the day of the press conference, which incidentally went off without a hitch, thanks to a thirty-minute tutorial on carbon 14 technique which I had the previous day from an expert at the University's Research Laboratory for Archaeology. Next day, another piece written by the archaeology correspondent of *The Times*, Norman Hammond, who will reappear in this story, announced: 'Science fixes date of Dead Sea Scrolls'. To add to the feverish chaos, various television crews converged on Yarnton in advance of D-day, and BBC 2's prestigious Newsnight team came along to film a high-profile current affairs item with Emanuel Tov and myself as the 'stars' – but as it turned out, with a sting in the tail.

The 'opening' ceremony[7] was attended by a distinguished audience.

Originally the only lecture of substance scheduled for the day was one by Emanuel Tov on Qumran 'Biblical Paraphrases', but since, despite the many other distractions, I had managed to write a paper on my recently received Scrolls assignment, I volunteered without delay to present some preliminary remarks on the Cave 4 fragments of the Community Rule. Such a prompt disclosure would show that a fresh spirit was blowing in the new editorial team. (The team was being considerably increased by Tov; from the original seven it rose to over sixty.) In the course of the lecture, the relevant manuscripts were shown by an overhead projector; every piece of information I possessed could be shared by any scholar who wished to know.[8]

The principal novelty I was able to reveal concerned the top level of leadership in the Qumran Community. According to the complete manuscript of the Rule from Cave 1, published in 1951, the overall government of the sect lay in the hands of the priests who were sons of Zadok, associated with the family of the Jewish high priests, whereas in two parallel Cave 4 texts dealing with the same topic the aristocratic Zadokite priests do not appear at all and their role is played by the more democratic 'congregation'. This significant difference was totally unknown up to that moment, which was all the more extraordinary since J.T. Milik, designated to edit these texts in 1953, failed to allude to it in his list of readings peculiar to the Cave 4 manuscripts of the Rule which he published in 1960. The presentation was warmly received and the audience was under the impression that a new era had started.

The broadcasting of BBC 2's Newsnight documentary on 4 July indicated that such optimism was unfounded. Neither Emanuel Tov nor I could guess what clever editing and the producer's preconceived story line would do to our filmed contributions. This story line was that although there had been some slight improvements, free access to the Scrolls was still some distance away. I was portrayed as well-meaning but imprisoned, prevented from doing what I wanted by the dark powers that be, symbolized by powerful boss Emanuel shown arriving in an enormous shiny black limousine. (The BBC offered to pick him up at London airport and he surely enjoyed the more than comfortable ride to Yarnton, fully ignorant of the use the producer would make of his emerging from the car and being greeted by me.) To sharpen the contrast further, Professor Norman Golb of Chicago, a vociferous critic of the policy of restriction, also appeared on the programme to state that visiting the Yarnton Qumran Room would be a waste of time for him as he would not be allowed to see what he needed.

To make things worse, a letter by Golb appeared in *The Times* on 10 July. He repeated his customary complaint that even after the recent changes, scholars (like himself) who did not assent to the official editors' views on the origin and nature of the Scrolls had not been invited to participate in the work. 'The Oxford Centre ... should clearly not have agreed to accept the photographs under such conditions.' I replied (16 July) that the texts allocated to me would form the subject of open seminars at the earliest opportunity, and that if in the meanwhile Professor Golb wished to consult them, he would be welcome to do so. Moreover I would continue to 'advocate and strive to bring about a *full* liberalization of access to all the Dead Sea Scrolls'.

This correspondence triggered totally unforeseen consequences both in Oxford and, unknown to me, 6,000 miles away in California. Both developments were part of what is usually referred to as the Scrolls revolution, the rumblings of which could be detected by perceptive ears in the late summer of 1991. It was through my constant contact with Hershel Shanks that I first learned that something was brewing across the Atlantic that might result in an imminent challenge to the monopoly introduced by de Vaux and maintained by the IAA. Towards the end of August, I knew exactly what was coming, namely that an attempt at breaking the embargo would be made.

I felt that the criticisms that arose after the opening of the Qumran Room, and in particular the BBC's charge that a 'closed shop' had been set up in Oxford, called for another warning. So I took Martin Goodman, my successor as University Reader in Jewish Studies, into my confidence and on 3 September 1991 we signed and despatched a memorandum to each Governor of the Centre. It contained an analysis of the current situation; a reminder that the imposition of a ban on bona fide scholars would breach Oxford custom;[9] and an outline of three possible courses of remedial action. These were a removal of restrictions 1. by negotiation with the IAA; 2. by a threat of returning the collection of photographs to Jerusalem in full publicity; or 3. through unilateral action. Of the three courses, experience showed that negotiation had only minimal chances of success, and a public threat to return the photographs would reflect badly on the wisdom of the Centre in accepting the collection in the first place. So by elimination, unilateral action in the defence of freedom of enquiry seemed to us the only *real* option, an action that would be acclaimed by the community of scholars, the general public and the world media.

These proposals, which promised to generate a heated debate, never actually came before a meeting of the Governors of the Centre. Regrettably, our initiative was overtaken by events.

The first rebellious act occurred on 4 September in Washington, DC. In typical American style, *The New York Times*'s headline announced on 5

September: 'Computer Hacker Bootlegs Version of Dead Sea Scrolls'. In plain language, the veteran Talmudic scholar Ben Zion Wacholder of Hebrew Union College, Cincinnati, helped by a doctoral student, Martin G. Abegg, who was handy with the computer, reconstructed several unpublished Cave 4 manuscripts from the privately issued Scrolls Concordance with the help of a computer.[10] The slim volume, 118 pages in all, entitled *A Preliminary Edition of the Unpublished Dead Sea Scrolls, Fascicle One*, was published by Hershel Shanks on behalf of the Biblical Archaeology Society. This created a head-on clash with the editorial team and its Israeli sponsors. For Scrolls officialdom, this was a pirated or 'bootleg' edition. Even the ex-editor-in-chief, John Strugnell, resurfaced and was quoted as saying, 'What else would you call it but stealing?' Threats of legal proceedings were muttered, but nothing materialized. We lived in suspense.

Just over a fortnight later came the real bombshell. In the evening of 20 September 1991, Norman Hammond, the archaeology correspondent of *The Times*, informed me of an imminent announcement by the Huntington Library of San Marino, California, that they would allow all qualified scholars to have free access to the Library's complete photographic collection of the Dead Sea Scrolls. Would I care to comment? I did and called the undreamed-of event 'absolutely grand'. This appeared next day (21 September) in a short article entitled, 'Dead Sea Scrolls embargo lifted'. It was a scoop for *The Times* over the US press. Next day, Sunday 22 September, the director of the Huntington Library, William A. Moffett, proclaimed to the world at a New York press conference the opening of the era of freedom in Qumran matters. The name-calling ('pirates', 'thieves', 'unethical action') restarted, and menacing noises could be heard from Jerusalem.[11]

How was the Huntington Library able to perform this coup? Its specialization in the study of the Renaissance, Shakespeare and English and American history did not *prima facie* qualify it to have a decisive role in the battle over Qumran. But here again we are dealing with a series of providential accidents.[12]

It all started with Mrs Elizabeth Hay Bechtel, a wealthy Californian philanthropist, who decided to create the Ancient Biblical Manuscript Center in Claremont, California. Accompanied by Robert Schlosser, the chief photographer of the Huntington, in a free-lance capacity, in 1980 she flew to Jerusalem, and obtained permission from the Israel Antiquities Department to take copies of all the Dead Sea Scrolls. On her return to California, she soon fell out with the Claremont Center and was removed from its board. Mrs Bechtel handed over one set of Qumran photographs to Claremont, but in 1982 she deposited the other set in the Huntington

Library and supplied funds for the building of an air-conditioned vault. In April 1982, an agreement was signed between Mrs Bechtel and the Huntington, specifying (clause 6) that only material for which Mrs Bechtel asserted the legal ownership of property rights would be deposited in the Library. In clause 9 it is stated that unless specific exceptions are made by Mrs Bechtel, all materials 'will be made available to use by scholars in accordance with the Huntington's general policies for its own materials'. I was formally assured that no such exception was ever made by Mrs Bechtel while the deposit was on loan, or when she donated the collection to the Library in 1986. Elizabeth Hay Bechtel died on 21 April 1987, four years before the Huntington photographs hit the limelight.

In 1990, the newly appointed director of the Library, William A. Moffett, was looking for space for an additional librarian's desk, and in doing so 'discovered' the Bechtel vault. Meanwhile the Qumran affair was hotting up. In June–July 1991 Moffett, whose name was unknown to me at the time, but who was soon to become a close friend, read the two articles in the London *Times* reporting on the Oxford Centre's Scrolls projects and the letters to the Editor by Norman Golb and myself. In an 'Internal Briefing' to the staff of the Library, dated 16 September 1991, William Moffett declared that his thinking had been influenced, among other things, by my interview with *The Times* on 24 June 1991. According to the Briefing, 'the Oxford Centre for Postgraduate Hebrew Studies would open an extensive collection of scroll photographs ... Although it could not be confirmed ... that Vermes's collection of photographs was as extensive as the Huntington's archive, there was reason for us to believe that the Oxford materials had in fact been duplicated from the set made by Bob Schlosser for Mrs Bechtel and given to the [Claremont] Ancient Biblical Manuscript Center.' Of course, this was pure imagination on the part of Moffett, since the Oxford Centre's archive came from the IAA, but if it helped with the decision-making, so much the better. Another stimulus towards action came from a letter, dated 23 July 1991, which was sent to the Huntington by one of the American official editors, requesting the Library to give up its Qumran photographs 'so that no copies of them be retained in your care'. In the light of the new circumstances Moffett advanced the date of the Huntington announcement to 22 September from the originally planned 16 October, when it would have been coupled with a NOVA television special on the Dead Sea Scrolls.

To return to the row provoked by Moffett's declaration. Soon after the first bellicose utterances, reported in the American press on 23 September, and no doubt in the light of legal advice, the Jerusalem establishment abruptly and unexpectedly changed its tune. I will never forget my excitement on receiving a fax from the IAA on 25 September, three days after the Huntington's declaration, stating that 'The Israel Antiquities Authority agrees in principle to facilitate free access to the photographs of the Scrolls'. This was a tacit acknowledgement of defeat. However, a final face-saving attempt followed. 'While all parties involved are in favour of free access to the photographs it is also felt that the work of scholars who in recent years have taken upon themselves to publish texts should not be harmed.' So a meeting was called in Jerusalem on 4 December 1991 to be attended by representatives of the institutions holding photograph collections and of the IAA, and members of the previous editorial team. By putting ten weeks between the issuing of the summons and the actual meeting, time would be gained, the dust would settle, and wounds could be licked in Israel.

Victory was in sight. In a fax to Bill Moffett I remarked that without his attendance the Jerusalem meeting would be a meaningless talking shop, and from his reply on 16 October it was clear that he did not intend to take part in the December conference: 'Unless there is an unequivocal surrender there is little point in going to Jerusalem (however much – as I've already said – I'd like to shake your hand at the Shrine of the Book).'

In Jerusalem resistance faded. Doubtless, on account of the bad international publicity heaped on the State by the charge of impeding free research, the IAA was summoned before the education committee of the Israeli Knesset in late October. They were told to cancel the embargo. On 27 October all the restrictions were lifted. On 29 October *The Times* reported: 'Israel opens access to the Dead Sea Scrolls'. The revolution triumphed, and opening of the photographic archive of the Qumran Room at Yarnton to all interested researchers quite naturally followed. My long-cherished dream came true.

During the remaining months of 1991 the press in Britain took a keen interest in the developments, and I was commissioned to write on the happy outcome of the war over the Scrolls for the *Times Higher Education Supplement* (9 November 1991), the *Church Times* (29 November), the *TLS* (20 December), and the *Jewish Chronicle* (10 January 1992). *The Times* itself published a piece of mine on its middle page under the title, 'Secrets of the Scrolls' on 27 December 1991 (printing a large Scroll photograph upside down).

The change that affected the circumstances of Qumran research was swift and beneficial. In November 1991 the Biblical Archaeology Society of Washington published a more or less complete set of photographs of the Scrolls, which anyone could purchase at the reasonable price of $195. By 1992, Emanuel Tov brought out a microfiche edition with the Dutch publishing house E. J. Brill. It carried the blessing of the IAA. And in the spring of 1997 a CD-ROM version of all the digitalized manuscript images, scanned at Yarnton, was issued on three compact discs by Oxford University Press and Brill in collaboration.[13]

The rate of publication of the official series, *Discoveries in the Judaean Desert*, has accelerated beyond all expectation. The output of the Cave 4 material between 1992 and 1996 under the Tov editorship already more than doubled the sum total of the previous thirty-nine years, and some seven new volumes were expected by the end of 1997. Qumran studies have never been healthier. The subsidies mediated by the Centre are being put to good use, and the completion of the *magnum opus* is truly in sight (in 2002).

How these changes have affected research can be illustrated by my own experience. Early in November 1991, two American scholars, Robert H. Eisenman of California State University at Long Beach and Michael O. Wise, then of Chicago University, announced to the press that a Cave 4 fragment speaks of a 'pierced' and executed leader of the congregation, possibly a slain messiah. As the full text was not issued by them and the press release contained no identification of the document, checking of the statement would have been impossible in former days. Could it be achieved now? The only factual information to start the search was that the text mentioned the 'prophet Isaiah'. So I turned to my (illegally acquired) copy of John Strugnell's Scrolls Concordance and looked for the two words in question. In fact I did the 'manual' version of the computer reconstruction pioneered on the basis of the same concordance by B.Z. Wacholder and M. G. Abegg. I soon tumbled on a text code-named 4Q285 with the corresponding Palestine Archaeological Museum photograph numbers. The rest was easy. In the Yarnton collection I found the relevant photographs. Study of them at once disclosed that the text conveyed the classic messianic doctrine, namely a triumphant, victorious 'Shoot of David', and not a suffering Messiah championed by Eisenman and Wise. On 20 December 1991 I called a special seminar of the Forum for Qumran Research, which had already spent a full term examining unpublished Scrolls, to discuss the (non-)'pierced' but rather 'piercing' Messiah document. It was attended by specialists from the Universities of Oxford, Cambridge, London and Reading as well as by a correspondent of *The Independent*, which published the story on the front page and an inside page on 27 December. The scholarly presentation followed in the Spring 1992 issue of *JJS*.[14] According to the standards prevailing before the 'liberation', my publishing of a document assigned to someone else would have been castigated as piracy or at least poaching. In fact, when I sent an advance off-print of the study to Professor J.J. Collins of Chicago, the designated editor of 4Q285, his instant and generous reaction was to offer the document to me for publication, as I had already done the homework.[15]

Those were the heady days of freshly discovered freedom of enquiry. Today, five and a half years after the war over the Scrolls, it is hard to understand the extreme foolishness of the previous four decades. I fought a good fight for a quarter of a century, and it was worth it!

Let me also add that the fact that we waged war on opposite sides of the barricades did not harm my relationship with friends on the official editorial team. Indeed, my most highly prized reward came when the Library of Congress invited me to give the keynote speech on 21 April 1993 at a symposium introducing the Scrolls exhibition organized in Washington by the Israel Antiquities Authority.

Access to the whole Qumran collection landed me with a great deal of work, the first tangible result of which was the publication in January 1995 of a 450-page fourth edition of *The Dead Sea Scrolls in English*, enlarged by 114 pages compared to the third edition. The *DJD* volume (Vol. XXVI) containing the Cave 4 manuscripts of the Community Rule prepared with Philip Alexander is practically ready. My latest contribution, *The Complete Dead Sea Scrolls in English*, a new hardcover edition of 668 pages, published in May 1997, marked the fiftieth anniversary year of Qumran. An extract from its preface provides an apt conclusion to this account of my life-long involvement with the Dead Sea Scrolls:

'Has the greatly increased source material substantially altered our perception of the writings found at Qumran? I do not think so. Nuances and emphases have changed, but additional information has mainly helped to fill in gaps and clarify obscurities; it has not undermined our earlier conceptions regarding the Community and its ideas. We had the exceptionally good fortune that all but one of the major non-biblical Scrolls were published at the start, between 1950 and 1956: the Habakkuk Commentary (1950), the Community Rule (1951), the War Scroll and the Thanksgiving Hymns (1954/5) and the best preserved columns of the Genesis Apocryphon (1956). Even the Temple Scroll, which had remained concealed until 1967 in a Bata shoe box by an antique dealer, was edited ten years later. The large Scrolls have served as foundation and pillars, and the thousands of fragments as building stones, with which the unique shrine of Jewish religion and culture that is Qumran is progressively restored to its ancient splendour.'

I am infinitely grateful for the part I have been privileged to play in conveying this splendour to the interested world.

FAREWELL TO BILL MOFFETT

Some friendships develop slowly; mine with Bill Moffett, my comrade-in-arms, was instantaneous. We just clicked. I especially valued his mordant wit, no doubt inherited from his Scottish ancestors.

A meeting of the Society of Biblical Literature at Kansas City on 25 November 1991 marked the official end of Scrolls hostilities. Bill, new to that club, attended the session which was to pledge, according to the grandiloquent jargon of the place, 'harmony and co-operation'. In a fax dated 3 December 1991 he called it a 'love-in'. The 'ebullience' of the meeting made him mischievous. His message to me reads: 'When it came time for me to speak I could not resist informing the gathering that as it was now clear everything worked out to the apparent satisfaction of all parties I could announce [tongue in the cheek, GV] that the Huntington's role had all along been an utter and complete hoax; that we never had any photographs at all and people should please stop pestering us for microfilm and take their requests to Claremont and Oxford. I confess I could not bring myself to see how [leading members of the official editorial team] took the joke, but the assembly loved it. As I say, I wish you could have been there.'

The funniest and most appreciated of Bill's light-hearted messages came out of the blue on 17 December 1992, occasioned by my review of Robert Eisenman's book, *The Dead Sea Scrolls Uncovered*, on 4 December in *The Times Literary Supplement*.

'To your earlier titles and honorifics, Emeritus professor, et al., it is apparent to me that you deserve to be styled Defender of the Faith, Lord of the Scrolls, and Teacher of Righteousness. At the very least, Defender of the Huntington! On what started out as a very ordinary day last week, the discovery of your demolition of the hapless Eisenman in *TLS* stirred some considerable admiration in these parts, and your persistent effort to establish a "correct" historical record of what happened last year provoked a hearty chuckle.' He then concluded, parodying Macbeth, 'Lay on, MacVermes!'

Next year we had a chance to meet. On 16 March 1992, Bill and his wife Debbie, on a tour of English stately homes with a group of supporters of the Huntington, succeeded in escaping for a few hours to pay a brief visit to the Vermeses on Boars Hill. We finally achieved the handshake which had been planned to take place at the Shrine of the Book in Jerusalem. The encounter was warm and delightful and we hoped that many more would follow. It was not to be. In 1993, I thought that Bill might come to the Scrolls exhibition at the Library of Congress, but I gathered that he had some health problems. By 1994, this turned out to be terminal cancer. I screwed up enough courage to write to Bill openly. Typical of the man, a fairly sanguine answer came: he hoped to be still around in the new millennium.

In December of that year I informed him of my forthcoming three-month stay at the University of California in San Diego and my plan to come to the Huntington and visit him. The letter was not answered and my San Diego friends were unable to contact him. Then in early March they faxed me his obituary notice from the local newspaper. William Andrew Moffett died on 20 February 1995 aged sixty-two years.

A few days later I received a message, as it were from beyond the grave. It was dictated by Bill to his wife on his death bed.

'I had so many things that I had to do, and I was so far behind in doing them, it seemed unthinkable that I should die this season. Unfortunately, it doesn't work out that way, and the old procrastinator finds himself out of energy and out of time. Even so, I did not want to go without saying goodbye. Thanks for your friendship.' He then appended with his own hand: 'Sorry I can't welcome you to Calif. as I had hoped. Bill.'

As the principal speaker at the Huntington Library's Chaucerian Feast on 19 November 1995, I was delighted to avail of this unique opportunity to pay William Moffett my heartfelt ultimate homage:

'Last year I learned about Bill's illness, and as one who had experienced bereavement, I felt it to be my duty to write to him a loving and honest letter. I assured him that his name, and what he did in 1991, would be recorded for ever and with golden letters in the annals of man's great fight for freedom of thought, inquiry and action.'

17

Jesus the Jew and his Religion

Had I been told in the 1950s that one day I would be known as an expert on Jesus, I would have been greatly surprised. Before specializing in the Scrolls and in post-biblical Judaism, I considered myself a student of the Hebrew Bible. The New Testament lay outside my sphere of interest. As an undergraduate in Louvain, I showed no liking for it. This lack of enthusiasm may be attributed to the local circumstances. At the Jesuit College, the Gospels were taught in the first year of the four-year theology course which in view of my previous studies I was allowed to skip. Even had I attended the relevant classes, the dry and technical discussion of the Synoptic problem – the literary relationship of Mark, Matthew and Luke – would no doubt have bored me to tears. Nor were the two years spent on St Paul in any way exciting. The lectures were aimed at expounding theological doctrine in the Letters to the Romans and the Corinthians rather than reconstructing the real world of Paul.

How then did I get involved with the New Testament? As a scholar, I first fleetingly encountered the Gospels when I began to focus on Bible interpretation at Qumran. As early as December 1951, I published a short essay in the *Cahiers Sioniens* (pp. 337–49), 'Le Commentaire d'Habacuc et le Nouveau Testament', investigating structural parallels between Qumran scriptural exegesis and the New Testament. A few similar efforts followed, but even in *Scripture and Tradition in Judaism* (1961), the New Testament section consisted only of the two final chapters.

My proper contact with the Gospels came in the mid-1960s when I switched to research in Jewish history in connection with the Schürer project. In an article published in the *Daily Telegraph* on 9 April 1966, on 'Neglected Facts in the Dead Sea Scrolls', I mentioned for the first time in the context of miraculous healing in the Gospels the example of the little known first-century AD Galilean charismatic, Hanina ben Dosa, who has since become, I suppose largely due to my studies, a household name among New Testament scholars. This was the first hint that was to lead to *Jesus the Jew*.

The idea of a book on the historical Jesus – and how revolutionary this idea was thirty years ago! – had a double beginning. In broad terms, it came as an offshoot of the Schürer project; that is to say, I intended to re-examine the Gospels as part of first-century AD Palestinian Jewish history and culture. I meant to portray Jesus against his genuine historical background, and not in the alien framework of Graeco-Roman culture *and* nineteen centuries of Christian elaboration. The second, more immediate, reason for launching into this search originated in an interview which I gave to the journalist and writer Colin Cross on the story of the birth of Jesus. It appeared in the *Observer Magazine* on 24 December 1967 under the title 'White Christmas, Black Christmas', anticipating the ideas which I later developed in *Jesus the Jew* on the Nativity story, the Gospel genealogies of Jesus, and the ancient Jewish understanding of the concept of virginity.

The article must have made some impact, for during my first return visit to Hungary in January 1968, a telephone call came from a London literary agent with the promise of a contract and a substantial advance (£500, a large sum in those days) for a book on Jesus along the lines of the *Observer* article. The agent kept his word, and I signed an agreement with a London publishing house, W. H. Allen, better known for its biographies and autobiographies of stage personalities than for historical and religious scholarship. I was then too inexperienced and naive to realize the mismatch.

As the manuscript was to be delivered within three years, I set out to work without delay. It was groping in the dark, but by the time I left for Brown University in Providence, Rhode Island, in January 1971, some chapters of the planned volume existed in written form. I gave several public lectures on the subject at various American universities, and as the echoes were encouraging I felt I was on the right wavelength. But when after my return to Britain I despatched about half of the book in first draft to the publishers, without hesitation they terminated the agreement. Mine was not a book they could sell. In despair, I consulted Colin Cross who, helpful as always, introduced me to his agents, A. D. Peters, to whom on 5 February 1972 my complete typescript was handed over. The final settlement with W. H. Allen (including the return of the advance payment) took a little while, but by the late spring the book was accepted by William Collins, a leading publishing house. I remember my first visit to Lady Collins, who was in charge of their religious publications. The centre of her office, an unused fireplace, was occupied by a dog basket, the throne of a much-loved poodle, who attended all the business discussions. Lady Collins let me know that when her principal adviser, Canon (later Provost) David Edwards was asked to choose the manuscripts he wanted to read, she heard a 'Ho, ho. What's this?' and away went what then was called *Jesus and*

Christianity. It was returned the next week with the reader's full endorsement. The only query was about the title, which they considered flat. 'Could it be re-titled 'Jesus and his Jewish background', I was asked. In that case, why not call it *Jesus the Jew*, I replied. That would be much stronger. Lady Collins enthusiastically agreed.

The book appeared on 20 August 1973, almost simultaneously with Volume I of the new English Schürer. The two together made something of a splash. The following year, a separate American edition followed under the imprint of Macmillan, New York.

Like most significant episodes of my life, *Jesus the Jew* was the product of a providential accident. Since it is generally believed that books on Jesus owe their existence more to the religious experiences of their authors than to problems surrounding the subject, it was automatically assumed by many that the same rule applied to me, too, especially in the light of my (presumed) spiritual wanderings. However, in my conscious knowledge, the purpose of writing the book had nothing to do with theological pre-occupations or with self-justification, a kind of *Apologia pro vita sua*, but was the unplanned outcome of the preliminary research which produced the first part of the revised *History of the Jewish People in the Age of Jesus Christ* (the new Schürer), coupled with an historian's desire at last to put the record straight. The present investigation, as I wrote in *Jesus the Jew* (p. 17), 'is prompted by a single-minded search for fact and reality and undertaken out of feeling for the tragedy of Jesus of Nazareth. If, after working his way through the book, the reader recognizes that this man, so distorted by Christian and Jewish myth alike, was *in fact* neither the Christ of the Church, nor the apostate and bogey-man of Jewish popular tradition, some small beginning may have been made in the repayment to him of a debt long overdue.'

The main problem facing a sympathetic, yet religiously detached, historian who confronts the New Testament results from the fact that the pocket book which contains the specifically Christian Scriptures offers two substantially different pictures of Jesus. All their subsequent theological colouring about Messianism and redemption notwithstanding, the Gospels of Mark, Matthew and Luke, the Synoptic Gospels, still allow a genuine glimpse of a first-century AD Jewish holy man, portrayed as a preacher, healer and exorcist, delivering special moral exhortations concerning the impending arrival of the 'Kingdom of God'. By contrast the Fourth Gospel, that of John, and the letters of Paul sketch an increasingly other-worldly saviour figure, the paramount centre of all the religious specula-tions of the primitive church. When one sketch is superimposed on the other, it becomes clear that they have hardly anything in common.

The purpose of *Jesus the Jew* was to rebuild the picture of the historical Jesus, a task considered to be beyond the scholar's means during the preceding half a century because according to the then current views hardly anything could be known 'concerning the life and personality of Jesus, since the early Christian sources show no interest in either'.[1] To achieve this aim, I endeavoured to explore the figure of Jesus as preserved in the Synoptic Gospels, in the framework of the political and social history of first-century BC – first-century AD Galilee, and especially in that of contemporaneous popular, charismatic Judaism of prophetic derivation. The hero of this type of Palestinian religion was not the king, the rabbi or the priest, but the man of God, believed to be capable of working miracles and mastering the forces of evil and darkness, namely the devil and sickness. In the first century BC, Honi the rain-maker was such a holy man, and so also was Jesus' younger Galilean contemporary, Hanina ben Dosa, renowned for curing the sick, even from a distance, and helping the needy. His many wondrous interventions earned him the title of protector, saviour and benefactor of humankind. The Galilean Jesus of the Synoptic Gospels is perfectly at home in such a company.

Having thus sketched the background and setting of Jesus' existence, I needed a checking mechanism, which I found in a historical and linguistic analysis of the titles borne by Jesus in the Gospels. Of these, three – 'prophet', 'lord' and 'son of God' – when examined in their Semitic (Aramaic/Hebrew) context are found in biblical and post-biblical Jewish literature applied to charismatic holy men.[2] Hence I concluded that the historical Jesus could be best situated 'in the venerable company of the Devout, the ancient Hasidim' (p. 223). I hastened to add, however, that compared to the portrait of minor charismatic figures preserved in post-biblical Jewish sources, Jesus stood out as incomparably superior. 'Second to none in profundity of insight and grandeur of character, he is in particular an unsurpassed master of the art of laying bare the inmost core of spiritual truth and bringing every issue back to the essence of religion, the existential relationship of man and man and man and God' (p.224).

Having produced a book on Jesus which I thought would be judged 'unorthodox' by Christians, Jews and New Testament scholars alike, I was greatly surprised by an overall lack of hostility. Of course, some unkind words were printed. A Jewish critic, violently resenting my refusal to classify Jesus as a Pharisee, put me among the anti-Semites. A well-known English Jesuit now deceased described the book's learning as 'at times ... oppressive'. He blamed the 'overcrowded' character of the volume on my 'apparent desire' to show off my familiarity with Christian biblical criticism! An American Bible expert, taking exception to my light-hearted remark that New Testament scholars often wear the blinkers of their trade, haughtily dismissed the book with 'Jesus the Jew deserves better than this'. A French woman writer, contributing to a right-wing magazine, settled for the double denunciation of 'scandal and blasphemy'. But on the whole the findings oscillated between warm approval and an open verdict. The former reached its pinnacle in a dithyrambic assessment published in the *Jewish Chronicle* (24 August 1973): 'In a field as well trodden as New Testament exegesis it is extremely rare to encounter a new book which can only be characterised as epoch-making.' As for the open verdict, I have always cherished the splendidly equivocal last phrase in the review appearing in Oxford's *Journal of Theological Studies* (1974, p. 489): 'The result is a valuable contribution to scholarship, but it is hard to assess exactly how successful it is.' But more explicitly, various reviewers, among them Henry Chadwick, then Dean of Christ Church in Oxford,[3] indicated that the absence of any treatment of the teaching of Jesus prevented them from arriving at any firm conclusion concerning my actual findings. Needless to say, I was fully aware of the need to tackle the problem of the sayings of Jesus and indicated in the Preface of the first edition that I hoped to deal with this important issue in another volume, entitled *The Gospel of Jesus the Jew*.

It took some time for the continuation of the Jesus project to reach the top of my writing agenda. It was preceded by the compilation of a volume of essays, entitled *Post-Biblical Jewish Studies* (1975) and consisting of three sections (Qumran – Bible Exegesis – Rabbinic History), a volume that was meant to mark, but missed, my fiftieth birthday in 1974. The second half of the 1970s was occupied by work on the second volume of the new Schürer, published in 1979, and from 1978 to 1980 I was chairman of the Board of Oriental Studies, which demanded much time for administrative and committee work. Some slight distraction was provided by lecture trips to Providence, Rhode Island (1976) and to Vancouver (1980), and especially to Israel in 1979, where I lectured at the University of Tel Aviv, paid my first visit to Qumran under Israeli control, and spent a couple of hours with Yigael Yadin, the deputy Prime Minister, who was convalescing after a first heart attack. We discussed his forthcoming English edition of the Temple Scroll, the Yadin *Festschrift* which the *Journal of Jewish Studies* was preparing for him, to appear in 1982, and my work on revising Schürer. Like most academics kicked upstairs to high administration, he seemed to be hankering after scholarly debate.[4] This was the last time I saw him alive. He died five years later, aged sixty-seven.

However, an unforeseen powerful impetus directing my attention to the dormant promise came from the Vice-Chancellor of the University of

Newcastle who, on the recommendation of the relevant committee chaired by my dear friend Colin Strang (cf. above, p. 129), invited me to deliver the 1981 Riddell Memorial Lectures. I had an instant title at hand, *The Gospel of Jesus the Jew*, and delivered the three addresses on 17–19 March 1981. The constraints of time and space imposed by the form of three one-hour talks meant that the Newcastle lectures could only be a succinct preliminary presentation of the piety preached and practised by Jesus. The opening lecture wrestled with the problem of how to distinguish the authentic message of Jesus from the many later accretions superimposed on it by the primitive church. Lectures two and three sketched the portrait of a person who, while remaining identifiable as a first-century Jewish holy man, nevertheless stands out as a teacher entirely inspired by faith-trust (*emunah*) and dedicated to a call for repentance (*teshuvah*) preparatory to the coming of the Kingdom of God. He also appears uniquely aware of his filial relation to the Father in heaven (*Abba*), and passionately to believe that his mission was to communicate the same sense of relationship with God among his fellow men and women.

It was a curious experience to be back in Newcastle. Both the city and the university had changed enormously since I left in 1965. In the staff club strange faces stared at me from every side. Nevertheless, at the lectures I met a few old friends. The former Vice-Chancellor, Charles Bosanquet, and his wife kindly came along to listen, and Colin and Barbara Strang offered me hospitality in their refurbished disused railway-station house in the back of beyond of the Northumbrian countryside. Those were delightful days.

In 1982 I tried out the Gospel lectures in Britain, in Ireland (North and South),[5] and during a three-week trip in the United States which included, in addition to Tulane University in New Orleans, where I was distinguished visiting professor in Judaeo-Christian studies, Emory University in Atlanta; Duke University in Durham, North Carolina; Rochester University, New York; and North Western University in Evanston, Illinois. The Riddell Lectures, reshaped in the light of the experience gained in the course of the exchanges at home and abroad, and enlarged by further studies previously published in *JJS*, resulted in 1983 in the second part of the trilogy, *Jesus and the World of Judaism*.[6] In a new preface, I attempted to respond to a frequently encountered objection: 'If Jesus was so steeped in Jewish piety and so fundamentally non-political in his outlook as you depict him, why did he clash with the representatives (or at least some representatives) of Judaism and with those of Rome?' My answer was that Jesus was seen, as according to Flavius Josephus was John the Baptist before him, as a *potential* threat to law and order and consequently to the well-being of the Jewish people, and in the authorities' judgment as such had to be eliminated for the common good. 'The trial ... of Jesus of Nazareth, a ... serious affair because of the affray which he caused in the Temple [in the merchants' quarter], and because of the suspicion that some of his followers were Zealots, led to a miscarriage of justice and one of the supreme tragedies in history' (pp. viii–ix). Ten years later, in the Preface of *The Religion of Jesus the Jew*, I reformulated this answer:

'The arrest and execution of Jesus were due, not directly to his words and deeds, but to their possible insurrectional consequences feared by the nervous authorities ... in that powder-keg of first-century Jerusalem ... Had Jesus not caused an affray in the Temple by overturning the tables of the merchants and money-changers, or had he even chosen to do so at a time other than Passover – the moment when the hoped-for Messiah ... was expected to reveal himself – he would most probably have escaped with his life. He died on the cross for having done the wrong thing (causing a commotion) in the wrong place (the Temple) at the wrong time (just before Passover). Here lies the real tragedy of Jesus the Jew' (p. x).

The Gospel of Jesus the Jew slightly advanced my argument, but I was still far from resting my case. Once more the Jesus subject had to be laid aside because of the urgency of the Schürer work. With the publication of Volume III, Part 2, this reached completion in June 1987, during the London symposium on the Dead Sea Scrolls. The whole assembled company of Qumran experts was invited by the publishers of the English Schürer to a celebratory party after more than twenty years of hard labour with speeches from Ramsay Clark, Fergus Millar, Martin Goodman and myself. The idea of a gaudy came from the Clarks (the publishers), but this did not prevent one of the senior Scrolls editors present from later reproaching me for using the Qumran symposium for self-aggrandisement. From 1987 onwards I got increasingly deeply involved in the Qumran war and the Yarnton Scrolls affair, so that the final instalment of the Jesus trilogy, contractually scheduled for 1989, was further and further postponed. Moreover, from 1991 Pam's deteriorating health added to the worry and delayed progress. I put in a big effort in 1992, perhaps urged on by my participation in the television documentary, *Jesus before Christ*, prompted by A. N. Wilson's successful book, *Jesus*, and filmed on location in Bethlehem, Galilee and Jerusalem.[7] By the autumn, the typescript of *The Religion* was finished and the publication of the final volume of the trilogy was fêted at Wolfson College on 1 March 1993. After days of hesitation,

Pam decided to attend and visibly enjoyed the occasion. This was her last appearance in public.

While *Jesus the Jew*, novel, even revolutionary, in its self-assurance that the historical Jesus is within the reach of scholarly research, combative in style and inspiration, is probably the part of the trilogy which made the deepest impact, *The Religion of Jesus the Jew*, more mature, mellow, constructive and 'spiritual', is my favourite of the three. It portrays Jesus as a faithful observer of Judaism and of the Jewish Law, 'perceived, primarily and essentially and positively, not as a juridical, but as a religious-ethical reality, revealing what he thought to be the right and divinely ordained behaviour towards men and towards God' (p. 45).

The exposition of the authentic Judaism practised by Jesus is followed by a sketch of the teaching of Jesus which took the form, not so much of Bible interpretation – most of the passages of polemical scriptural exegesis originated in the early church – as of authoritative statements by a master possessing spiritual power. 'It was the people's belief in the heavenly origin of Jesus' ... teaching, reinforced ... by his apparent mastery over corporal and mental sickness, that dispensed [him] from the need to demonstrate the truth of [his] teaching' (p. 74). In short, the words of Jesus were endowed with authority not because they were backed by Scripture, but because he was revered as a prophet, inspired by the spirit of God.

If the form of the message of Jesus was charismatic, its literary style was that of popular proverbs and parables. The latter, particularly typical of the teaching of Jesus, had focussed on three radical topics: repentance, confidence in God, and total self-dedication to the kingdom of heaven.

The two main topics of Jesus' preaching concerned his particular perception of the Kingdom of God and of God as Father. As regards the Kingdom, his approach was oblique and his outline hazy; he never distinctly spelled out his concept of 'Kingdom'. Two features stand out: 1. The God of Jesus is not a regal figure but rather 'a well-to-do landowner and paterfamilias of rural Galilee'; and 2. The expectation of, and work for, the Kingdom took place in an atmosphere of eschatological enthusiasm. Jesus 'and his disciples entered whole-heartedly into the eschatological age and recognized a fundamental difference between their own time with no future, and the centuries that preceded it. From the moment when Jesus obeyed the Baptist's call to repentance, time for him became the end-time demanding a decisive and irrevocable *teshuvah* [return to God]' (p. 148).

The Father image is at the heart of Jesus' representation of the Deity. It is a characteristic Jewish concept which, as usual, has gained personal and individual colouring in the mind of Jesus. 'Needless to say, the picture of a loving and solicitous Father does not tally with the human experience of a harsh, unjust and cruel world. Then as now, fledglings fell from the nest, little ones perished and, as Jesus himself was soon to experience, the innocent suffered. It would be a mistake to imagine that he offered to his followers a kind of sentimentally anthropomorphic image. But what lies at the heart of his intuition and gives individuality and freshness to his vision is the conviction that the eternal, distant, dominating and tremendous Creator is also and primarily a near and approachable God' (p. 180).

All this naturally leads us to 'Jesus, the religious man'.[8] This religious personality was characterized by an all-pervasive eschatological spirit, one imparting enthusiasm, inspiring urgency and absoluteness in action. It also stimulates the individual to a constant imitation of God.

Through his three ancient witnesses, Mark, Matthew and Luke, the real Jesus, Jesus the Jew, challenges traditional Christianity as well as traditional Judaism. Jesus cannot be represented as the founder of Christianity. 'For ... if he meant and believed what he preached ... namely that the eternal Kingdom of God was truly at hand, he simply could not have entertained the idea of ... setting in motion an organized society intended to endure for ages to come' (pp. 214–5). Only the future will show if and how Christians and Jews will respond. Standardized bodies usually shy off such confrontations. But there is one constituency which is earmarked for Jesus in the present as it was in the past. The 'magnetic appeal of [his] teaching and example ... holds out hope and guidance to those outside the fold of organized religion, the stray sheep of mankind, who yearn for a world of mercy, justice and peace lived in as children of God' (p. 215).

Always foreseeing the worst, I was amazed by the warm reception granted to *The Religion of Jesus the Jew* in all shades of public opinion. On 2 March 1993, the day after its publication, in a full-page piece in the *Evening Standard*, headed 'The scholar who found the real Jesus', A. N. Wilson wrote : 'Of Jesus the man, perhaps we still know very little – but of the kind of teacher and healer he was, the kind of religion he preached, the kind of audience he addressed, we now know infinitely more, thanks to Vermes; and once one has absorbed the message of Vermes's books, it is impossible ever to view Christianity in the same light.' In a different vein, but no less encouragingly, the renowned Cambridge theologian, Don Cupitt, summed up the book's challenge to Christian scholars. They have 'to accept that Jesus' own religion was simply Jewish, and he had no thought of stepping outside it. So a Jewish account of Jesus is bound to be the best – which leaves Christians permanently one down.' Also, though here and there he himself finds fault with the book, he declares that 'Vermes in effect wins the main argument' (*The Guardian*, 27 March 1993). Again, to follow A.E. Harvey, a friend, a former Oxford colleague, and now

Canon and Sub-Dean of Westminster, who strongly disagrees with my thoroughly eschatological approach, 'many readers may find that Jesus comes freshly alive' and in *The Religion of Jesus the Jew* his essential portrait appears 'credible – even, at times, arresting' (*TLS*, 9 April 1993) .

As could be expected, there were some dissenting voices in the confraternity of transatlantic New Testament scholars, particularly quibbling with my lack of 'methodology' in the use of rabbinic literature in the interpretation of the Gospels. Missing the humoristic tone in the characterization of my approach to the issue as 'true *British* pragmatism', with a distinct preference for 'muddling through', because 'innovative [research] should not be bound by fixed, predetermined rules' (*Religion*, 7), a recent critic of the Jesus trilogy, John P. Meier, felt entitled to deliver a little sermon in my direction and for my benefit: 'Any scholarly investigation that is not totally erratic operates by certain rules.'[9] If Meier had taken the trouble to glance at 'Jewish Studies and New Testament Interpretation' referred to on the same page as an account of my method in Gospel exegesis, his readers could have been spared such a pompous (not to say asinine) remark.

Jewish reactions have also been essentially positive. In the *Jewish Chronicle* (6 August 1993), Tessa Rajak, a friend and former pupil, provocatively presents Jesus as 'probably the most famous Jew of all time. Yet [he] is a Jew who rarely gets discussed in (Jewish magazines).' 'Geza Vermes gives us a Jesus who is ready to claim his place in the line of the great Jewish people of God, irrespective of what later became of his teaching. The low-key, meticulous, fair-minded – positively British – investigations of the now emeritus professor of Jewish studies at Oxford have a way of shaking things up, so that they never look the same again.' A powerful revolutionary echo came from Israel, too. Reviewing *The Religion of Jesus the Jew* in the country's leading newspaper, *Ha'aretz*, Magen Broshi, director of the Shrine of the Book, called the age-old ban by virtue of which the name of the Nazarene was never to pass through Jewish lips 'patently absurd'.

The tangible proof that the trilogy made some mark was provided by the fact that between 1977 and 1995, *Jesus the Jew*, was translated into Spanish, French, Italian, Japanese, Portuguese, German and Hungarian.[10] *Jesus and the World of Judaism*, already extant in Portuguese, reached the Hungarian market during the Budapest book week in June 1997, and *The Gospel of Jesus the Jew* has been included in *Jesus der Jude*, the German translation of *Jesus the Jew*. As for *The Religion of Jesus the Jew*, it has already appeared in Spanish and Portuguese, and translations into Korean and Hungarian are in the making.

Twenty-five years ago, anyone foolhardy enough to confront the problem of the Jesus of history appeared an innovator. Since then an increasing number of scholars have ventured in that direction, first in Oxford, and more recently in the United States, too.[11] When Lady Collins and I decided to call my original contribution to the Jesus story 'Jesus *the Jew*', the title enunciating what should be patent to all still sounded striking and pioneering. According to Paula Fredriksen, it caused a 'small revolution' (*JJS* 44, 1993, p. 319). During the intervening years the phrase 'Jesus the Jew' became more and more familiar. Ten years after the publication of the book, a long leader of *The Times* published on Easter Saturday (2 April 1983) was entitled 'Jesus was a Jew'. This progressive headline was far ahead of the more conventional theological views expressed in its correspondence column by a world-famous Cambridge New Testament scholar: 'Jesus was indeed a Jew, but one whom his own fellow-Jews could not tolerate. This is a fact' (*The Times*, 7 April 1983). This was a yesterday's theologian's fact. *The Times* signalled the way of the future. Today 'Jesus the Jew' almost ranks as a cliché.

The same *Times* leader foresaw another new line of development by announcing that 'Jesus the Jew may become a symbol of some ultimate unity in the quest for truth between Christian and Jew, just as he is between Christian and Christian'. The admirable progress shown during the last twenty-five years in the Christian-Jewish dialogue constitutes the fulfilment of the dream of Jules Isaac concerning *friendship* (*amitié*) between individual Christians and Jews and, who knows?, one day between church and synagogue.

In Britain, the Council of Christians and Jews, established during the war against Hitler, has been remarkably revived in recent years. The Oxford branch may be a good illustration. The late Anglican archdeacon Carlyle Witton-Davies, closely associated with the running of the national Council over the years, unsuccessfully tried a number of times to set up a local branch. He made a fresh effort in 1980 and encountered an enthusiastic response. He proposed me as chairman, an office which I held until 1985, and the Oxford branch, a kind of Fabian Society, organized *avant-garde* debates on all aspects of Judaeo-Christian relations in Wolfson College. The Council, both the national and the international, is flourishing and slowly paving the way towards the recognition of the 'real' Jesus by Christians and Jews.

Have *Jesus the Jew* and its sequels played a small part in the developments that took place over the last couple of decades in both Christian and Jewish circles? A change in the attitude of the churches to Judaism and the Jews is noticeable. It is particularly welcome that the new spirit of the dialogue is concerned not only with fighting Christian antisemitism, but also with the study of the Jewish understanding of the Bible and of the figure of Jesus of Nazareth. It is particularly significant that the Christian stand is now expressed not only in the work of enlightened theologians, but also in official documents.

Thus, in its statement on inter-faith dialogue, issued in 1988, the Lambeth Conference of the Anglican Communion formulated the new outlook with characteristic clarity:

'Modern biblical scholarship is increasingly becoming a joint enterprise between Jews and Christians ... Some Jews have become very aware of Jesus as part of their own history, and their writings have brought home to Christians his Jewishness. Renewed study of Jewish sources by Christian scholars has led them to see first-century Judaism in a new and more positive light.'

The 'conversion' of the Roman Catholic Church is if anything even more noteworthy. Its new stance is put forward by none other than the Pontifical Biblical Commission, which in the first half of the twentieth century was the mouthpiece of the most fundamentalist and retrograde opinions on all matters pertaining to the Bible.[12] In a document agreed by its learned members in 1983, and written up by one of them, Professor Henri Cazelles, whom I knew well in my Paris days, the Biblical Commission set out to outline the church's teaching about the Christ-Messiah under the title *Scripture and Christology*. Published in Latin and French in 1984, it has also been available also in English since 1986, thanks to the work of my former classmate from Louvain, the Jesuit Joseph A. Fitzmyer, now himself a member of the Commission.[13]

In its survey of methodologies used today in christology, the Commission dwells on historical research (quite necessary, we are told, but never neutral or objective), and more specifically on 'the approach to Jesus from Judaism'. It is there that a point of view, inconceivable just a few decades ago and no doubt still shocking for backwoods Christians, expresses itself with clarity and vigour.

'After the First World War some Jewish historians, abandoning centuries-old animosity – of which Christian preachers were themselves not innocent – devoted studies directly to the person of Jesus and to Christian origins (J. Klausner, M. Buber, C. G. Montefiore, etc.) ... Some Jewish historians ... have set in relief certain lines of his personality; they have found in him a teacher like the Pharisees of old (D. Flusser) or a wonder-worker similar to those whose memory Jewish tradition has preserved (G. Vermes). Some have not hesitated to compare the passion of Jesus with the Suffering Servant, mentioned in the Book of Isaiah (M. Buber). All these attempts (at interpretation) *are to be accorded serious attention by Christian theologians engaged in the study of Christology'* (p. 9, my emphasis).

A little later, the same point is repeated with equal stress: 'The diligent study of Judaism is of the utmost importance for the correct understanding of the person of Jesus' (p. 23). Not even the *caveat* that follows[14] – the Commission seems to have come to the realization that it had been carried away too far by scholarly enthusiasm – can undo the massively positive effect of this epoch-making church document. Incidentally, I find it quite comforting that, although at least half a dozen members of the Commission, among them Pierre Benoit and Dominique Barthélémy from the world of the Scrolls, knew me and my Catholic and priestly past, they did not shrink from including my name among those *Jewish* experts whose views 'are to be accorded serious attention by Christian theologians engaged in the study of Christology'.

Since Judaism has no institutions similar to the Lambeth Conference or the Pontifical Biblical Commission, it would be useless to look for a Jewish authority to issue official statements on Jesus. Nevertheless, here too signs of a thaw may be detected. Naturally, sympathetic utterances are more often heard from progressive Jews than from Orthodox quarters, but in academic circles one witnesses a notable metamorphosis. For instance, when in 1965 Professor Shmuel Safrai of the Hebrew University, a strictly observant Jew, devoted a fascinating study to the *Hasidim* (or Devout) in early rabbinic literature, it never occurred to him to include Jesus under this heading. Yet when three decades later he returned to the same subject, Jesus figures prominently among the ancient pietists from Galilee.[15] Moreover, when – as I have noted earlier – one can read in the leading Israeli daily, *Ha'aretz* , in a review of *The Religion of Jesus the Jew*, that the age-old, traditional ban on Jesus is 'patently absurd', it is difficult not to sense there the beginning of a wind of change.

So we can look forward with burning expectation to the new millennium. If, as Pope John Paul II has promised, the Catholic Church will belatedly express her sorrow over Christian injustice inflicted on the Jewish people, the people of Jesus the Jew,[16] and if, by a miracle, *any* modern book on Jesus is offered in modern Hebrew to Israeli readers, I will begin to believe that the hope formulated in the Introduction of *Jesus the Jew* will have come true and 'a small beginning [will] have been made in the repayment to [Jesus] of a debt long overdue' (p. 17).

Shortly before I had to relinquish my Oxford University post in 1991 due to age, I received an invitation from the late Dr John Sykes, one of the general editors of *The New Shorter Oxford English Dictionary*, to act as an adviser on all matters relating to Judaism. I gladly accepted this retirement job: the pay was a pittance, but the task intrigued me. So for about a year, batches of entries – hundreds of them – taken from the previous edition kept on reaching me. My task was either to approve them, or to suggest alterations. I quite enjoyed the challenge, but foolishly failed to record for myself the changes I put forward to the editors, who made the final decision. So at the end I could not check the number of my proposals which ended up being accepted.

The work progressed fast, the two gigantic volumes (3,801 tightly set pages) were completed, and a monumental press launch was scheduled at Claridge's on 7 September 1993 with a luncheon party arranged for editors, guests, leading media personalities, and us humble advisers. I found myself sitting at a round table in the company of a dozen people, all unknown to me. To make conversation, I asked the white-haired lady on my right about her connection with the *Dictionary*. 'Oh, I'm Burma,' she declared without hesitation, having dealt with all the words of Burmese origin. I could not think anything better to reply than 'How d'you do? I'm Judaism.' Emboldened, I enquired from the septuagenarian on my left what his line was. 'I'm snooker,' he said. 'A famous player?' 'No, no, I'm the author of the rule book. Mind you, I can play, but my highest break was fifty-eight, which I managed on my fifty-eighth birthday.' Further to the left a familiar-looking woman with large glasses turned out to be 'wine'. She was Jancis Robinson of TV fame, and in the process of completing *The Oxford Companion to Wine*. I even discovered an academic, a Cambridge professor of linguistics, in charge of all the grammatical terms of the *Dictionary*. The meal was sumptuous, but when we left Claridge's, I assumed that this was the end of my involvement with *The Shorter Oxford English Dictionary*. I was mistaken.

What I did not realize was that my suggestion regarding the name Jesus had been adopted by the editors, and this in turn provoked quite an outcry on the part of old-fashioned Christians and much hilarity in the editorial circles of *The Times*. Instead of the old definition 'The name of the Founder of Christianity', the new one runs '(The name of) the central figure of the Christian faith, a Jewish preacher (c.5 BC–c.AD 30) regarded by his followers as the Son of God and God incarnate.' 'Jesu, joy of man's defining', was the front page headline in *The Times* (9 October 1993), which reported, among other things, that the Reverend Tony Higton, a senior evangelical and a member of the General Synod [of the Church of England] found 'the idea of Jesus as a "Jewish preacher" to be a rather derogatory term'. Since someone no doubt made him aware of the possible antisemitic connotations of his statement, the unfortunate clergyman then tried to extricate himself from the mess of his own making by welcoming the fact that the *Dictionary* 'helpfully records for the first time that Jesus is Jewish', but objecting to the designation 'preacher' (letter to *The Times*, 13 October 1993)! But the third leader of *The Times* (9 October), under another humorous headline, 'The game of the name', came out firmly in my support: '*The New Shorter Oxford English Dictionary* ... has defined the name of Jesus accurately and more economically than before.'

I have the strange feeling that my best known and most lasting contribution to a better perception of the historical Jesus may be this dictionary definition which does not carry my name.

18

Harvest Time

(1985–1993)

The golden years of Oxford with their multifarious challenges gave me much gentle satisfaction, but for many years failed to produce any external recognition in the form of promotion. I arrived among the dreaming spires in 1965 as a University Reader, and by the 1980s it began to look as though I would bow out in the same position. The magic title of Professor seemed to elude me. Of course, I knew that in Oxford such things did not really matter. Besides, a readership bestowed on its holder professorial status and consequently qualified me to be a 'professorial fellow' of Wolfson College. During the earlier years of my Oxford career, the University counted among its staff a handful of Readers on whom, according to the official jargon then in force, 'the title of professor was conferred by decree'. The great G.R. Driver was one of these: formally Reader in Semitic Philology and until his retirement drawing a reader's salary, in 1939 he was granted the privilege of calling himself 'Professor', apparently to reward him for his unwillingness to leave Oxford, not even for the Regius Professorship of Hebrew in Cambridge.

I believe that in the late 1960s or early 1970s the University decided to abolish this 'anomaly'. In those days it was thought improper to give the title without the stipend; so it was resolved to discontinue the giving of the title. Edward Ullendorff sat one day at a dinner next to the head of the General Board of the University, the body in charge of academic appointments and (theoretical) promotions, and enquired why Oxford deprived so many distinguished dons of the professorial accolade. 'Such trifling things don't matter here,' was the haughty reply. This was indeed true in local thinking, and of course no one would have hinted in public at the difference in salary. Such mundane matters were to be ignored. But in a non-Oxford context the nomenclature could be embarrassing. I once overheard an American friend explaining to another who had no idea what my title of 'Reader' meant: 'Oh, you know, he's just one below full professor.'

In a kind of childish dream, which I openly admit here for the first time, I used to long for three further accomplishments: I hoped one day to become a Professor, a Fellow of the British Academy, and to be listed in *Who's Who*. After two earlier failures in Britain over a professorship, a totally unexpected chance arose on 3 December 1984. 'Would I be interested' – wrote the chair of the search committee – 'in a newly endowed chair in Judaic studies attached to the History department of the University of California at San Diego?' I would be the sole candidate and the salary would be 'above-scale'. Since my British stipend was only a fraction of the sum indicated, the offer seemed unbelievable.

However, more or less at the same time, applying the Thatcherite policy of competitiveness to the academic world, the government compelled all British universities to introduce regular (in Oxford four-yearly) exercises of promotion to personal professorships. Faculty boards were to select candidates for consideration by a specially constituted body consisting of eminent professors. As in the case of the Regius chair of Hebrew seven years earlier, my colleagues on the Oriental Studies board did me the honour of putting only my name forward for promotion.

But long before the University Committee for *ad hominem* professorships got anywhere near to picking their winners, I had to decide what to do with the invitation from San Diego to pay them a visit and give them a chance to persuade me. I was promised great freedom and very attractive conditions from both the personal and the departmental points of view. For instance, I was assured that after the mandatory retirement at seventy, professors of my standing would be recalled to active duty every year *indefinitely*. And, oh yes, several new departmental appointments would follow. In belt-tightening British academia this sounded paradise. So, after much debate at home, it was decided that I ought to go and see for myself, which I did between 24 February and 1 March 1985.

The trip was a unique experience. In February the sun was shining in San Diego, the Pacific was blue and the day-time temperature was in the seventies. I received VIP treatment from the President, the Vice-Chancellor for Academic Affairs and the various deans. My two lectures, one for faculty members (on Jewish history in the Graeco-Roman age), the other for the general public (on the historical Jesus), were very successful. My negotiations with the Vice-Chancellor could not have been smoother. The standard answer to any difficulty I raised was, 'If money can buy it, don't worry.' 'O yes, housing in the neighbourhood of the University campus at La Jolla, the most select district of San Diego, formerly inhabited largely by retired admirals, is rather expensive, but one of our donors has an interesting idea which we can work out if you accept the offer.' I was overwhelmed by friendliness and generosity.

Fortunately, since the University of California is a mammoth organization and San Diego is one of nine constituent campuses, the local and central administrative machine took a couple of months before a written offer reached me in May, so I did not need to arrive at a decision in a hurry. Meanwhile I made discreet inquiries about the state of the personal professorship exercise in Oxford and soon learned that my name was not among those which had been pulled out of the hat. The disappointment might have given me the final prompting to opt for San Diego, but then along came another of those providential accidents which seem to have ruled my whole life.

On 14 May 1985, while opening my mail at the Oriental Institute, I came across a medium-size impersonal-looking envelope marked Private and Confidential. Another request for a reference, I thought. Instead, it contained a letter from the Secretary of the British Academy, who wrote: 'I have the honour to inform you that the Council has resolved to propose you for election as a Fellow of the British Academy at the Annual General Meeting on 2 July 1985.' This came totally out of the blue; I hardly could believe my eyes. The most cherished of my three unfulfilled dreams, the one theoretically the most difficult to achieve, had suddenly come true. (The second, entry into *Who's Who*, was automatically to follow shortly, since FBAs are included as it were *ex officio*.) Still trembling, I rang Pam. 'Here is the sign from heaven. We're staying. San Diego is off.' I felt relieved and she was more than delighted. I politely turned down the offer from the University of California, cherishing British recognition more than American comfort.[1]

Although being a Fellow of the Academy does not mean much in practical terms, it was noted at home and among friends that it made me a visibly happy man. Fully aware now, after years of experience, of the difficulties of getting someone elected, I remain deeply grateful to those who enabled me to affix to my name 'those three golden letters', as one of my well-wishers phrased it.

The Academy was the first, and probably the biggest, step up the ladder of academic honours. The next came in 1988 when Oxford 'granted me leave to supplicate' for the title of DLitt, the higher doctorate of Letters. The degree was conferred on 21 May amid pomp and ceremony. The Sheldonian Theatre, the regular venue of such proceedings, displayed its usual splendour and my elevation was witnessed by my family – my stepdaughter Tina flew over specially from the States – many of my Oxford friends and a large number of pupils.

I was quietly pleased that after more than twenty years of service I had became a *real* doctor, for in Oxford's eyes my previous Belgian DTheol was just a kind of fiction which was tolerated. In official listings until then

I had been a mere MA, since in this university, apart from its own degrees, only degrees conferred by Cambridge and Trinity College, Dublin really count. I also found it gratifying to be secularized, to belong to Letters rather than to Theology. Oxford's higher doctorates have also their fun side: the holders of such degrees are invited yearly by the Vice-Chancellor to 'partake in Lord Crewe's benefaction' and remember the financial patrons of the University by eating strawberries with cream and drinking champagne. This little feast takes place just before the grand Encaenia ceremony in the Sheldonian, where the *crème de la crème* of the world of arts and sciences receive honorary doctorates in the presence of a multicoloured gathering.[2]

Finally, in 1989, two years before retirement, my last unfulfilled dream, promotion to a chair, also came my way. On 21 February, on my way home at the end of a long afternoon spent in my college, for no special reason I decided to stop at the Oriental Institute to check the mail. There it was, a letter straight from the Secretary of Faculties, dated 20 February 1989: 'I am very pleased to inform you that the General Board has agreed, on the recommendation of the Ad Hominem Promotions Committee, that you should become an *ad hominem* Schedule A professor with effect from 1 October 1989.' Somehow I was neither surprised nor elated. I felt it was my turn. I quietly drove home without telephoning the news. After dinner, I sat on the bench facing the back garden and watched my foxes having their supper on the lawn. Suddenly I was filled with silent contentment.

The University magazine *Oxford Today* (Michaelmas issue, 1989, p. 47), which defined the *ad hominem* professorship as a sort of academic 'life peerage which ceases to exist when the person retires', chose me out of the twelve successful candidates as the subject of its 'Profile of a Professor'. At the end of my interview with the editor of the magazine I was quoted: 'I am the first Professor of Jewish Studies at Oxford University. I hope I won't be the last.'

The fulfilment of my wish was not delayed for too long. Making a complete U-turn, in 1996 Oxford reverted to the former system of granting the professorial title without remuneration, but whereas in the old days this kind of generosity was an exception reserved for a handful, this time – very justly – it was showered in one fell swoop on a large number of lecturers and readers, on one-hundred and sixty-two to be precise. My pupil, friend and successor, Martin Goodman, was one of them, and became the second Professor of Jewish Studies in the more than seven-hundred-year-long history of this University.

It is almost embarrassing to carry on, but twenty years of stasis gave way between 1985 and 1990 to a flood of accolades. It was truly harvest time.

After the Academy and the professorship came two honorary doctorates in Divinity. The first was all the more pleasantly surprising as it was granted by Edinburgh, a university with which I had no direct association beyond a public lecture given there some years earlier. The second honorary DD took me to Durham, where on account of my years spent at King's College, Newcastle, while it was still part of Durham University, I continued to count as 'one of us'. The ceremony was made particularly graceful by the presence of the Chancellor, prima ballerina Dame Margot Fonteyn. In spite of her grave illness – she died a few months later – she was still charm and delight personified. The other unique feature of the occasion was my first reunion after twenty-three years with my former pupil, Crown Prince Hassan of Jordan, also recipient of an honorary doctorate, not in Divinity but in Law. It was a warm and happy encounter.

Another distinction of a new kind was awaiting me in the same year, 1990. To mark my sixty-fifth birthday, friends and former students, twenty-one of them, produced a magnificent Festschrift, entitled *A Tribute to Geza Vermes: Essays on Jewish and Christian Literature and History*.[3] It was meant to be presented at the meeting of the European Association for Jewish Studies in Troyes in July 1990. Indeed, I received a proof copy from Philip Davies during the general assembly of the Conference, but the finished volume was handed over at a dinner party at Wolfson College on 27 November 1990, attended by the majority of the contributors.

Thanks to the providential timing of these honours, Pam was still able to join in and share my pleasure. She was present in Edinburgh and Durham, and even managed to travel to glorious mediaeval Troyes, but only just. The decline set in early in 1991 leading to the end already recounted in the Prologue.

Looking back with gratitude and amazement on my harvest-time, I would like to believe that these honours were a reward for a life devoted to the search for truth and to the service and dissemination of learning. When on 30 September 1991 I had to vacate my chair and move out of the Oriental Institute, my home for twenty-six years, the undeniable feeling of loss was fully compensated for by the profound satisfaction that one of my former pupils, Martin Goodman, was succeeding me in my University post, and another, Philip Alexander, my first DPhil. student, was soon to become the president of the Oxford Centre for Hebrew and Jewish Studies. 'You've founded a dynasty,' a friend commented with a smile.

But if I had to single out from among all my deeds one as more portentous than all others, it would be my saying 'no' to California, a decision which enabled me to remain faithful to Britain and Oxford, the two homes where I have been made what I am. Last but very definitely not least, had I fallen for the lure of the sun and other attractions of the West Coast of the United States, the most unpredictable and blessed of the many providential accidents still in store for me would have had no chance to turn into reality and help me to renew my life.

Epilogue: Late Afternoon Sunshine

(1993–)

The days and months which followed Pam's departure passed in semi-darkness and mourning, with the burden of solitude on my shoulders. I lived at a slow pace and from day to day. Loving family (my two step-daughters) and friends stood by me and helped to prop me up. So did Pam's parting advice: 'Get on with the unfinished business, and who knows what will happen.' I made a great effort and tried to lose myself in work. Without delay I proceeded to pay my three final debts: I commissioned a tombstone, and arranged for a memorial service and for Pam's poems to be published.[1] Then I set out to prepare the fourth edition of *The Dead Sea Scrolls in English*, working the whole day and often until midnight. On photographs taken at that time I look stooped and dazed, but I was not in despair.

Then unexpectedly, as always, the miraculous accident suddenly struck. I cannot describe it, as it is too marvellous and private. It is allusively revealed in the dedication of the first major work finished in the new era, *The Complete Dead Sea Scrolls in English*: 'For M. and I. with love'. M. is Margaret, a scientist with degrees from Cracow and Oxford. She is now my wife. I., Ian, is her son, now seven years old. I have known Margaret for fifteen years; she and her then husband, a former very special student of mine, were much loved young friends of both Vermeses. They split up; Margaret and I met again, and the rest followed. We found, needed and comforted each other. She introduced me to the glories of her native city, Cracow, reminiscent of the happy days of the Austro-Hungarian empire. I took her to visit the places where I spent my childhood and youth in Hungary. We visited together in Budapest my last living relation, the vivacious widow of my great-uncle, aged ninety-three. Margaret was with me in Sheffield when I received another honorary doctorate, this time a DLitt; in Budapest, where the American Society of Biblical Literature organized a little celebration of my work on Jesus; and in Jordan, in April 1997, where we enjoyed the dream-like hospitality of my former pupil, Crown Prince el-Hassan bin Talal. She was with me on the occasion of the first of the annual 'Geza Vermes Lectures in the History of Religions' which I delivered at the University of Leicester on 28 May 1997.

Margaret is the blessed providential accident that transformed my life. Visibly. When I first revealed the secret to a close friend, who turned out to be very observant, he surprised me with his answer: 'Now that explains it. I've noticed that lately your steps have become springier.'

Present happiness is not divorced from the past. Tina and Anna, my two stepdaughters, did not hesitate a second to embrace us, and we have all become one loving family. Also, Margaret and Ian regularly join me to perform our weekly ritual of visiting Pam's grave, to pray there for all those whom we love and for the world. They are the source of my still flowing energy in the late afternoon sunshine. Now that my reminiscences have come to an end, I keenly look forward to the next challenge, *The Changing Faces of Jesus*, which I would like to complete for the turn of the millennium.

As for dear little Ian, the new experience of living with a small child fills me with infinite delight. He calls me Geza at home, but at school refers to me as his daddy. He wants to watch the news on television because he has noticed that I am an addict. And yes, he knows a lot about the Dead Sea Scrolls. At the age of five, he gave a lecture to his class about the shepherd boy who, looking for a lost sheep, found a treasure. 'Was it gold?', asked the children. 'No, very, very old books written in Hebrew.' He surprised Emanuel Tov, editor-in-chief of the Qumran Project, who was our dinner guest, with a present of several maps, drawn by him, of caves where more scrolls can be found ... provided you avoid the clearly marked trap doors. But the star episode happened during our visit to the Huntington Library. While Margaret and I attended a Chaucerian dinner, Ian stayed with Bill Moffett's daughter and her children. She overheard Ian and one of her boys competing: 'My grandad found the Dead Sea Scrolls,' boasted Bill's grandson. 'O yeah,' retorted Ian, 'but my daddy wrote them.'

To epitomize the lessons of an eventful life, here is my secret philosophy – for what it is worth:

Trust your intuition; it rarely deceives you.

Act on it, and with a whole heart do what you are meant to do.

Having done your best, wait for providential accidents which, if my experience is anything to go by, quite often follow.

Notes

1. Roots

1. I still have the nonagenarian widow of one of my mother's uncles among the living.

2. Quite recently I learnt from a friend that the author of the letter, Etus (Ethel) József, was still alive and in June 1997 I visited her in Budapest. I didn't know what to expect from a lady aged ninety-four, but I was very pleasantly surprised. She was vivacious and delightful and clearly remembered my parents, great-granny, and the old house in Makó. She gave me her blessing when we parted and promised to come next day to my book-signing session during the Hungarian Book Week. She actually turned up, and gave me a copy of an English edition of her brother's *Selected Poems and Texts*; she wanted to know whether the translation was reliable. It was a deeply moving occasion, a link with a small world of which Etus József is probably the last living witness.

2. Childhood Memories

1. My 1994 visit to Makó and to our home, which still has the old street number plate (41 Szeged Street) next to a more recent one, has confirmed the correctness of my childhood memory. When two years later I last passed in front of the family house, a poster proclaimed that it was up for sale. I resisted the urge to enquire about the asking price.

2. This newspaper still exists. In fact, it carried a report on my public lecture given at the Attila József University in Szeged in October 1996.

3. During my pilgrimage to the synagogue of Makó in 1996, I saw her name and those of her husband and two children on the inscription commemorating the victims of the Holocaust. I remembered her with warm emotion.

3. Unread Signs of Doom

1. In pre-war Hungarian 'democracy' no newspaper could be published without ministerial authorization. Indeed, a proof copy of every issue had to be submitted to the office of the public prosecutor for approval. This was a mere

formality and the censorship took only a minute or two, but without the state *imprimatur* the printers were not allowed to produce the paper.

2. Both left Hungary in 1956. One lives in Phoenix, Arizona, and the other in Vienna.

3. Hungary actively entered the war in 1941 as an ally of Hitler's Germany.

4. I learned from *The Times* of 10 June 1995 that post-Thatcherite 'competitive' Britain was catching up with pre-war Hungary. Even universities, including Cambridge, were introducing special measures to prevent cheating. According to a recent report, 13% of undergraduates confessed to copying from a neighbouring candidate; 8% had slipped crib-sheets into the examination hall; and 5% said they were helped by whispers and notes.

5. The marks obtained in every subject in the final year were printed in the school yearbook. One of these, physical education, did not count in the general classification. To spoil the appearance of my otherwise faultless result, I was given a 2 (not a 1) by the notorious sports instructor responsible for pre-military training. I was a borderline case, so this was not strictly unjust, but since he awarded a top mark to someone less good in athletic performance than me because of his excellence in the irrelevant military drill, I felt cheated.

4. From Boredom to Nightmare

1. In 1996 I revisited the district, which by then had virtually no Jewish inhabitants.

2. This advocate, Dr Zoltán Keszt, together with another lawyer friend who usually handled my father's legal business, Dr Julius Hraskó, a Christian with a Jewish wife, were made supreme court judges in 1945.

3. After 1944 I lost all contact with my colleagues from Szatmár, apart from Miki Frank. So imagine my astonishment when sometime in the late 1970s a letter written in Hungarian arrived in Oxford from Romania, signed by a fellow-student from those remote days. Since he suffered from insomnia, he was apparently in the habit of twiddling the knobs of his radio during his sleepless hours, searching for Hungarian programmes. One night he suddenly heard a seemingly familiar voice on the BBC World Service giving a talk on the Dead Sea Scrolls. He persevered to the end and thus discovered the name and address of the speaker.

4. Despite the dissolution of the Austro-Hungarian monarchy, Hungary remained (until 1945) a kingdom without a king, and to make the oddity even more blatant, the Regent of the country, by then completely landlocked, was an admiral.

5. This branch of the Catholic Church admits married priests, but marriage has to precede ordination. For those seminarians who were prospective celibate priests, it seemed extraordinary that their Eastern colleagues' chief topic of

conversation was their wedding plans. I remember the consternation caused by the break-up of the engagement of one of their number. Not only was the future bridegroom emotionally devastated; he had also to postpone his priestly ordination until a suitable and willing new fiancée had been found!

5. From Darkness to Light

1. Andy, as will be seen in the next chapter, left Hungary in 1946. first for Rome. He then engineered a transfer to Rabat in North Africa, where he was ordained priest. In Morocco, still under French rule, he sided with the Arabs and was promptly expelled by the authorities. He wrote to me in Paris, where by then I was living: could I do something to reverse the expulsion order? An influential French journalist friend of mine approached the French Home Office, only to receive a letter from the Minister, François Mitterand, stating that the matter had been looked into, but since the Abbé Villányi was a proven troublemaker, Mitterand saw no reason to rescind the decree. Andy spent the rest of his life in Rome, complaining that the church authorities kept him on the breadline. He visited me once in Newcastle in the early 1960s, arriving with a large bunch of roses for my wife, Pam. I remember taking him with me to the library of the Oriental School in Durham where we were welcomed by the late I.C.I. (Jack) Foster, the most remarkable academic librarian I ever knew. 'And what is your speciality, Dr Villányi?', he asked. Dear Andy had no speciality, but in order not to let me down, he said he was interested in the history of Christianity in North Africa. 'We are fairly well equipped in this field,' Jack told him, 'Is there anything you would like to consult?' With some difficulty, Andy suggested a title, and in no time a large volume was placed on his desk by Jack. Andy hardly knew which way to hold it. Jack, discreetly observing the scene, enquired whether he could find what he needed. Once more Andy had to improvise and name a topic. I will never forget the sight of Jack, sinking to one knee, pushing his glasses to his forehead, and with one brusque movement opening the folio volume... exactly on the right page! Andy remained a dear and most amusing correspondent, source of much clerical gossip from Rome and Hungary, until he died in 1973, aged seventy-two.

2. The name of Szobel, who was my father's look-alike, brings a delightful anecdote back to me. One day Father arrived home visibly amused. Apparently he had been accosted in the street by an unknown young woman who confided intimate medical details to him, as though he had been fully in the know. After a few moments of perplexity, the penny dropped. 'Madam, I am sure these matters were intended for the ears of Dr Szobel, the gynaecologist, and not for the journalist that I am.'

3. Having accidentally met our last landlord's daughter in Gyula, I learned from this honest woman that she had taken various pieces of furniture from our

flat. I had more difficulty in persuading a 'friend' of my mother's to hand over to me the small amount of money which was entrusted to her for safe-keeping.

4. He was an expert in the Ugaritic language and literature which had been discovered some fifteen years earlier at Ras Shamra in Syria. When later in the early 1950s I sent him an offprint of one of my early publications with greetings from a former pupil, he honestly, and unsurprisingly, admitted in his thank-you note that he could not remember me; I never had the opportunity to re-introduce myself because by the time of my first return to Hungary as a scholar in 1968, Aistleitner was no longer alive.

5. This failed benefactor, whom I never met, had been a famous man in his time. Dr Dezső Földes (1880–1950) won two Olympic gold medals in fencing as a member of the Hungarian sabre team at the 1908 London and 1912 Stockholm games. Four out of the five victorious 'Hungarian' fencers were Jews, including the winner of the individual title. Sporting excellence was one of the side effects of assimilation. Andrew Handler's *From the Ghetto to the Games: Jewish Athletes in Hungary*, East European Monographs CXCII, Columbia University Press, New York 1985, makes amazing reading.

6. *The Fathers Of Notre-Dame De Sion: Prelude*

1. These ten points may sound commonplace today, but they were revolutionary in 1947. They proclaim that *Christians should be reminded*: 1. that the same God speaks to all in the Old and the New Testaments; 2. that Jesus and his mother were Jews; 3. that Jesus' apostles were Jews; 4. that the precept of the love of the neighbour allows for no exception; 5. that post-biblical Judaism must not be disparaged for the sake of exalting Christianity; 6. that the term 'Jews' must not be used exclusively to denote the enemies of Jesus; 7. that the story of the Passion must not be so presented that its odium is directed to all the Jews, including present-day Jews; 8. that the curse, 'Let his blood be on us and on our children' cannot prevail over Jesus' prayer of pardon, 'Father, forgive them'; 9. that the opinion which holds the Jews cursed and rejected is irreligious; 10. that the first members of the church were Jews.

2. The dedication of the volume speaks for itself: 'To my wife, to my daughter, martyrs – killed by Hitler's Nazis – killed simply because their name was ISAAC.' The author describes the work as 'the cry of an indignant conscience, of a broken heart'. It addresses the conscience and the heart of men. I pity those who refuse to listen to it. Two Popes, Pius XII and John XXIII, learned from his passionate wisdom, and his influence on the work of the Second Vatican Council's decree concerning the Jews was considerable. A second book of his, *L'enseignement du mépris* (The Teaching of Contempt, 1962), contains copious mentions of the writings of Paul Démann. I was fortunate to have met and experienced the magnetism of Jules Isaac. Indeed, I

assisted again and again this tall, erect, noble-looking man when he worked in the library of the Fathers of Sion in Paris, preparing a revised edition of *Jésus et Israël*. I am proud that he considered my youthful work on the Dead Sea Scrolls worthy of repeated quotations in the supplementary notes appended to the later 1959 edition of this great book.

7. Discovery of the Bible

1. Only one of my colleagues, Joseph A. Fitzmyer, an American Jesuit, several years my senior in age but one year behind me in study, was to make an international name for himself. By coincidence, he also became a Dead Sea Scrolls expert and a specialist on the Semitic background of the New Testament. We had a number of academic clashes over the years, but, like experienced gladiators, we were always respectful of each other's fighting skills.

2. The same anti-progressive spirit ensured that New Testament exegesis would fare no better. A single illustration will suffice. When dealing with the 'Synoptic problem', i.e. the relationship between the Gospels of Matthew, Mark and Luke, no Catholic exegete was free to adhere to the so-called 'two-source' theory which had for many decades dominated (and still largely dominates) critical scholarship, namely that the compilers of the Gospels of Matthew and Luke relied heavily on the Gospel of Mark (source 1) and on another anthology of Jesus' sayings, no longer independently extant, so-called Q, from German *Quelle* = source (Decree of 26 June 1912). By the way, the Fourth Gospel had already been firmly declared, against an almost unanimous critical consensus, the genuine work of the apostle John, containing historically authentic speeches of Jesus (Decree of 29 May 1907).

3. In this respect the Holy Office, predecessor of the Biblical Commission as guardian of orthodox doctrine about Scripture, showed itself more flexible (if this is the right word to use about a body formerly called the Sacred Congregation of the Roman and Universal Inquisition). On 13 January 1897 it promulgated a decree declaring that the so-called *Johannine comma*, i.e. I John 5. 7, is authentic, that is to say, that the sentence 'For there are three that bear record in heaven, the Father, the Word and the Holy Ghost: and these three are one' belongs to the original Greek text of the New Testament. However, the persons responsible for formulating this decree of the Holy Office were ignorant of the fact that the words in question do not figure in any of the ancient Greek manuscripts and derive, not from the authentic New Testament, but from a late fourth-century Latin work, and were inserted several centuries later into the Latin New Testament. Thirty years had to elapse before the Holy Office half-heartedly and in its own inimitable style revoked the earlier pronouncement: 'The decree was meant to control the audacity of learned individuals who arrogated to themselves the right either completely to reject or at

least to question the authenticity of the Johannine comma. It did not in any way wish to prevent Catholic writers from investigating the matter more fully and, after carefully weighing the arguments with the moderation and self-control required by the gravity of the matter, arriving at a conclusion which is against authenticity, as long as they profess themselves ready to stand by the judgment of the Church, to which alone the office not only to interpret but also faithfully to preserve Holy Scripture was entrusted by Jesus Christ' (Decree of 2 June 1927).

4. Loisy's expulsion from the church did not diminish, but if anything enhanced, his standing as a scholar, since almost at once he was appointed to a chair in the illustrious Collège de France, where he taught from 1909 till 1930.

5. It would be both invidious and unkind for me to express an opinion, but publication statistics strangely support the rumours. Between 1949 and 1952, coinciding with my undergraduate and graduate years at the College St Albert, Father Lambert wrote a dozen articles on the Scrolls, some of them substantial, but after my departure from Louvain until his death in 1961, I can trace only two more titles, only one of them on Qumran.

6. Contrary to the normal course of events, Father (later Cardinal) Bea was transformed in his old age from an ultra-conservative into a liberal. He played an important part in the Second Vatican Council's debates on the church's attitudes towards the Jews and during the last years of his life became a leading figure in circles promoting Christian-Jewish understanding.

7. A few years later, when I lived in Paris, I met Cardinal Tisserant a number of times in circumstances worth recording. He used to leave Rome during the summer and return to France, where he regularly summoned my friend Paul Démann for a discussion of Jewish-Christian issues. Démann must have told the Cardinal about me and my research. From then on, each year I was called to meet 'Eugène', as we used slightly disrespectfully to refer to him, to put him in the picture about current developments in Dead Sea Scrolls studies. He visibly enjoyed our conversations and declared them more entertaining than the affairs of the college of cardinals.

8. Meeting the Dead Sea Scrolls

1. The oldest scrolls found on the north-western shore of the *Dead* Sea do not predate the second half of the third century BC.

2. In 1883, a Jerusalem antique dealer, Moses William Shapira, offered the British Museum fragments of a scroll of Deuteronomy allegedly some two and a half thousand years old. The experts first pronounced the fifteen leather strips authentic, but soon recanted, and the exposed Shapira committed suicide.

3. I hardly could have imagined at that time that fragments belonging to the

latter document, better known now as 'The Community Rule', would be found in another Qumran cave and that some forty years later I would be invited to become their official editor.

4. 'La Communauté de la Nouvelle Alliance', *ETL* 27, 1951, 70–80.

5. *Comptes rendues des séances de l'Académie des Inscriptions et Belles-Lettres*, 1952, 174–5.

6. *Observations sur Le Commentaire d'Habacuc découvert près de la Mer Morte*, Paris 1950, 29.

7. (Wilhelm) William Kahle became a Catholic priest and until his recent death was attached to Westminster Cathedral in London. He plays a minor role in this story.

8. I was sent a complimentary copy of the book and hardly could believe my eyes when I discovered that I was a frequently quoted 'authority' in the work of this famous scholar.

9. *Jerusalem and Qumran*

1. They were reissued under the title *The Scrolls from the Dead Sea* in 1955 by Oxford University Press, New York. I warmly recommend the book for its delightfully accurate vignettes not only of Flusser but also of Roland de Vaux, who explained to Wilson how to make a good meal out of hyena meat, which tastes 'like wild boar', and Dupont-Sommer, who, 'round-faced, short and rotund, bland and urbane and smiling', resembled his hero, Renan, 'just as biographers sometimes look like their subjects and ornithologists are often birdlike'.

2. The work, completed in association with my former student, Professor Philip Alexander of Manchester University, is due to be published by Oxford University Press as Vol. XXVI of *Discoveries in the Judaean Desert* in 1998.

10. *Paris and the* Cahiers

1. A supplementary survey of liturgical education by the same authors followed in nos. 2–3, 1953 of the *Cahiers*, entitled 'Formation liturgique et l'attitude chrétienne envers les Juifs', 115–78.

2. I wonder how the teachers reconciled this with the creation of the State of Israel in 1948?

3. The details are given in *Cahiers Sioniens* 7, 1953, 77–105, 215–18. A summary account may be found in Bernard Wasserstein, *Vanishing Diaspora*, London 1996, 133–5.

4. *Textes rabbiniques des deux premiers siècles chrétiens pour servir à l'intelligence du Nouveau Testament*, Rome 1955.

11. The Turmoil of Transition

1. This is his real name, but not the one under which he is known. I do not wish to give a positive identification.

2. The last two numbers of the 1955 volume were delayed until well into 1956, and the quadruple issue planned for 1956 to serve as a Renée Bloch memorial never appeared. All the solicited contributions arrived in time except one, that of Paul. He was still mentally and spiritually paralysed. With Renée's death and my withdrawal the journal ceased publication. Its last issue is dated December 1955.

3. John's cherished nickname from schoolboy days.

4. A biography of John was published by John Dove, a Jesuit friend of his, under the title, *Strange Vagabond of God: The Story of John Bradburne*, Ward River Press, Swords, Co. Dublin 1983, and a sample of his poetic outpouring, *Songs of the Vagabond*, was edited in 1996 by David Crystal.

12. Finding my Feet in Newcastle

1. Five years later, he asked me to visit his father who, in his last years, felt lonely and depressed. Gone were the days when his home was full of guests and the postman arrived with a bagful of mail. I spent three days with him in the glorious month of May in 1962 when Oxford looks at its best. It was almost entirely a sad occasion. Physically and mentally exhausted, Paul Kahle was unable to converse for more than a couple of minutes at a time. The main reason for this failure was his continuous insomnia. However, the night before my return to Newcastle he had a good sleep and next morning he was nearly his old self. This was the last time I saw him alive and he seemed happy. I believe that the following year his sons repatriated him to Germany, where he died in 1965, aged ninety.

13. Laying the Foundations

1. Friendship was renewed between them during the last few years of Pam's life. We visited him and his second wife Anne once or twice in London and they were our guests in Oxford several times. Charles came to pay a moving last visit to Pam a month or so before she died, and attended her funeral.

2. Pam also qualified as a driver later in 1959. The day on which she *passed* the test happened to be the last occasion on which she touched the steering wheel. I kept renewing her licence in the hope that she might change her mind, but she preferred to leave driving, and the posting of letters, to me. She was a very active correspondent, writing in longhand, but once she had signed her missive, she considered that the communication was finished and the menial act of dropping the envelope into a letter box was left to me.

3. See my short article, 'New Light on the Sacrifice of Isaac from 4Q225', *JJS* 47, 1996, 140–6.

4. Typical of his punctilious attention to detail, Vajda pointed out in his six-line notice of the 1973 reissue of the book that I had failed to correct an erroneous reference which he had indicated in his earlier review. I am ashamed to confess that it was forgotten again in the 1983 reprint of *Scripture and Tradition*.

5. One of the items in the new agreement concerns possible strip-cartoon rights of *The Changing Faces of Jesus* (!).

6. Originally 255 pages, in its 1997 incarnation – *The Complete Dead Sea Scrolls in English* – it has grown into an almost 700-page hardback, selling at £25.

7. Quite soon after its appearance as a cheap paperback, *The Dead Sea Scrolls in English* moved to a much higher class, being selected as the text for one of the 1966 volumes of The Limited Editions Club.

8. The *Habilitation* is an advanced doctorate required by the German higher education system as a qualification for holding a university chair.

14. The Wonderland of Oxford

1. The same item of university news also carried the appointment of my French Scrolls friend, Dominique Barthélemy, to the Grinfield Lectureship on the Septuagint, an illustrious special lectureship tenable usually for three years, established in the middle of the nineteenth century.

2. On one occasion a common friend (Fergus Millar), in happy ignorance of Stern's dislike of me, invited both of us to an after-dinner party. He soon realized that something was wrong when on my arrival S.M.S. picked up a book, took his chair to the corner of the room, and spent the remainder of the evening reading with his back turned towards the rest of the company.

3. The MA by decree is another Oxford quirk. In order to qualify for membership of the Congregation, composed of the teaching members of the University, one has to be a Master of Arts. This degree, which in most universities is gained through hard work, is granted here to any well-behaved Oxford Bachelor of Arts who, 'with the approval of his society [so] supplicates … in or after the twenty-first term from his matriculation' (*Oxford University Examination Decrees and Regulations*, 1997, p. 545). In short, the most important qualification, that which introduces one to the academic parliament, is based on a fictitious degree, which in my case was conferred by an additional legal fiction. I may have been the last one who had to pay (five guineas if I remember correctly) for this honour. Since 1966 it has been given free of charge to those who receive it by decree.

4. Another quasi-uniform which I had to buy was a dinner jacket, more often

needed thirty years ago than it is now. I am still wearing the same one, though in the meanwhile the waist of the trousers has had to be increased.

5. This ridiculously low requirement becomes less outrageous when it is borne in mind that traditionally Oxford instruction takes the form of tutorials. Ordinary tutorial fellows may have to teach considerable number of hours in their colleges in addition to their university lectures amounting to no less than 1.5 hours per week over a twenty-four week academic year. As a University Reader, I was permitted to undertake no more than six hours weekly tutorial teaching.

6. Not long before he died in 1975, aged eighty-three, I saw him arriving in the Institute with a bad limp. He explained that a day or two earlier he had been to the memorial service for C. H. Dodd, his co-editor of the *New English Bible*, held in a non-conformist chapel in North Oxford. After the service, he decided to go home along the Cherwell as he used to when he was a child, but did not know that in the meanwhile a gate had been built across the path and it was locked. So without hesitation he climbed over it, but slipped and hurt his leg. Perhaps a little earlier, on my return from a trip overseas, one of my graduate students, now holding a senior post at the School of Oriental and African Studies in London, asked me whether I had seen the interview with the Scrolls maverick, John Allegro, in *Penthouse*. To my negative answer came the offer: I will steal it for you from the barber's shop where I saw it if you promise me that you will show it to Professor Driver. A deal was struck and, equipped with the issue in question, I knocked on Driver's door. 'Here is Allegro's latest,' I told him, and put the girlie magazine on his desk. He had to page through a fair number of naked bosoms – with an absolutely straight face – before finding the article. He returned the copy with a note which I still have: 'Thanks, but I take a very poor view of the literature that you read! G.R.D.' Some years after his death, I found behind the drawers of my (formerly his) desk in the Oriental Institute the copy of a letter written by Driver in 1964 to the Vice-Chancellor of Manchester University, commending me together with two others for the vacant chair in Semitic Studies. Fortunately, as it turned out, I was not chosen, but nor were either of the two other Driver nominees.

7. In the early 1980s, I spent a few weeks at Tulane University in New Orleans, and on one occasion sat next to the President of the University at dinner. Having learned that previously he had held high office at the Ford Foundation, I used the grant to Wolfson College as my opening gambit in our conversation. Apparently Isaiah Berlin's coup had provoked a near revolution, because the Ford president's decision on the spur of the moment to give away $3,000.000 completely upset the budget planning of his senior colleagues.

8. The publication of this nineteen-page article, 'The Use of *bar nash/bar*

nasha [=SON OF MAN] in Jewish Aramaic', is a story in its own right. When it was almost complete early in January 1965, I mentioned it to Matthew Black, Professor of New Testament at St Andrews, who immediately offered to include it in the form of an appendix, under my name, in the forthcoming third edition of his well-known book, *An Aramaic Approach to the Gospels and Acts.* I agreed, and Matthew informed the publishers, Oxford University Press, of the matter. Along came a letter from OUP in mid-January requiring the typescript by the end of that month, as the book was scheduled to appear in September. Not before late February, I replied, and my deadline was accepted with a groan. In fact, the book was not published until 1967, and to my dismay contained a two-page partly critical appendix stuck to my own appendix by Matthew Black without my prior knowledge or consent. At the first opportunity, I reissued the paper independently in *Post-Biblical Jewish Studies*, Leiden, 1975, and brought it up to date in 'The Present State of the SON OF MAN Debate' in *Journal of Jewish Studies* 29, 1978, 23–134.

9. Quite recently I learned that Tom died as he always hoped he would, not in his bed, but 'on the job'. The people for whom he worked found him lying on the lawn: he had a heart attack.

15. The Journal and the New English Schürer

1. One day during the retreat I was prevailed on to join the so-called 'historical tour', i.e. a visit to Hitler's bunker. The German guide reminded us three times during his much rehearsed spiel that Hitler was an *Austrian*.

2. While in New Orleans, I was invited to address the professors of the Southern Baptist Seminary on the Qumran scrolls. Each of them warmly greeted me with identical words: 'I'm mighty glad to welcome you on the campus.' But when I had finished my talk, I was asked only one question, 'What do the Dead Sea Scrolls say about Jesus Christ?' When I replied 'Nothing', they ceased to be interested.

3. Today just under 1,000 copies of *JJS* are distributed, which is reasonable for a periodical of its kind, but in my view it still could do better.

4. Over the years, the *Journal* produced three special volumes. The first celebrated the sixty-fifth birthday of my friend and sponsor, David Daube (*Studies in Jewish Legal History*, guest-edited by Bernard S. Jackson, 1974); the second also commemorated a sixty-fifth birthday, that of the great Israeli archaeologist and Scrolls scholar, Yigael Yadin, *Essays in Honour of Yigael Yadin*, edited by G. Vermes and J. Neusner (1982); the third was the *Special Issue to Commemorate the Twenty-Fifth Year of Geza Vermes as Editor*, edited by Philip Alexander & Martin Goodman (1995).

5. Today, a quarter of a century later, the Oxford Centre for Hebrew and Jewish Studies is an impressive institution, occupying beautiful premises at

Yarnton, outside Oxford, devoted to research and teaching not just in Hebrew literature since the end of the eighteenth century but in the whole field of Jewish studies.

6. Some fifteen years later, the same Stella, by then married with four children, came to my assistance and for a while administered the *Journal* with enthusiasm and competence.

7. I have kept these heavily annotated proofs among my memorabilia, but would gladly donate them to any library interested in such a curiosity.

8. I subsequently published the original version in *JJS* (1973, 88–91).

9. On the occasion of the opening ceremony of a conference at Christ Church, Oxford, Edward was asked to represent the President of the British Academy. The organizing secretary of the conference, an anxious middle-aged lady, asked me to introduce her to Edward. 'Professor Ullendorff, how very kind of you to take the trouble to travel from London. It is extremely generous of you,' I heard her saying. 'Madam,' replied Edward with aplomb, 'that's no trouble at all. I have my chair in London, but my bed is in Oxford.'

10. After some years in Brighton, Michael, who was a priest in the Church of England, applied for a chaplaincy in one of the Cambridge colleges. Would I be willing to referee for him? 'If they ask my opinion,' I replied, doubtful that my views would count much in appointing a chaplain. Fairly soon a delighted Michael was on the telephone warmly thanking me for my support. Yes, he got the job. I did not have the courage to tell him that my opinion was never solicited.

11. Earlier I had played a passive and almost unwitting part on the occasion of the honorary degree proposed for the then President of Pakistan, Zulfikar Ali Bhutto. Our young Orientalist colleague, Richard Gombrich, now Boden Professor of Sanskrit, was so incensed by this proposal that he decided formally to oppose it. Most of the inhabitants of the Oriental Institute turned up to support him, but one of our experienced colleagues who sat next to me did a quick head count and realized that those present did not constitute the quorum necessary to make a decision binding on the Hebdomadal Council, the inner cabinet of the University. So he turned to me and said, 'Geza, when I stand up do the same. Don't ask questions, just do it. You don't need to open your mouth.' So when Richard finished his speech, my neighbour and I rose to our feet, to the visible consternation of the Vice Chancellor presiding over the proceedings. Unknown to me, our gesture meant that we were requesting an adjournment for two weeks, I think, which had to be granted according to the rules. By then enough publicity had been marshalled and the Bhutto honorary doctorate, like the one planned for Mrs Thatcher some years later, was officially cancelled.

12. A friend of Cheslyn Jones drew his attention to the usefulness of this book, and Cheslyn in turn informed me.

13. She remained in season much longer than expected and was caught *in flagrante* with Simon, an inveterate roamer who spent his time fathering puppies on Boars Hill.

14. It was posthumously reissued, taking into account Pam's corrections and supplements, by the Littman Library of Jewish Civilization in 1994.

16. The Battle over the Scrolls: A Personal Account

1. With hindsight we know that during the 1980s only one volume was added to the series, edited by the French priest Maurice Baillet, whose work was delayed by spending an inordinate amount of time on trying, and failing, to make sense of heaps of useless scraps. The pathetically lacrymose ending of his preface makes curious reading to British ears. *'Vus ses imperfections, cet ouvrage trouvera peut-être des censeurs sévères. Au moins aurai-je la satisfaction d'y avoir mis le meilleur de moi-même. Ami lecteur, n'oublie jamais qu'il est écrit avec des souffrances, et parfois avec des larmes.'* [On account of its imperfections, this work may perhaps find severe critics. At least I will have the satisfaction of having put into it the best of myself. Friendly reader, never forget that it has been written with suffering and sometimes with tears.]

2. *The Dead Sea Scrolls: Qumran in Perspective* (1977), 23–4. At one stage the preparation of this series of lectures ran into serious trouble and was saved by more than the customary amount of help from Pam, which was acknowledged on the title page.

3. I last met Pierre Benoit in Strasbourg in 1983 at a congress organized by the Association Catholique Française d'Études Bibliques. In the course of the brief private conversation I had with him (in French), he lamented the passing of French as an international language at conferences dominated by *l'impérialisme linguistique anglo-saxon.*

4. *JJS* 39, 1988, 3–4. In the lead letter published on the same day in *The Times* (11 June 1987), Edward Ullendorff advanced an identical proposal: 'The most urgent task is the immediate publication, by photographic reproduction, of all the available fragments ... Let us have the raw material, and there will be no shortage of willing hands to attempt a decipherment.'

5. *The Greek Minor Prophets Scroll from Nahal Hever* [*DJD* VIII], 1990.

6. 'For the Man, Compassion; for his Views, Contempt', *BAR* 17, Jan.–Feb. 1991, 64.

7. Of course, the *opening* affected only the published photographs. A senior Israeli expert gave a particularly apt and succinct assessment of the Yarnton collection under the imposed restrictive clauses: 'The published material is unnecessary, the unpublished is useless.'

8. The paper appeared in print together with the photographs three months later in the Autumn 1991 issue of the *Journal of Jewish Studies*: 'Preliminary

Remarks on the Unpublished Fragments of the Community Rule from Qumran Cave 4', *JJS* 42, 1991, 250–5.

9. I was assured that the policy followed both by the Bodleian Library and by the Ashmolean Museum was to give free access to their unpublished documents, even if they were in the process of being edited by someone.

10. This concordance, based on a handwritten card-index of words cited in context, was completed by 1960. In 1988 it was reproduced in twenty-five copies for the exclusive use of the editorial team. But one copy was left at Hebrew Union College, Cincinnati, where a whole collection of Scrolls photographs was deposited sometime after the 1973 Israeli-Arab war for safe-keeping. No doubt by inadvertence, the Concordance was placed on the open shelves of the library of the College.

11. Even from as far as Australia, his home base, Alan Crown, the itinerant administrator of the Oxford Centre's Qumran Project, was reported by the *New York Times* as expressing 'anger at the Huntington's release of the photographs'. However, by adding that he also doubted 'that the Israeli authorities would carry out the threat to sue the library', he simultaneously succeeded in annoying both the freedom fighters and the IAA.

12. Thanks to two visits to the Huntington in November 1995 and to the generous assistance of its President, Robert A. Skotheim, I am now in possession of documentary evidence clarifying the part played by the Library in the 'liberation' of the Scrolls.

13. The disks are marketed by Brill at £1,500. When I was first consulted by the electronic publishing division of OUP, the price contemplated was reasonable: £350 to 400.

14. 'The Oxford Forum for Qumran Research Seminar on the Rule of War from Cave 4 (4Q285)', *JJS* 43, 1992, 85–94.

15. It will be edited by Philip Alexander and myself with the full blessing of the editor-in-chief, Emanuel Tov.

17. Jesus the Jew and his Religion

1. Rudolf Bultmann, *Jesus and the Word*, 1934, 14. (The original German edition, *Jesus*, appeared in 1926.)

2. Of the other two designations investigated in the book, on the basis of my earlier research (cf. pp. 163–4 above) I excluded 'son of man' from among the original titles during the lifetime of Jesus, although I accepted it as a Christian midrash, a theologico-exegetical product of the Greek-speaking early church. As for 'Messiah', I argued that because of its most generally held sense of a liberating king of the last days, Jesus was disinclined to apply the notion to himself and that the so-called 'messianic secret' of the Gospel of Mark, i.e. the prohibition by Jesus to be proclaimed Messiah, was inspired by his unwilling-

ness to be seen as fulfilling that role. And when questioned, his elliptic reply, 'It is you who say so', needs to be completed by 'but not I'.

3. He first voiced his unease in a conversation, and repeated it in an evaluation of the book on the BBC's Third Programme under the somewhat depressing title, 'A rather pale Galilean'.

4. I had already made a similar observation about Cardinal Tisserant (cf. p. 238 n.7), and remember Robert Shackleton's comment that he infinitely preferred talking about Voltaire, on whom I consulted him, to discussing the hourly wages of cleaning women which he, *qua* Bodley's Librarian, had ultimately to decide.

5. In Belfast, my hosts were nervous that the followers of the Reverend Ian Paisley might disturb the lectures (which for them were anti-Christian). Their fears were unfounded. In Dublin, by contrast, the large Roman Catholic audience insisted that I should not fudge my answers: 'Did I think Jesus was God? Yes or no, no double talk, please!'

6. By that time I had new publishers, SCM Press in London, who also rescued *Jesus the Jew* from Collins, and Fortress Press in the United States.

7. The trip was made possible by the kindness of my stepdaughter Anna, who, together with her husband, came to Oxford to look after Pam during my absence.

8. 'We are so accustomed ... to make Jesus the object of religion that we become apt to forget that in our earliest records he is portrayed not as the object of religion, but as a religious man,' T.W. Manson, *The Teaching of Jesus*, 1935, 101.

9. J.P. Meier, *A Marginal Jew* II, 1994, 14 n.7.

10. Apparently the book was a publishing success in Hungary and the first printing was sold out on the day it reached the bookshops.

11. To name a few: A.E. Harvey, *Jesus and the Constraints of History*, 1982; E.P. Sanders, *Jesus and Judaism*, 1985; *The Historical Figure of Jesus*, 1990; M.J. Borg, *Jesus: a New Vision*, 1987; J.H. Charlesworth, *Jesus within Judaism*, 1989; *Jesus' Jewishness*, 1991; J.D. Crossan, *The Historical Jesus*, 1991; J.P. Meier, *A Marginal Jew*, I–II, 1991–94, etc.

12. Since 1971, the Commission has been associated with the Sacred Congregation of the Doctrine of the Faith, and is presided over by the head of that Congregation, Cardinal Joseph Ratzinger.

13. *Scripture and Christology: A Statement of the Biblical Commission*, translated with a commentary by Joseph A. Fitzmyer, SJ (1986).

14. 'If to understand Jesus studies are conducted *only* along these lines, there is always the danger of mutilating his personality, precisely at the moment when stress is being put by such studies on his Jewish background and character' (p. 23).

15. S. Safrai, 'The Teaching of Pietists in Mishnaic Literature', *JJS* 16,

1965, 15–33; 'Jesus and the Hasidim', *Jerusalem Perspective* 42–44, 1994, 3–22.

16. The French Catholic Bishops' 'repentance' at the end of September 1997 for their church's failure to condemn the persecution of the Jews during the Second World War preceded the statement by the Pope promised for the end of 1997.

18. Harvest Time

1. I could jokingly report to friends that I had just declined a job which carried a salary double that of Mrs Thatcher. (In 1985 the dollar was almost equal to the pound.) 'Aren't you a bit silly?', a fellow Wolfsonian commented, but even with hindsight I remain persuaded that my choice was correct.

2. Until quite recently the procession formed at the end of the 'benefaction', established by Nathaniel Lord Crewe, an eighteenth-century Bishop of Durham, was the only occasion when academic achievement palpably took precedence over College administrative authority. The beadle invited the participants to to line up in the following hierarchical order: Heads of Houses (= colleges) who were holders of a higher doctorate were to be followed by Doctors of Divinity, Civil Law, Medicine, Music, Letters and Science. Finally the tail of the procession was formed by those Heads of Houses who were *not* doctors. This worthy distinction between doctors and non-doctors fell victim to that trend towards modernization which also turned the splendid 'Sibthorpian Professorship of *Rural Economy*' into that of dull '*Plant Science*'.

3. The *Festschrift* was edited by two ex-students, Philip Davis and Richard White, and published as volume 100 of the Journal for the Study of the Old Testament Supplement Series by Sheffield Academic Press.

Epilogue: Late Afternoon Sunshine

1. *The Riddle of the Sparks*, Foxcombe Press, Oxford 1993. Pam seriously began to write poetry during the last ten years of her life.

Index